FRIENDSHIP
LOVE
AUTISM

COMMUNICATION CHALLENGES AND THE AUTISM DIAGNOSIS THAT GAVE US A NEW LIFE TOGETHER

MICHELLE AND ANDREW PRESTON

Copyright © 2022 BELLAMIMA LIFESTYLES INC.

All Rights Reserved. This book contains material protected under International and Federal Copyright Laws and Treaties. Any unauthorized reprint or use of this material is prohibited. No part of this book may be reproduced or transmitted in any form or by any means, electronic or mechanical, including photocopying, recording, or by any information storage and retrieval system without express written permission from the author/publisher.

ISBN: 978-1-7387354-0-2 (Paperback)
ISBN: 978-1-7387354-3-3 (Hardcover)
ISBN: 978-1-7387354-2-6 (EBook)

This book is dedicated to all autistics who feel misunderstood.
We stand with you as you embrace your differences
and celebrate your uniqueness.

TABLE OF CONTENTS

Acknowledgments..vii
Introduction..ix
Chapter 1 - The Big Discovery......................................1

FRIENDSHIP..23
Chapter 2 - A Lucky Swipe Right...................................25
Chapter 3 - Friendship Beginnings.................................44
Chapter 4 - The Friendship Continues..............................56
Chapter 5 - The Shift to Romance..................................71
Chapter 6 - Our First Real Date...................................88

LOVE..99
Chapter 7 - The Small Stuff......................................101
Chapter 8 - Some Learning Curves.................................122
Chapter 9 - Randomness...142
Chapter 10 - More Learning Curves................................159
Chapter 11 - The Slightly Tough Stuff............................177

Chapter 12 - The Tough Stuff............................195
Chapter 13 - The Toughest Stuff - What Nearly Broke Us......214
Chapter 14 - Living Together 230
Chapter 15 - The Bedroom............................243

AUTISM...................................259

Chapter 16 - November Has Arrived....................261
Chapter 17 - Robot Man, Period Girl,
     and their Love Languages..................277
Chapter 18 - The Diagnosis 295
Chapter 19 - The Aftermath of the Diagnosis..............317

Conclusion 323
Endnotes..331

ACKNOWLEDGMENTS

We would like to extend our deepest gratitude to our social media followers, who inspired us to write this book series. Your kindness and emotional support have kept us going when we've doubted ourselves. We would also like to recognize the invaluable support of Teresa De Grosbois, our writing coach, who never lost patience as she turned two wannabe writers into authors. Lastly, we would like to express our deepest thanks to all of our beta readers for taking the time to read drafts and provide feedback. Each and every one of you contributed to the success of this book. We felt like we had an army behind us, and this improved our process more than words could ever express.

INTRODUCTION

Our love story unfolded opposite to everything I'd ever imagined. My knight in shining armor didn't swoop in and do all of the right things. He wasn't popular or charismatic. There were no sparks or magic, and our first few dates were full of awkward moments. He was the furthest thing from a smooth talker and didn't express his feelings in any of the ways I was accustomed to. On top of all that, he never wore anything remotely stylish.

Growing up, I loved fairy tales and romantic comedies. Many of us watched these movies thinking, *Surely only an idiot would think any of these stories could play out to be true.* But I think it's safe to admit that subconsciously, we hoped they would play out to be true.

Personally, I know I was looking for love in all of the wrong ways, and a large part of the reason is because of what society portrays to be important.

My knight in shining armor is, in fact, terrible at all the things that are portrayed in society to be the most important. So you can see why I friend-zoned him. He didn't have any of the qualities I thought I was looking for.

My name is Michelle Preston, and this book is about me and my husband, Andrew. The more I talked about our story on social media, the more it became evident that the world needed to hear about everything we went through to get to where we are today.

This book is our love story, and it's not about the popular guy. It's about falling in love with a nerd and seeking to understand him.

When I began writing, I decided to write the only way that made sense to me. As if you are my best friend, and I'm sharing my story with you over some delicious beverages. Andrew and I agree that we aren't going to leave out details that make us look bad. The only way we can do this book series justice is to speak freely by telling our stories as they happened. So, since you're my bestie, getting all of the juicy details of our lives, I trust you will play your part as the best friend and reserve your judgments.

This book has "autism" in the title, but it's not just about that. And it's not just about my own knight in shining armor. It's about all the nerds out there. The underdogs, who I am forever rooting for. And the partners who could be so happy with them.

All it takes is opening your heart to the possibilities that are right in front of you and a little understanding. We share our story in the hopes of giving you a new perspective because everyone deserves a fighting chance at being in a happy, fulfilling relationship.

* * *

Hi, I'm Andrew, Michelle's nerd in shining armor, and I am terrible at the dating thing. A few months before I met Michelle, I went on a date. The date was going well, as far as I could tell, and she accepted my invitation to continue enjoying the evening after dinner. We found a pub and had some beverages over light conversation. At one point, as she was unlocking her phone, my subconscious caught her pin number as I glanced in her direction. Because I have a visual mind, her pin was locked in my mind.

Minutes later, she passed me her phone to look something up for her. She gestured for her phone back as she realized I didn't know her code. I had already unlocked her phone. My explanation was honest and nonchalant: "When you entered your pin, I happened to be glancing in the direction of your phone, and I saw the pin through the corner of my eye." To me, this was no big deal. I was honest and told her exactly what had happened. No harm, no foul, right?

Wrong.

The date felt awkward after this moment, and I couldn't understand why. Our hug at the end of the night felt like she was begrudgingly hugging me. It felt weird. *What did I do?* I thought to myself.

Days later, I mentioned to a friend that I unlocked her phone without her knowing I knew her pin. He told me that it might have spooked her. In hindsight, I realized that I severed the date or the potential of anything more at that moment.

Oh God, I thought. *What else in this world do I have to pay attention to so that I can avoid upsetting people?*

Growing up, I knew I was different. In school, being labeled "one of the weird kids" would follow me to adulthood. During my early teenage years, I considered myself to be weird, underachieving, and dumb. I wrote myself off from living a normal life or having a good job. The best I could ever hope for would be a happy life with my interests, a few friends, and maybe a girlfriend. I was comparing myself to everyone else, and to how life will (or should) play out through guidance from teachers, parents, and other students. Turns out, they and I were wrong.

During my twenties, I went through a lot of emotional and spiritual changes. This momentum has not changed. It kept getting harder, but I fought and got stronger with it. In my own nerdy way, life has unfolded in ways I would have never imagined.

When Michelle and I first met, I knew she was special. Spending time with her made me happy. Hanging out with her was something I always looked forward to. She was my first girlfriend that felt like a teammate who was with me. Michelle had to help me realize what I was feeling. I could feel something positive, but it was hard to understand because past relationships weren't based on true friendship and companionship. *Why am I so happy?* I would wonder. Until I realized that it was because of my relationship with Michelle. Wow.

This kind of life-changing learning has not stopped, and I don't want it to stop. Knowing how far we have come and how many people on social media resonate with our story brings me a lot of joy. This book is to help others to see relationships and communication differently. Please take the ideas and feelings from this book and use them to better yourself and others.

* * *

1

THE BIG DISCOVERY

Watching Andrew play computer games is usually something I enjoy. But not tonight. It's Wednesday evening, and I'm curled up in my favorite reclining chair at his place. I'm watching him while in a heavy brain fog from my post-concussion syndrome. Negative thoughts occupy my headspace, and I can't seem to shake them.

I'm happy to be at Andrew's place. We've been dating for nearly five months. Andrew is kind to me when my concussion symptoms flare up. He makes sure I'm comfortable, kisses my forehead, and then leaves me to sit alone. He never makes me feel bad about it or gets impatient. If only I could be that kind to myself.

Andrew doesn't play computer games like anyone I've met before. His keyboard lights up like a rainbow, and his headset has a microphone attached to it. Pair that with his fancy gaming chair and the fact that his computer screen curves to the shape of his desk, and it kind of looks like he's about to launch himself into outer space.

Watching any computer screen can feel overstimulating with post-concussion syndrome. Andrew's screen is flashing with frenzied movement, so I keep having to close my eyes. Every time I do this, my inner voice shames me, telling me I'm weak and useless. My concussion symptoms have been flaring up a lot lately, and I'm tired of it. My recent return to work, after having a year off, is proving too much for my bruised brain to handle. Depression looms as I question everything about my life. Will I ever be able to train in martial arts again? Play baseball? Or work in the classroom that I used to love? Or have I permanently damaged my brain by getting punched in the head during one too many kickboxing fights?

Andrew's book collection is twice the size of mine, and he reads more than any man I've dated. His bookcase is across from me against the wall, and it becomes a welcome distraction from my thoughts. My gaze moves across each shelf, looking for a book that may help explain my moods.

My emotions don't seem to have a gray area; I'm either on top of the world and full of confidence or down in the doldrums. This has become more evident during my brain recovery as I don't have many distractions. Sitting alone for hours at a time on a daily basis is a surefire way to get to know yourself, and I don't like what I've been seeing.

Books about investing and economics fill the first two shelves. I ignore those. My gaze moves across the middle shelf as a book catches my eye. It's called *Shadow Syndromes, The Mild Forms of Major Mental Disorders That Sabotage Us*.[1] It catches my eye because Andrew has mentioned it before. I'm too lazy to remove myself from the comfy chair, so I wait until his game is finished to ask him about it.

"Andrew, can you pass me *Shadow Syndromes*?" Andrew turns around to look for it on the shelf.

He hands it to me with a smile and says, "This is the book I told you about. My psychologist recommended it to me."

As soon as I get my hands on it, I feel the urge to read it. "Can I borrow it?" I ask.

"Of course," Andrew answers. "Let me know what you think. It's pretty interesting."

It's getting late, and my dog Baxter is alone at my condo. We cuddle for a few minutes before saying goodbye.

I walk out the door, clueless about the fact that I'm holding a book that is about to completely change our lives.

---

[1] By John J. Ratey M.D. and Catherine Johnson, Ph.D. 1997

Shadow Syndromes

There is a popular quote by Dr. Stephen Shore that highlights how diverse autism is. That quote reads, "If you've met one person with autism, you've met one person with autism." I share this quote because I want to emphasize that autism presents differently in everyone.

This book talks about the traits I noticed most in Andrew. You may relate to many of them and not be autistic. You may be autistic and not relate to Andrew's traits at all. But by telling you about our discovery process and how our relationship was able to flourish through it (and because of it), we hope to inspire you to go on your own journey.

Shadow Syndromes was published in 1997, and some of its terms are out of date. For this, I apologize. It didn't feel right to misquote the information I read when I made my discovery, so you will be reading everything as I did. This means you'll be getting a lot of information all at once, and it may be tough to digest (I know it was for me). Don't worry, bestie. There's still an entire book ahead that will help these things sink in, and you can always revert back to this chapter afterward once you know our story.

Shadow Syndromes captivates me right away. By the end of the first chapter, I'm hooked. It's called "The Noisy Brain." The fascinating analysis helps me realize why so many people continue to make the simplest of mistakes in their day-to-day lives. It reads, "*What... stress is to the body, noise is to the brain.*" It goes on to explain that "*Invariably, people overwhelmed by noise make mistakes; their processing capacity falls apart. ...A person on overload, in other words, is a person operating at the far low end of his capabilities.*"

This chapter speaks to me because it puts things so simply. Stress is such a huge issue in society. Many of us are constantly overstimulated without realizing it. We are operating at the lowest end of our capabilities because our brains are overloaded.

I enjoy this chapter, but it's no match for what is coming up.

So, here's how it all goes down...

With a chamomile tea in hand, I'm snuggled up in bed reading *Shadow Syndromes*.

My entire world flips upside down as I begin reading Chapter 6, "Autistic Echoes." My poor highlighter nearly runs out of ink as everything is suddenly sounding so familiar. It's as if I'm smacked on the head with a 2x4 full of much-needed information.

Andrew has also used his highlighter throughout the chapter and has written numbers beside some of the paragraphs. I highlight the words, *"Who is the person with a hidden form of autism? He is the odd duck. His difference from 'normal' people is readily apparent to all of us; we recognize him as being somehow off."*

Memories flash through my mind like a movie scene. First, when my roommate Gabriel said to me, "Andrew's missing something? What's he missing?" Followed by my many conversations with our good friends Jackson and Caleb about how Andrew usually "seems awkward."

I continue to read: *"He suffers overwhelming troubles with communication; it is difficult for him to ask or answer questions, difficult for him to use the word 'yes.' Even if he possesses language… he only rarely grasps the back and forth of a conversation; instead, he monologues or sits silent as a stone while others speak to him. He cannot read body language or facial expressions; if he can, he cannot do so well as other children his age. He cannot play games unless he is painstakingly taught every step involved."* That last line makes me remember the time we tried to play Scrabble and how impossible it seemed for him to grasp which way to put the letters.

Can't read facial expressions—check. Can't read body language—check. Socially awkward—double-check. I begin thinking about Andrew sitting alone on the floor at Gavin and Chelsea's, reading his book while the rest of us chatted for hours. Our many small miscommunications flash through my mind. Everything begins to make sense.

Adrenaline fills my body in such a way that it is impossible for me to remain horizontal. Without a thought of it being after midnight, I jump out of bed and turn my lights on. No amount of chamomile tea is going to put me back to bed now. A tranquilizer dart couldn't do the job.

After moving to my living room table, I continue to read what feels like an entire chapter about Andrew. *"At present, the classic autism shadow syndrome is undeniably male.[2] And, social stereotyping aside, the most recognized embodiment of this shadow syndrome is the nerd. He is the computer programmer hunched over his monitor at all hours of the day and night, a pocket protector lodged permanently in his rumpled shirt. He has few or no friends; often has no wife. He is a geek."*

The chapter has many points that are nearly word-for-word things I have thought about Andrew. My mind is comparing everything to him as I continue to read.

"...usually speak somewhat differently from the rest of us: often their diction is formal, their affect somewhat flat." That's Andrew. His tone is so flat that it's hard to tell if he's being serious or joking.

"...cannot make small talk."
Definitely Andrew. The thought of having to make small talk will ruin his day.

"...monologuing, not allowing anyone else to speak."
Also Andrew. He sometimes talks so long that I have to interrupt him because I can't listen anymore.

"...ability to welcome criticism as being merely useful feedback."
A hundred percent Andrew. I love how he takes criticism; he listens without getting defensive.

"...trusting nature."
Totally Andrew. He takes people at their word, even when they've proven many times over that they don't keep their word.

"...does not intuit hidden motives."
Yup, also Andrew. In his mind, everyone else is just as honest as he is.

---

[2] More and more women continue to be diagnosed autistic every single day.

"...great difficulty picking up on the unspoken."
Most definitely Andrew. He can't take a hint even if you smack him over the head with it.

"He experiences himself as an open book, and, in his dealings with other humans, he has only one option, to be honest."
Again, a hundred percent Andrew. His honesty is unlike any I've ever experienced.

The more I read, the more I am convinced.

This part is my favorite as it makes my heart smile: *"...all of the shadow syndromes bring their blessings, mixed though they may be, and the autistic person, loath to change and not much of a mind reader, is as loyal, steadfast, and fundamentally honest as he is socially unaware."*

One wife speaks of her husband fondly even though she has many struggles with him: *"Children love Dan. They instinctively like him. He's childlike, simple; Dan is uncomplicated. What you see is what you get. That was one of the things that attracted me to Dan, and that is still the case today. Dan is a man of integrity."*

This woman is speaking my language. I relate to everything she is saying about her husband. That is exactly how I feel about Andrew—after many years of dating men who were often keeping secrets in an attempt to hide their insecurities. Andrew's integrity is impressive and refreshing.

I keep reading.

"The autistic person's real problem may be not so much with emotion as with empathy—with perceiving and comprehending the feelings of others."
That's Andrew. It's so hard for me to explain to him why something he did hurt my feelings.

"...literal-minded; they will typically interpret a question or a remark in its most concrete sense."
Totally Andrew. We've gotten into some funny situations because of this one. I need to watch my words because he takes them so literally.

"He needs things spelled out; he needs people to be direct. But when people are direct, he can get it. And that makes all the difference."
Definitely Andrew. If I don't explain things in detail, he will have no idea what I expect from him.

"...ability to shift their attention quickly from one thing to another."
Could not be more like Andrew. He shifts his focus quickly and is very impulsive. It's tough for me to keep up.

"...the need for sameness and routine, the limited interests, the repetitive behaviors."
Also Andrew. He follows a pattern for everything he does.

"...difficulty following social rhythm."
Totally Andrew. He definitely marches to the beat of his own drum. It feels as though he is in his own world.

"He is 'mind-blind'; he cannot read minds."
Omg, that's a thing? That's so Andrew. When I tell him how I'm feeling, he seems so surprised by it, even when it's obvious.

"Once an autistic person is on track to do something, he needs to stay on track."
Again, it's Andrew. If I talk to him while he's in the middle of doing something, it completely throws him off.

"Visual thinking..."
Yup, Andrew thinks in pictures. He once described a picture to me to explain a story.

There have been many times when I have been baffled by Andrew's ability to "miss the point" in something that is obvious to me. I will think, *How can he possibly not understand? It's so obvious.*

Reading this next part helps put this in perspective for me. *"...the autistic person, they believe, suffers from a deficit in the ability to bring unity to the perceived world. Instead of seeing the world as a world, or the room as a room, or the carpet as a carpet, he sees the world in pieces. The normal person automatically, unconsciously, assembles his perceptual world into wholes. We see a face, not a nose, mouth, and two eyes."*

I have to stop and take that in before I continue because it is so much to unpack.

Does Andrew see the world in pieces? What would it be like to have your brain work that way? It must be difficult to see the fragments of the world so clearly when most people are looking at the whole.

It's almost as if Andrew is watching an entirely different movie than the rest of us, yet he is in the same room. Wow.

MIND BLOWN.

Once I begin to grasp the idea that Andrew sees the world in pieces, so many things start to make sense. Why he thought to pack all the little things we needed for our camping weekend but didn't make sure we had enough time to get there before dark, that is a big picture thing.

It explains how he neglects to see that certain people are obviously affecting his life in a negative way. Why he never understands the major role someone can play in completely ruining his day.

Or, on the flip side, for him to realize who plays a role in improving his life. I've often felt the need to remind him who his high-quality friends are, who should be getting more of his time, and those who maybe didn't deserve so much of it. Why I've needed to do this is something I've never understood, and I don't like doing it. No one I've previously dated has gotten any speeches about who they should hang out with, but with Andrew, it's so needed that I can't help myself.

Andrew is one of the smartest people I know, so I've never understood how he could be incapable of comprehending something so obvious to me. But if he sees everything in pieces, as individual events, then I can begin to fathom it. If he can't connect the dots of events together, it makes sense that he doesn't realize which dots are coming from certain people.

"...he becomes very good at perceiving the world in parts," I continue to read. *"This is a strength of autism, perhaps the key strength and the source of the autistic genius we see in the so-called idiot savants: an autistic person, while far worse than the normal person at grasping a whole, is often far better at perceiving the parts. In embedded figure tests, tests in which a child is asked to find a hidden picture in a picture, autistic children far outperform normal children; often they outperform the experimenters as well."*

This helps me put the spotlight on Andrew's obvious genius qualities, and there are many of them. He is gifted when it comes to noticing details many of us will miss, especially when it comes to mechanics. He never cuts corners or rushes a job.

It's nearing 2 a.m. by the time I finish the chapter. It ends by saying, *"...focus exclusively on their narrow fields of interests; they cannot do otherwise. And they succeed brilliantly. Some are geniuses, some are near geniuses. The rigidity of autism, the narrowness of interest, the need for sameness: these same qualities can produce a miserably unhappy...child, or an isolated genius whose work will alter the world as we know it. The strange and bewildering disorder we know as autism can move a person either way."*

As I put the book down, fireworks begin going off in my brain. I sit motionless in my living room. It feels like my head is exploding with information. Many dots connect to paint one obvious picture: Andrew is autistic in some form that I don't understand.

I don't have much experience with autism, not with anyone I've been close to anyway. It's my thirteenth year teaching cosmetology in the high school system. Eleven of those years have been spent working specifically with students who have various learning disabilities. I've met many students diagnosed as autistic throughout the years. But those students have never taken my class. Cosmetology is pretty much the most social trade there is, as it involves working on clients. Naturally, this will not be appealing to them in most cases.

As I sit and ponder, I don't know what to do with myself.

The thought of calling Andrew pops in my mind, but instinctively I know better. This isn't something I can just blurt out to him. I'll really have to research and think about it further to come up with a planned approach. Also, calling him at 3 a.m. on a workday would really throw off his routine, a terrible idea in itself.

Is there any way I could be wrong about this? It seems highly unlikely. There are qualities in the chapter that Andrew does not possess, but he has most of them.

For nearly an hour, I sit and process what I just read. Researching further is what I feel like doing, but my brain is already overloaded with more than enough new information.

I'm restless, so I keep picking up the book to read a few things I've highlighted, then I put it back down again.

Then, I notice something. It's a blue sticker on the side of the book. It's slightly worn out, so I have to bring it closer to my face to see what it says.

It's not often that I laugh out loud when I'm alone, but this is one of those moments. I burst into laughter as I read, "Clearance, four dollars."

That's the best four dollars Andrew's ever spent, I think to myself. I cannot stop laughing, not just because it's funny but because I'm relieved. So much about being with Andrew makes me happier than I've ever been. But there are also things that frustrate me to no end. Gaining perspective and understanding where these things are coming from feels like a possible solution to many of our problems.

Further Research into Autism

The next few days are a whirlwind as I attempt to cram as much knowledge into my brain as possible. I order five books off of Amazon that are related to autism and start stalking Pinterest pins. Pinterest is pretty foreign to me, so I'm pleasantly surprised when I easily find many helpful pins and small articles.

The first pin I find reads – Asperger's syndrome[3]
Children and Adults with Asperger's syndrome might:

- Have a hard time understanding body language
- Avoid eye contact
- Want to be alone; or want to interact but not know how to
- Have narrow, sometimes obsessive, interests
- Talk only about themselves and their interests
- Speak in unusual ways or with an odd tone of voice
- Have a hard time making friends
- Seem nervous in large social groups
- Be clumsy or awkward
- Have rituals they refuse to change, such as a very rigid bedtime routine
- Develop odd or repetitive movements
- Have unusual sensory reactions

That last point makes me feel like an absolute jerk. Sensory issues? All this time, I've been teasing Andrew about how picky he is with clothes, and it's an actual sensitivity he has. Oh man, do I feel terrible.

This pin makes me research sensory issues further. The "Autistic Echoes" chapter didn't say much about them. Google teaches me a lot on the subject. I learn that sensory issues related to autism could include sight, sound, taste, smell, touch, and body awareness. Understanding what body awareness means is a challenge for me, but I know it likely explains why I hate giving Andrew massages because he can't tell if he is enjoying them or not.

Andrew loves his noise-canceling headphones and is often complaining about things smelling bad (including me on occasions) when I don't notice a smell. He is so picky about airflow and temperature that he packs our portable air conditioner for weekend getaways just in case our Airbnb doesn't have one. It hardly fits in my car, but Andrew insists. Sometimes, he forgets to take his sunglasses off inside.

---

[3] Asperger's syndrome is no longer the term used. People are now considered autistic. With the understanding that autism presents as a large spectrum.

I mention it to him, and he says he wants to leave them on. Is that because of light sensitivity? Does everything sound louder to him? And feel scratchier on his skin?

More fireworks go off in my head. OF COURSE...all of his senses are heightened! He's not just being difficult. This is something I can now understand and work with.

Many of Andrew's traits have been confusing to me, so I've already begun taking notes. This week I've added several traits to the list.

There is no doubt in my mind that Andrew is autistic, but I still need to decide how I will approach him about it.

After some deliberation, I decide that if I'm going to approach Andrew about something I think he has, I better decide what I think I have. Or at least what I'm the closest to having. If I'm going to ask him to learn more about himself, it's only fair that I venture down the same path. We are a team, and the better we understand ourselves, the stronger we will be to support each other throughout life.

Before bringing anything up to Andrew, I'm going to finish *Shadow Syndromes*. It seems like the logical thing to do. It'll give me time to digest the information and make sure I don't miss anything. It'll also give me time to figure out more about myself, which is the whole reason I decided to read it in the first place.

Learning about Myself

The chapter I relate to most is about women who are hypomanic. It's a milder form of bipolar. There is a chapter about a woman named Mary Ellen, "The Mad Housewife," that I feel is the most similar to me. In the book, they describe her as being *"at risk for becoming manic-depressive."*

She explains the following: *"I think I had mildly manic episodes in college, where I'd stay up all night and memorize whole books—entire books—and then write wonderful essays. I'd be wide awake, and I didn't have to take drugs to stay awake the way all my friends did when they needed to pull an all-nighter. The deadline would just suddenly hit me out of the blue, I'd be up all night, get A's on the exams, and the essays I stayed up for. It was a weird way to go to school. The aftermath would be exhaustion, and I would get sick after finals. And the material was just in short-term memory; I'd forget everything I've learned."*

Mary Ellen's story sounds similar to my high school days. Stimulants were never something I needed to pull all-nighters, and I pulled them often. Memorizing entire books is not in my skill set, but I can easily learn all I need to in one evening to ace a test. Information never sticks with me for long, but I've hardly failed any tests in my life.

Mary Ellen talks about how she will all of a sudden feel the need to paint the entire house. She will unpack two closets, rearrange the furniture in all the rooms, and have the house painted in twenty-four hours by herself without sleeping. My first thought is, *Yup, I've been there.*

"The soaring self-confidence, the quick-wittedness, the flirtatiousness, the lack of sleep: these are all signs of a hypomanic episode. And, like most hypomaniacs, Mary Ellen felt suffused with purpose and drive." This really sticks out to me, feeling a purpose. Whenever I feel a surge of energy to do something, I will be overwhelmed with purpose and the feeling of "it's meant to be."

Mary Ellen feels familiar on many levels. Packing my schedule to the max while hardly sleeping is my go-to lifestyle choice. Soaring confidence would be all I felt while booking a bunch of martial arts competitions, only to question myself later as to how I could possibly fit them all in. It felt like such a high to be able to take on so much, but there was always an inevitable crash. The aftermath was usually quite the dumpster fire and not worth the accomplishments. Yet, I kept repeating this pattern until concussions forced me to stop.

Balance is tough for me to achieve; I suppose it is because it feels somewhat boring. At my high points, I felt like I was on top of the world, chasing ambitious goals. At my low points, I struggled to look in the mirror or leave the house. The rush was something I needed and craved, and it was damn near impossible for me to sit around and do nothing until I was forced to.

Seasonal depressive disorder is also something I relate to in the book, which is another very mild form of bipolar. The more I think about it, the more it makes sense that many in my family could be somewhat manic-depressive or bipolar. There aren't many diagnosed, but that's mainly because they cope with alcohol rather than therapy. I write down some notes that I believe to be true about myself and pair them with my notes about Andrew.

It's been nearly two weeks since I've read the "Autistic Echoes" chapter, and I now feel ready to approach Andrew about it.

For those of you who are curious to see them, I've included the notes I wrote about Andrew in the back of the book.[4] Many of those notes are likely to make you say, "That's all men" or, "So many people are like that," and of course, you'd be right. Many people have these traits, but the severity of which I observed them in Andrew was quite a bit higher than I had previously observed in any one person.

Approaching Andrew

On social media, I frequently get asked how nervous I was to approach Andrew about possibly being autistic. The truth is, I wasn't overly nervous. People are usually surprised to hear that. He would have a lot of questions, so I made sure to be well prepared, but I wasn't nervous. Andrew and I are no strangers to talking about therapy, mental breakdowns, and needing professional help from time to time. Life is going to throw some nasty curveballs at you, and having support systems ready seems like the only logical choice for both of us.

We've had a few miscommunications, so Andrew is well aware that I'm struggling to understand certain things about him. Approaching him about a possible answer to our struggles seems exciting. I know that he won't feel attacked as I will also explore my own potential diagnosis of hypomania or mild bipolar.

The Big Moment

Andrew arrives for dinner at 5. The book is sitting on the table with my notes inside. After he sits down, I get right to the point.

"I just finished reading *Shadow Syndromes*, and I can't wait to talk to you about it."

---

[4] My notes about Andrew are in the Endnotes on page 331

Andrew looks enthused.

"A few of the chapters really stood out to me."

"Sounds good," Andrew replies, as he seasons his food.

"One chapter that really interested me was 'The Noisy Brain.' Do you remember reading it?"

Andrew nods with a smile and reaches for the book.

As he skims through it, he says, "I highlighted a few passages in this chapter. I feel like some of it applies to me, for sure."

We discuss "The Noisy Brain" chapter until we are finished eating.

As I clear our plates, I shift the conversation toward myself.

"The chapter I relate to most is about hypomania. It got me thinking that forms of manic depression or bipolar disorder may run in my family."

Andrew looks up at the ceiling for a moment and pauses before speaking. He nods his head as he answers, "Yeah, I suppose that could be true."

I continue, "I only know of one cousin that is diagnosed manic depressive, but I don't think anyone else has been to therapy to find out. It could help explain the heavy alcohol use."

As I begin putting our dishes in the dishwasher, I say, "I'm going to ask my doctor for a referral to see if I can get assessed. Some days I feel so down on myself I can hardly look in the mirror, and I'd love to understand why. At the very least, I'll learn more about the subject."

Andrew doesn't skip a beat as he answers, "That sounds great."

It seems fitting to wait until I'm done cleaning the kitchen to shift the conversation toward Andrew. This way, we'll be sitting down with no distractions.

Soon after we sit down, I lay it out there.

"The chapter that reminds me of you is called 'Autistic Echoes.' I wrote down some notes of the similarities between your traits and the things I learned in this chapter."

My entire body gets hot as I open my notes. Maybe I am a little nervous after all. I pause to give Andrew a chance to speak, but he says nothing.

Showing him my highlights from the chapter, I begin going over my notes. Andrew listens intently until I finish speaking. His body language leaves me no clues as to what he is thinking, but I'm used to this by now.

Once finished, I'm pleasantly surprised by how nonchalant Andrew is as he says, "You've made some valid points, and it sounds like it's a definite possibility. You've noticed things in this chapter that I missed."

His tone is as calm as ever; I'm impressed that he isn't getting defensive. Now is the perfect time for the speech I rehearsed all week in my head.

This is it. This is the big moment that can change everything.

As I begin my speech, I feel my tempo speed up and my pitch rise slightly. Suddenly I sound like a teenager who is trying to talk her way out of being in trouble.

"I would love for us to seek an autism diagnosis together. I think it could help us understand each other better. If you are autistic, it would help me take things less personally. Maybe you're not capable of expressing your feelings the way I've been wanting you to, and if I knew that, it wouldn't hurt me so much. I don't understand you, and to make our relationship work, I need to be able to understand you."

I pause to take a breath before continuing.

"I think if we both look into the more challenging aspects of ourselves and explore them, we can better support each other. If we do this together, it will make us a stronger team. Regardless of the outcomes, we will have a better understanding of the traits that cause us so much confusion. We could put the hard work in now and then benefit for the rest of our lives. It would help me better understand how I can make you happy and communicate with you. I really think having a diagnosis could help us. I'll book it and everything; you just have to come."

As soon as I am done talking, I need to take a deep breath in.

Andrew looks at me and says, "Yeah, I'm open to it. Make an appointment." Instantly, I know that I overdid my speech. Andrew didn't need nearly as much convincing as I anticipated.

"Really?" I ask. "I'm so happy you're up for it."

"Yeah, I'm up for it," Andrew replies. "I was diagnosed with ADHD as a child, but then my psychologist told me I'm not ADHD, so I've always kinda wondered."

"Great, I'll make the appointment," I reply with a smile.

This night couldn't have gone better. It feels like we are finally going to be building a more solid foundation for our relationship.

* * *

ANDREW'S TAKE

A few months before Michelle approached me about being autistic, I skimmed *Shadow Syndromes*. I highlighted many things throughout that book. Michelle had a great list of traits from the "Autistic Echoes" chapter that she noticed in me. I didn't mind when she approached me about it. It helped that I was very much in the mindset for self-discovery.

Michelle highlighted some points in *Shadow Syndromes* that I found interesting, and I couldn't deny the similarities.

"…cannot make small talk."
I've never enjoyed small talk. It feels weird.

"…monologuing, not allowing someone else to speak."
I love to talk and talk deeply and enthusiastically about an interesting topic. I try to tell if the person that I'm talking to is interested in what I'm talking about and then end the conversation if they seem uninterested. But if the person shows any interest, then I will push the conversation deeper and deeper. I truly love having a deep engaging conversation. When you get to have this kind of conversation with someone else who is also as interested as you are, it is one of the most entertaining things there is to do in life.

"…does not intuit hidden motives."
It takes so much mental energy to try to figure out someone's hidden motives.

"He experiences himself as an open book, and, in his dealings with other humans, he has only one option, to be honest."

Throughout my life, I have found it difficult to lie. I get an uncomfortable feeling inside, a tenseness. Because of this tension, I try to make sure the person I'm talking to has all the information and understands it well. This can cause problems because I will feel an urge to over-share. If I feel like I'm under-sharing, then I will get this tense feeling and be compelled to give more information.

"...literal-minded; they will typically interpret a question or a remark in its most concrete sense."
I struggle with this and feel as though I always will.

"...the need for sameness and routine, the limited interests, the repetitive behaviors."
I didn't realize how much I needed sameness and routine until Michelle brought it to my attention. When a rhythm gets interrupted, it causes me stress. At work, I was told to make sure my audible alarm was enabled for email. During the day, the office will send out emails, and they want you to respond right away. I can't do this. If I'm in the middle of repairing machinery, and my phone is going off two to twelve times an hour, I go crazy. When my mind is in a rhythm, and I hear a ring that derails my train of thought, it feels painful.

"...difficulty following social rhythm."
I've never been able to follow the social rhythm. Unless the social rhythm is to have fun, joke, and enjoy myself with other like-minded people, in this setting, it seems that I can thrive. Workplace social norms can be so hard to follow. Such as dealing with time pressure at work. Time pressure is such a hard thing for me to stop from taking so much of my mental energy.

"Visual thinking..."
When Michelle is explaining something to me, I can understand what she is saying the majority of the time. But this does not imply that it will stick, and I will be able to retain the knowledge that she's trying to explain to me. Pictures make so much more sense and they stick in my mind.

In 2008 I learned that I was misdiagnosed with ADHD as a child. This kept my inner journey alive and made me even more curious about who I am. Then in 2013, I had a bout with panic attacks. I was able to overcome this difficulty with the help of a psychologist.

It's great to look at this journey in a proactive way. Learning more about myself helps me understand how I can better help myself and Michelle.

I was up for learning more because I could see how much it would help us.

Also, Michelle mentioned that Shadow Syndromes was, "The best four dollars Andrew's ever spent." Well, to be clear, it was not four dollars. It was thirteen dollars. I ordered it as a used copy from Amazon. The four-dollar sticker is still on the book to this day.

* * *

Michelle Seeks an Adult Diagnosis

It's the following day, and I'm excited to get to work. Over my morning coffee, I book myself a doctor's appointment and then begin searching online for how to get an adult autism assessment. The first doctor who comes up in Calgary is Dr. Baker. His website explains that he specializes in adult autism diagnosis and that it is covered by Provincial Health Care (meaning it's free). There is an intake session coming up that I try to apply for, but it's full. I keep searching.

The other specialists I find online do not feel promising. They say that they offer adult diagnoses but that it can likely take 10–14 sessions. Andrew and I both have health coverage, but we would still be looking at around $3,000–$4,000. That's a lot of money, but it isn't so much the money that bothers me. The way I see it, this is an investment into our future.

The lack of enthusiasm I feel from the professionals toward doing the assessment is what disappoints me. Not one person I call seems eager to diagnose Andrew. I'm excited about this, and I want the professional providing the assessment to have somewhat of the same enthusiasm. Over the next hour, my continued searches online don't find any promising prospects.

Just as I begin to lose hope, I notice that the Autism Calgary Association is located fifteen minutes from my condo. Baxter needs a walk, so I figure I'll drive down there to ask questions on my way to the dog park.

As I pull up to the Autism Calgary Association, the parking lot is pretty much empty. I'm greeted by a girl at the front desk as I walk in. She has beautiful long red hair and funky thick-framed glasses that suit her well.

"What can I do for you?" she asks in a friendly tone.

"I'm looking for information on how to receive an adult autism diagnosis," I reply.

"Is it for yourself?" she asks.

"No, it's for my boyfriend."

"We don't perform those here, but Dr. Baker does, and he works alongside us." She hands me his card with a large smile on her face. "Dr. Baker performed my diagnosis, and I really enjoyed talking to him. He's also autistic and is extremely knowledgeable on the subject."

Recognizing his name, I reply, "Yes, I tried to sign up for an intake session on his website, but it was full."

She lets out a mild sigh. "Yeah, Dr. Baker's intake sessions often fill up in one day, and he only holds two or three per year."

My enthusiasm begins to dwindle.

"Do you know anyone else in Calgary who specializes in adult diagnosis?" I ask eagerly.

"I'm not sure if there's anyone else, but you can check the Autism Calgary website," she replies.

It's obvious from her tone that I'll be hard-pressed to find anyone else.

I thank her and go on my way.

As I get in my car, there is no doubt in my mind that Dr. Baker is the guy for Andrew. Getting an appointment with him is my mission. Over the following days, performing daily checks on Dr. Baker's website becomes as natural as having my morning coffee.

Weeks pass before there is any change, but one morning I click to find a new advertisement on the home page. My face lights up as I read the words, *New intake session in February 2019, registration opens in November.*

To get into this intake session, I will have to be clever. November is weeks away. This gives plenty of time for people to see this registration opportunity, and it makes me nervous.

As I mark the date in my day planner, I realize it's the same day we are flying to Ontario on the red-eye to visit Andrew's family.

Perfect, I think to myself. *I'll just stay up all night and keep refreshing the website until I can click "sign up." I'll make sure I'm first.'*

My plan feels solid. Now, all we have to do is wait for November.

Rewind to when we first met…

FRIENDSHIP

Many of us repeat the same patterns and mistakes over and over, hoping for a different result. We all know this doesn't work (intellectually, at least). But that doesn't mean we are capable of shifting gears.

Me, well, I was making the obvious mistake of chasing that tingly feeling. You know the one. That initial feeling when you meet someone, and you get butterflies because you feel so attracted to them. You have a certain nervousness that flows through your body as you interact with each other, and it feels exciting.

As it turns out, I would say that the feeling I was chasing is, in fact, a red flag to run away and date someone else if you want something long-lasting. Feeling nervous around someone is your body's natural way of warning you that you are in danger of being hurt. That tingly feeling is lust, and it often blinds us to making horrible life choices. It is impossible to be yourself around someone who makes you nervous or look at them objectively.

Life was smart to disguise my partner as a friend. This allowed me to be my authentic self without overthinking everything like I usually do when I'm dating. I had zero hesitation in saying exactly what I was thinking around Andrew from the very first day I met him. Without trying to, I broke my pattern and found something authentic.

This section is all about our friendship and how it slowly grew into something I never expected. Most of us assume we know what we are looking for in a partner, but what if life knows better than we do? I know this was the case for me. I never imagined myself having a friendship that would unexpectedly and slowly blossom into love. I always assumed that when I met my person, I would know immediately.

Boy, when I'm wrong, I'm wrong. And thank goodness I was.

2
A LUCKY SWIPE RIGHT

It's the end of March 2017, and I'm spending my spring break visiting my good friend Jackson in Puerto Vallarta, Mexico. Jackson and I met in grade 8 and immediately bonded. I was attracted to his chocolate skin, killer dance moves, sexy smile, and sense of humor. We dated for forty-eight hours and shared a few passionate french kisses before he dumped me in a voicemail, telling me he'd rather be friends. Fast-forward to today, and we are still close. Only now we share a similar taste in men.

Jackson is one of my favorite humans. He's one of those people that gets along with everyone because he's always fun to be around. I was sad when he and his boyfriend Caleb decided to move to Mexico for two years to switch things up. I've missed him dearly. They are only months away from moving back to Calgary, and I have finally fulfilled my promise to come visit. It's six weeks shy of my thirty-third birthday, and I haven't been in a serious relationship since the age of twenty-six. Rather than love, my life is filled with travel and martial arts competitions. I currently have a crush on an Olympian I've been in talks with since Christmas Eve, and I'm optimistic about our connection.

Caleb is Jackson's boyfriend of five years, and I've never spent much time with him. Caleb is shy in group settings, and previous to this trip, I had only met him in large groups while we were in Calgary. On this trip, we bonded while Jackson was at work. It's been fantastic to gain a new friend who is a great listener and an even better tour guide.

I've always known it would take a special man to get Jackson to settle down. Caleb is that and then some. He looks like he stepped off a *GQ* magazine cover, is good at pretty much everything, and yet he resists the spotlight. I have no idea how someone with such a solid jawline can come across as timid, but that's just Caleb's style. He wears it well, and it is somehow the basis for his charisma. Caleb is athletic, speaks Spanish, and can decorate a cake as well as any professional, yet he remains humble. He has a quiet charm to him that is a rare find in this world.

This trip to Mexico is exactly what I need to help me unwind in between my kickboxing fights. So far, it's been filled with delicious tacos, belly laughs, and nights out clubbing. Jackson and Caleb are by far my favorite people to go clubbing with. They are fantastic dancers and always know where the good music is playing.

Puerto Vallarta is filled with ridiculously good-looking gay men. And when I say good-looking, I mean downright gorgeous. This is a new experience for me. I have never been in a bar so full of scrumptious bottoms and chiseled abs. It's been fun to enjoy the eye candy while busting a move on the dance floor. A buff guy pinches my ass at one point and tells me I'm beautiful. It is the most action I've had this entire trip, and I'm completely okay with it.

THE TRIP TAKES AN INTERESTING TURN

While out for a walk, I see a kickboxing poster near Jackson's place. The IKF logo is one I recognize. It stands for International Kickboxing Federation. I have two title belts with the same logo.

I competed at the IKF world classic in Orlando, Florida, three years in a row. When I returned to defend my title for the second time, my opponent pulled out at the last minute. The IKF officials felt terrible that I had traveled all that way for nothing, so they tried to make it up to me. They put me through judge training so I could judge some of the fights that weekend, and I was grateful to learn from some of the best. Through this experience, I became friends with many of the officials.

Finding an IKF poster in Mexico seems odd. I have never even seen one in Canada before. I take a selfie with the poster and upload it to Facebook.

Within the hour, I'm receiving multiple messages from IKF officials telling me to go meet the chairman of the IKF in Mexico. Minutes later, I get a friend request from him, along with an invitation to meet for lunch at his pub tomorrow. Jackson and Caleb have to work, so I accept his invitation. I'm not one to turn down opportunities, as I believe they present themselves for a reason.

When Jackson returns home from work, I tell him about my afternoon.

"So I had an interesting day. I took a picture with a kickboxing poster and put it on Facebook. Now I'm going for lunch tomorrow with the chairman hosting the event."

"Oh, we kind of know him," Jackson chuckles. "He owns the hotel down the street and the pub you're going to. We are friends with his son."

"Small world," I reply. "That's so random."

"Yes, that is random. They are a nice family; you'll enjoy lunch," Jackson explains, "It's a nice pub."

The IKF chairman and I meet at his pub the following afternoon.

It turns into a three-day ordeal. He has friends in town for the Muay Thai event. He plans to take them on a road trip tomorrow to show them "the real Mexico," as he likes to call it. He offers to take me as well, and I jump at the opportunity.

Three gentlemen in their fifties and I embark on a road trip through Mexico. We drive over an hour outside of Puerto Vallarta to go eat some crawdads. We have a blast listening to classic rock while sharing our life stories. The entire drive there, no one will tell me what a crawdad is, and I don't have data to look it up. All they keep saying is, "The food is so fresh it's being caught as you order it. This is the real Mexico."

Upon arrival, I learn that crawdads resemble small lobsters, and they are tasty.

After a delicious lunch, we do some sightseeing. Then we are off to the press conference and the weigh-ins for the fights. For those of you who aren't familiar with the sport, weigh-ins typically take place the evening before the fights. This gives the fighters time to eat, rest, and rehydrate after their weight cut.

THE WEIGH-INS

Once we arrive at the weigh-ins, the chairman introduces me to the fighters before I go take my seat. There are tables full of boxing gloves and trophies, along with a large assortment of snacks. I'm impressed at how large and well-organized this event is. Many of the fighters' family members have come down to support them, and there are television cameras.

The weigh-ins are in Spanish, so after a while, it becomes tough for me to pay attention.

While enjoying some chicken wings, I text Jackson, *Hey, the day is running long so it's looking like I won't be back for dinner. Let me know if you guys decide to head out and I'll meet you.*

After I hit send, I start devouring a chicken wing.

Mid chicken wing, I start getting multiple elbow taps from the man beside me.

I look up to realize that the room has gone completely silent, and all eyes and cameras are on me.

The chairman had introduced me as "the Canadian champion," who will be an honorary guest at the fights. This was announced in Spanish. I'm oblivious.

Everyone is expecting me to stand up and smile while everyone claps. Instead, I am completely buried in my phone eating chicken wings (palm to face).

In an attempt to redeem myself, I stand up, take a bow, smile, and wave at the room. The chairman continues to talk about me, but I have no idea what he's saying. The crowd is surprisingly kind, giving me a huge round of applause.

After I sit down, I look at the man beside me. "Was that as bad as I think it was?" I ask.

"Yeah." He smiles as he doesn't spare my feelings. "The only way it could've been worse is if there would've been an actual chicken wing stuck to the side of your face as you stood up."

"Also, just so you know," he laughs and points at the cameras, "all of these cameras are broadcasting nationally, so half of Mexico just saw that."

"Fantastic," I reply.

I'm so embarrassed that I can't wait to get out of here. I text Jackson, *Actually, I'm on my way now,* and I leave without finishing my chicken wings.

As I walk back to Jackson's, I'm telling myself that the embarrassment will wear off by the time of the fights the next day.

Fights on the Beach

As I arrive at the Muay Thai fights on the beach, I notice the chairman has reserved a seat front and center for me. I take my seat and enjoy the view. Seven o'clock comes and goes, and the fights haven't started yet.

Eventually, the chairman comes to say hello, "Hello, nice to see you. Sorry we can't start, one of our judges is late. We haven't heard from him, so we are not sure when he is coming."

The chairman seems worried as he looks at me and jokes, "I wish you could be a judge."

I chuckle and say, "Well, I did take the judge's training in Orlando with the IKF."

He cracks a huge smile. "Are you serious? They trained you to judge?"

"Yes, for the world classic. Is it the same?" I ask.

Things shift quickly. The chairman doesn't answer my question. Instead, his eyes light up as he walks away. He returns in minutes with a judge's shirt and introduces me to the other two judges.

"You seriously want me to judge?" I ask. "I don't speak Spanish."

"I'll have someone sit with you who can translate the form," he explains.

Before I know it, I'm sitting ringside with a pen in my hand. It's a televised event, so I'm as nervous as I am excited. There are twelve fights on the card, so I'm going to be here until well after midnight.

At intermission, the chairman comes to thank me.

"Thank you so much for judging," he says, "I'm going to try to find you an opponent so you can come back and fight on one of my cards sometime."

"Sounds fun to me, but at five foot ten, it's tough to find girls my size," I explain. "I'm a heavyweight."

"Oh, I'll find one," he says as he walks away. "Mexican girls love to eat."

Sweet, I think to myself. A paid trip to Mexico to fight on a beach? Yes, please!

The plan was to go meet Jackson and Caleb after the fights, but I'm too tired to go clubbing. Judging takes a lot out of you. I walk back to their place to relax and watch some Netflix on my computer. They come home drunk just after 2:30 a.m. Caleb makes us all food, and we enjoy some laughs at Jackson's expense. He's had a few more drinks than usual, and Caleb wants to make sure he eats enough and drinks some water.

"Tomorrow is your last day, right?" Caleb asks after he escorts Jackson to their bedroom.

"Yes, I need to be at the airport by 5 p.m.," I reply.

"How about we have a late lunch around two before you leave?" Caleb suggests as he brushes his teeth.

"Sounds perfect," I reply. "Goodnight."

As I crawl back into bed, I am feeling particularly lonely. It's been an amazing week in so many ways. But sometimes it's even tougher to be alone when you are happy. Jackson and Caleb are the perfect match; it's rare to see two people click as they do. It makes it a little harder for me to be alone tonight. I want what Jackson and Caleb have, and it seems as if it's drifting further and further away from me.

When I got here, I was optimistic about a new love on the horizon, but I have hardly heard from my Olympian crush all week. Even worse than that, his text messages are beginning to resemble small talk.

My Last Day in Mexico

After breakfast, I go for my last jog along the beach. The most important thing I do at the end of all my vacations is meditate and assess where I'm at emotionally before I begin the journey home. There is no better time to reflect than when you've had some time away from your usual routine. The clarity I need to make long-lasting changes often comes when I'm on an airplane, and I journal intensely at airports.

Until last night, I hadn't realized how lonely I've been feeling. At the start of this trip, I was telling Jackson all about my Olympian. Explaining how I had spent the previous three months thinking I was falling in love with him. We chatted long-distance, but it always felt as though he was with me. It was as if I had a best friend in my pocket at all times. My instant connection with him felt so strong that it convinced me he was "the one."

When I left Calgary, I was sure that things would eventually fall into place for us. But after a week of hardly texting, I'm beginning to question everything. He is still checking in from time to time, but he is no longer asking about my day like he used to. I think it's time to face the fact that our connection has faded.

After finishing my morning jog and meditation, I sit down on some rocks near the beach. Loneliness overwhelms me. Tears begin to flow down my cheeks and onto my chest as I watch the waves roll in. I want to reach out to my Olympian to see if I am right. Would he answer me right away? Or would it take a day or two? I take a selfie of myself sitting on the beach and send it to him. He immediately responds with, *You look so happy. You must've had a great trip.*

Something breaks inside me as I realize he doesn't know me at all. Happy!? How can he think I am happy? I'm yearning for the connection I felt with him that seems to keep dissipating further and further. There's an emptiness inside me, and I'm lonely.

Something about that text message makes me feel like we are never going to reconnect in the same way. This devastates me, but he is clueless. *Yes, it has been a fantastic trip,* I text back. I'm not ready to tell him the truth about how I'm feeling.

For weeks I have been telling myself that after his next competition we will reconnect and talk like we used to, but deep down I know he is slipping away.

When it comes to men I genuinely want to be with, I'm much too proud to be vulnerable. The Olympian never knows of the heartbreak he causes me. I suffer in silence, as I always have, expressing none of my pain, sadness, or fears to him.

After this exchange, I sit and cry for an hour, reflecting on the past few years and my patterns with men. I'm closing in on thirty-three and have not been in a meaningful relationship since my "almost marriage" at the age of twenty-six. I had thought things were different with the Olympian. We had such a powerful connection in the beginning and had opened up to each other in ways I hadn't thought possible. When we were talking daily, he was across the world, but it felt as though he were right beside me. Now, I feel alone. We are no longer connected; we are small-talking like strangers. He is still being polite, but I feel like an afterthought. I know this pattern. I know this pattern all too well.

Wanting to take some of my power back, I make a rash decision to put an online dating app on my phone. It's been months since I've put myself out there, and it's a big step in admitting that I'm giving up on the Olympian. It needs to be done now before I get off this beach.

As I set up my dating profile, I vow to break my pattern and try something new. This time has to be different. I have been meeting a certain type of guy for years, and it keeps leading me back to this same place. It's time to switch it up. No more intense chemistry that is bound to fizzle in three months. I'm over it, so over it. This time I will avoid charismatic athletes that I feel instantly attracted to and meet several other types of men. I vow to swipe right on the guys whose profiles don't look instantly appealing. It's time I try dating guys who are into things I've never tried before.

Yes, this will be fun, I think to myself. *If a guy looks as if he is my usual type, I'm not allowed to swipe right. I need to find a new type.*

I create my profile, having no idea that this small decision will soon change the course of my life. Once my profile is set up, I put my phone away, wipe my tears, and walk back to Jackson and Caleb's. It's nearly time for our final lunch before I catch the bus to the airport.

"So, I put a dating app back on my phone," I tell them over lunch.

They both laugh as they twirl their spaghetti.

"What? Giving up on the Olympian? You just spent the whole week talking about him," Jackson says in surprise.

"Yeah, I feel like he's drifting away. I could sense it this morning. I need to get over him," I explain.

"Well, that was fast," Caleb chimes in.

"Yeah, it just hit me this morning. I think he drifted away weeks ago, but I'm just now admitting it to myself," I respond.

"I really need to stop dating athletes," I continue. "I'm going to try dating guys that aren't my usual type."

Jackson smirks. "This should be interesting."

"It's the perfect time to experiment," I explain. "I'm starting my fight camp next week, and this will keep me entertained. If nothing else, it should at least give me some interesting stories to tell."

They both laugh and say, "Well, we look forward to updates."

After lunch, I hug Caleb goodbye, and Jackson walks me to the bus stop.

"I hate saying goodbye," I say as I give him a huge bear hug.

"I'll be back in Calgary in a couple of months," Jackson replies.

"I know, but I'll still miss you," I explain.

Once I board the bus, I open the dating app. It feels fun to be swiping again instead of waiting for text messages that are becoming less and less frequent.

The hour-long bus ride to the airport feels like ten minutes because I'm so entertained. Scrolling through profiles is such a fun way to pass the time while you are traveling by yourself.

It's a Match

Andrew is one of my first matches. His profile catches my attention with how genuine and honest he seems. It is obvious to me that he is a decent guy who is likely looking for a relationship. He has pictures of himself scuba diving in Thailand, so I can tell he also likes to travel.

Andrew's profile reads, "I've been told I'm an intelligent, confident, handsome man with my shit together. (Siri is too nice sometimes) Pros: Healthy lifestyle, snowboarder, I own a pair of rollerblades (don't judge me), travel, hike. Adventure. Cons: leaves the toilet seat up occasionally."

What Andrew wrote was adorable. I feel like I am not allowed to complain when he leaves the toilet seat up (which is all the time) because he disclosed it before we met.

Half the fun of online dating is talking about it, so I often took screenshots of men I planned on meeting or of profiles I wanted to make fun of later with friends. If it weren't for the screenshot I took, I would have completely forgotten what Andrew wrote on his profile. Don't worry, bestie, of course I'm going to show you his profile photos. There will be a treat waiting for you at the end of the chapter.

Thank goodness for screenshots. It excites me that one day I'll be sixty and still be able to look back at old pictures and remember random dating stories.

This next part is going to accentuate my shallow side. But remember, besties withhold their judgment. The truth is, Andrew is not the type of guy I would have ever swiped right on because of the way he dressed.

In one picture, he was wearing my least favorite sunglasses of all time. Those popular Oakleys from the '90s that have orange lenses. You know the ones; they are so thick-framed that they take up half of someone's face. They are called Oakley Juliets, and to me, they look like giant bottle caps.

To say they are "not my style" is an understatement. I think they are hideous. They instantly kill any chance a guy has of getting my attention. I mean, they were bad enough in the '90s, and it's 2017.

Naturally, I text pictures of Andrew to Jackson once I get to the airport. *Hey, thanks again for a fantastic trip. I already matched with a nice guy. He seems cute, but it's tough to overlook the glasses.*

Jackson immediately shares my disgust. "Yeah, cute, but you're definitely going to have to burn those sunglasses."

"I'm hoping it's an old picture," I reply. "Maybe he doesn't have them anymore."

I wish I could tell you that the glasses were my only turn-off, but they were just the beginning. In another picture from Andrew's profile, his pants are obviously too short. Another big no-no for me. He's also wearing a ball cap in two of the photos. I usually love a man in a ball cap, but not the way Andrew is wearing it. It's much too small for his head, the rim is bent in an awkward way, and it has a leather strap at the back that needs to be tightened. It reminds me of an elementary school kid's ball cap. It's not sexy.

Pre-Mexico Michelle would have most definitely overlooked Andrew's profile, but because of the promise I made to myself, I swipe right. He has everything I vowed I would start to look for. Kind eyes, an adventurous spirit, and a genuine demeanor. I take my experiments seriously, at least for the first two weeks after I start them. Sexy is no longer needed. In fact, I am trying to avoid it. After I swipe right, we are an instant match. It's on the Bumble app, which means I have to message first. Andrew is polite and easy to chat with.

Hi Andrew, how are you doing? I write.

I'm good. Nice to meet you Michelle. It's cool you're into martial arts, I'm into powerlifting, Andrew writes back.

It seems we both have a healthy addiction, LOL. What are you up to? I reply.

I'm just putting together an Ikea dresser, Andrew answers.

Ouch, that doesn't sound fun at all. So many pieces. I'm about to board a plane. I just spent spring break visiting friends in Mexico, I message back.

It's going really well, I saved so much because I'm doing the labor, he continues.

That's fun, must have been a great trip.

Well, good luck with that :) It was a fantastic trip, but I'm happy to be going home, I say.

Would you like to play squash sometime? Andrew asks.

Sure, sounds fun. I've only played twice many years ago, but I enjoyed it, I reply.

Great. I'll book us a court then. When is good for you? he asks.

Next weekend works. How's Saturday afternoon? I suggest.

I'll let you know once I reserve a court, Andrew texts. Followed by, *Have a safe flight.*

In my many years of online dating, no one has ever asked me to play squash. It feels refreshing. I like that we planned it so promptly.

We do not text much after we set the plan to meet. This is also refreshing, as he does not come across as needy or bored. Talking too much before meeting someone is not something I'm a fan of, as it's easy to build up unnecessary expectations. This is a mistake I've made one too many times. It's better to have little to no expectations when meeting someone new.

THE SQUASH DATE

As I get ready to meet Andrew, I feel exhausted. The first week of my fight camp has been tough, and I'm stressed about the twenty pounds I have to lose before my fight. All those street tacos in Mexico certainly didn't help this situation. On my way to play squash, I tell myself that no matter how the date goes, I am not spending time with him afterward. Rest and an Epsom salt bath is what I need. A night of good sleep is mandatory if I am going to make it through my next week of fight camp.

As I walk up to the squash court, I spot Andrew from a distance. He is exactly as I pictured him. He is well-groomed, pleasant-looking, and has a big smile on his face as he turns to greet me. As predicted, my first thought is, *Yup, not my type.*

He is wearing sports shorts that are pulled up just a little too high for my liking, and his socks are pulled up to his mid-calf even though he is wearing shorts. Ankle socks certainly would have been the wiser choice. He is also wearing safety glasses, and he immediately points out that he has brought a pair for me.

"I brought you a pair of safety glasses. I took a dodgeball to the eye and scratched my cornea. I always wear safety glasses now because you really don't want to take a ball to the eye," he explains as he hands them to me.

"Thanks," I say as I grab them and put them on. It takes quite a bit of willpower not to burst out laughing at that one.

Andrew is adorable and pleasant to talk to, but not the type of guy I typically date. I'm just going to say it... He looks like a nerd. His clothes are enough to send my attention toward the two cute guys playing on the court beside us. I have no idea if they are single or not, and I don't speak to them. But I keep glancing in their direction after I can sense that they notice me. They move in a certain way that gets my attention. They have that style that I always go for, as opposed to Andrew's nerdier style. It feels like they are more my rhythm.

There is a certain awkwardness that has always repelled me away from guys like Andrew. Maybe it's his nervousness or the way he stands upright, but it just doesn't feel sexy to me. To be fair, I'm not sure any nerds have ever tried all that hard to get my attention, but there is nothing about them that initially draws me in. I emphasize this because I want everyone to realize that there may be a fantastic potential relationship right under your nose that you don't notice for this very same reason.

"I brought my speaker so we can listen to music," Andrew says as I lace my court shoes.

"Perfect," I reply as we enter the court. "I love music." His muscular legs make it evident that he keeps active, and I know I'm in for a challenge.

Andrew puts his speaker down and turns it on. I'm pleasantly surprised when 90s music starts playing. I love the Counting Crows. As I look around the court, I'm expecting the rules of the game to come to me, but I'm at a loss.

"You'll need to explain the game," I say as I turn to Andrew. "I haven't played in years, and nothing is coming back to me."

Andrew explains the game to me in detail. He is respectful, knowledgeable, and patient. He even gives me some pointers.

"Okay, I think I got it," I say as I bob to the music in my safety glasses. "You can serve first."

Andrew serves and is quite good with his racket. Racket sports are not my forte. I'm often throwing the racket back and forth because I have never quite figured out which hand to use. Most people never notice this, but Andrew picks up on it pretty quickly.

"I think your other foot needs to be in front if you're holding the racket with your left hand," he says to me after he wins yet another rally.

"Thanks, I'll try that," I reply. "I write and throw with my left hand, but I play hockey, golf, and bat right-handed. I haven't quite figured out which hand is better to play with in racket sports. That's why I keep throwing it back and forth."

"Maybe try keeping it in your left hand, but switch your feet," Andrew suggests.

"Yeah, that makes sense. I'll try that," I reply. "I think I need to keep my right hand behind my back so I stop using it. I'm all over the place."

Andrew's suggestion helps a little, and I manage to win a few rallies. Andrew is by far the superior player. He is not the type to go easy on me or let me win, which I appreciate. He may have beaten me on the scoreboard, but I won in the smack-talk department. I love smack-talking during sports; it is half the fun. I'm happy I managed to dump a few in the corner that he couldn't get to.

"Shall we go for a swim?" Andrew asks as he wipes the sweat off his forehead.

"A swim sounds perfect," I reply as I attempt to catch my breath.

We pack our things and head toward the changing rooms.

"Meet you on the other side?" I ask as I head toward the women's locker room.

"Yup, see you there," Andrew says as he grabs a drink of water.

Once in the locker room, I go to the washroom, change into my swimsuit, lock up my things, and head toward the pool. Once I get to the other side, there's no Andrew.

Five minutes go by, and I'm confused. I don't feel like I was overly fast. As I look around the pool, I notice the large water slide. Memories of swimming here in my childhood come flooding back to me.

Another ten minutes go by.

I'm now pacing back and forth. I'm thinking to myself, *This guy takes the longest poops*. I consider putting my clothes back on and leaving the pool.

Finally, Andrew walks out of the locker room.

"What on earth were you doing?" I ask.

"Oh, I forgot my swim trunks, so I went to the front to buy some," Andrew explains.

"When I got to the till, I realized I forgot my wallet in my locker, so I had to go back to get it. There was a long line both times."

"Well, at least they are nice swim trunks," I say as I look him up and down. He looks much better in these ones than he did in his squash shorts. They are a little baggier and aren't pulled up as high.

"Yeah, I like them," Andrew says. "Shall we go swim in the waves?"

"Sure," I respond as we walk into the pool.

We swim in the waves and go on the waterslide a few times before retiring to the hot tub. We enjoy some impromptu laughs with a couple sitting across from us. It seems that Andrew enjoys random conversations with strangers as I do.

Once the couple leaves, I ask Andrew, "How long have you been single?"

"Ten months," Andrew replies.

"How long were you together?" I ask.

"Nine years," he answers.

This surprises me. You don't often hear that number from someone who's thirty-one, and it doesn't seem as though he is fresh out of a major breakup.

Once the Tarzan rope opens up, Andrew jumps out of the hot tub and runs toward it like a 5-year-old boy. He swings on the Tarzan rope and flips into the deep end a few times while I watch from the hot tub.

As I watch, I am confused by Andrew. I can usually feel a guy's attraction to me, or lack thereof, easily on a date. With Andrew, I have no idea if he is interested in me or not. I find him easy to chat with, but other than that, I have nothing to process. I simply cannot read him.

It is clear that he is a nice guy, but I feel no romantic attraction to him. A part of me is still holding out hope that I will reconnect with my Olympian crush, so Andrew doesn't really stand a chance, even if he were a good dresser. My heart is closed off.

Andrew is not the type of guy you want to hurt. If he does feel attracted to me, I want to be honest with him right from the start.

Before we leave the hot tub, I say to him, "You've basically been in one relationship your entire twenties. I think you should explore the dating world before you commit to another relationship. Maybe travel a little and see what's out there. Ten months isn't a long time to be alone after nine years with someone."

"Yeah, you're probably right," Andrew says with a small smirk on his face. "That makes sense."

"It's tough to know what you want before you explore what's out there," I continue.

Andrew nods in agreement.

"I'd be down for playing squash or hiking occasionally if you want to be friends. I can get my workouts in, and you can tell me about how your dates are going," I continue.

"Yeah, that sounds good," Andrew replies.

"I have unresolved feelings for a guy that's traveling, so I'm not looking for anything either," I continue.

Andrew seems relieved by my honesty and forwardness, but other than that, I cannot sense any kind of disappointment or emotion. Again, I find him impossible to read.

"Would you like to go watch the UFC with me tonight?" Andrew asks as we walk toward the changing rooms.

"Sure, " I reply, completely breaking the promise I made to myself about resting and staying away from food temptations. "There are some good fights lined up. I'm a huge Daniel Cormier and Patrick Cote fan."

We decide to each go home and shower, then meet at the Boston Pizza in between our two places.

WATCHING THE UFC FIGHTS

I arrive at Boston Pizza just as the fights are starting. When I walk in, Andrew is already sitting down at a table. I am impressed with his clothes as he is wearing a white long-sleeve shirt and jeans that fit him well. His hair seems longer and is all spiked up, which is a change from the afternoon. In an attempt to limit my calories, I order water and oven-roasted wings with veggies.

My roommate Gabriel and some training partners are a few tables over, also enjoying the fights. A few people I know are fighting on the card tonight. I have spent a few camps training at Tristar in Montreal, Quebec, and many of the fighters tonight are people I trained with there.

Andrew is asking lots of questions about the rules. He loves how much I can tell him about the fighters' strategies and who I think is going to win. We enjoy friendly conversation and good entertainment.

When the fights are over, we split the bill and walk outside toward our vehicles. What happens next is something I still tease Andrew about to this day. He shakes my hand with a big smile on his face and loudly says, "It was great to meet you. You have an awesome personality." It isn't so much what he says but the tone that he says it in that makes me laugh. He says it so loud and matter-of-factly, "YOU-HAVE-AN-AWESOME-PERSONALITY."

Then we hug before going our separate ways. As we hug, I realize that he smells good.

"Yes, this was fun. Let's hang out again soon, maybe go for a hike," I suggest as I wave goodbye.

"For sure," Andrew says. "See you soon."

As Andrew walks toward his truck, I notice how good his butt looks in his jeans. For a brief moment, I think to myself, *Oh, maybe I am attracted to him.*

As I drive home, I don't put much thought into meeting Andrew. The only thing on my mind is how I'm going to fit my entire to-do list in tomorrow, as well as training.

"How was your date?" my roommate Gabriel teases me when he gets home.

"Nice guy, but no attraction, really," I reply.

He chuckles and says, "Yeah, that's what it seemed like. We were all talking about it in between fights. It was just so funny to see you on a date."

Gabriel is a jiujitsu training partner who has been renting out my spare room for a few months. In my ten years of training martial arts at various gyms, I have never dated a single training partner. My gym is my safe place, so I present myself as one of the guys. This is important to me, especially being one of the only females on the mats.

"Everyone is going to be teasing you about your date tomorrow," Gabriel says as he heads off to bed.

"I'd expect nothing less," I reply back with a chuckle. "I'm sure it's weird for them to be seeing me on an actual date."

MICHELLE AND ANDREW PRESTON

* * *

ANDREW'S TAKE

Since my nine-year relationship, before meeting Michelle on Bumble, I had only gone on a few dates. A few months prior to this, I was on Tinder and had one of my first "friends with benefits" relationships. These kinds of relationships are exhausting. Trying not to "catch feelings" with someone is hard. Having sex with someone frequently and not developing feelings for them is a paradox.

Once Michelle and I matched on Bumble, I thought to myself, *She has some interesting martial arts photos and a great big smile on her face. Seems like a really interesting person. I'd like to meet her.* Once we began talking, it wasn't long before I asked her on a date. An uncommon date. A squash date. I like inviting people to do activities that I find fun. When I first saw her, I was greeted with a warm smile and friendly nature.

The squash game went well, or as well as it could, considering it was Michelle's second time ever playing squash. I made sure to bring extra eye protection for Michelle. This is because I've worked in the oil field and currently have a dangerous(ish) job. Plus, I've been hit in the eye with a dodgeball. I didn't want her to suffer a detached retina on our first date.

After squash, we went for a swim. We were in the hot tub when I realized THE TARZAN ROPE IS OPEN! I wanted to impress Michelle, time to show off my stuff. In my mind, I hoped to look spectacular, but in reality, I was probably average at best. Although I did nail one backward dive from the Tarzan Rope. *Dusts off left shoulder.*

Michelle was into MMA, and I knew there was an exciting UFC event later that night. During this time in my life, I enjoyed watching these competitions. Because of my powerlifting background, I really respect athletic competitions where athletes spend two months of hard training for one day of competition. I was grateful to watch the UFC with Michelle and be able to ask her questions and listen to her perspective.

While watching the fights, we chatted quite a bit. I was captivated by how Michelle spoke about herself, her experiences, traveling, MMA training, life, the future, and me. It quickly occurred to me that Michelle had a special gift. This gift can be best described as the embodiment of the word providential. Fortunate as if through divine intervention.

How special and rare to meet someone who has this gift. I knew that I wanted to be friends with her, but I also felt I wasn't in her league. There were still many things that I had to work out in my life. I needed to regain my confidence and recover from my recent breakup. Michelle even told me that I should not be dating and that I should be traveling and gaining new experiences while I was healing. She was right.

As the night ended and we were parting ways, I really wanted to let her know how special I thought she was. I did what made the most sense to me, and I told her, "You have an awesome personality," then I shook her hand. I meant it. I truly meant it. Turns out this was a very unique way of ending a nice evening.

At the end of the night, Michelle told me that she wanted to stay in touch. At that moment, I felt special, knowing a great new friendship was forming. Even if we would become just friends, I was already grateful.

* * *

Photos for Chapter 2
Bellamimalifestyles.com/bookphotos

3
FRIENDSHIP BEGINNINGS

Our First Hike

Two weeks later, Andrew and I plan our second activity. The plan is to go for a hike on Saturday morning. Andrew ends up running behind, so we decide to walk around Fish Creek Provincial Park in Calgary instead of making the eighty-minute drive out to the Rocky Mountains.

I'm taken aback once I see him. Out of all the clothes I've seen him in, this outfit takes the cake.

I'll start from the ground up because I want you to fully experience it...piece by horrid piece. His shoes are brown and quite worn out. They are not runners or hiking shoes. They kind of look like clunky old work shoes that are no longer fit to be worn in public. The laces are tied so tight that it causes a slight curve upward toward the toe, making it look like they are too big. Just above his shoes, you can see his gray socks. They are thick and slightly bunched up around the ankles.

You might be wondering why I can get such a good view of his socks. Well, that, my friend, is because his pants are two inches too short. And what are these pants, you ask? Prepare yourself. They are stonewashed jeans. Yes, that's right, stonewash jeans. They wouldn't be overly terrible if they were long enough for him or if they were paired with a half-decent shirt. The one thing they do have going for them is that they make his butt look good, but any pants could make Andrew's butt look good.

This brings me to the worst part: the T-shirt. He is wearing the ugliest shirt. The only reason anyone should be wearing a shirt like that is if they are about to do some painting. It is orange, or at least it used to be before it got so faded. It is too short for his frame and is so worn out that there are a few small holes in it near the armpit. There are remnants of a label that used to be written across the chest, but it is tough to make out what it says. It has clearly been washed more times than anyone could count.

It is a grave injustice for a good-looking powerlifter to have such unfashionable clothes draped over his obviously muscular frame.

Okay, enough about the outfit.

Just give me a minute to get that out of my mind so I can tell you about the rest of the afternoon.

Deep breath...exhale...moving on.

As Andrew pulls up to my condo, I grab my dog Baxter and head outside to meet him. Baxter is my Yorkshire terrier who weighs five pounds and looks like a black and brown teddy bear. It's a sunny day in Calgary, and the smell of spring is in the air. It's the perfect day for a walk.

Andrew gets out of his truck and comes around the passenger side to clear some papers off the front seat to make room for me to sit. He drives an old 2001 white Toyota Tundra that he has put a lot of work into, so it runs perfectly. It feels like a tradesman's truck through and through.

Andrew leans the passenger seat forward to make some space in the back to put Baxter's dog carrier. As I hop in the front seat, I notice those hideous gray Oakleys with orange lenses on his dashboard. The sunglasses that I hoped were no longer in his possession.

After securing Baxter in the back, Andrew walks around the truck and gets in the driver's seat. He immediately picks up the sunglasses and puts them on his face...further solidifying his friend status. They look even worse in person than they did on his Bumble profile. How is this possible?

Andrew has gotten a haircut since I met him to play squash. It is not a bad haircut, but it is quite short, nearly a buzz cut. Having less hair really adds a bigger spotlight to the fashion disaster that takes up half his face. Andrew has fantastic hair, so to buzz it all off seems like such a crime.

On our way to the park, Andrew earns some serious bonus points for his driving skills. Not enough to take my mind off his outfit, but certainly enough to soften the blow. I care more than the average person about how someone conducts themselves behind the wheel. It can be an instant deal-breaker for me if someone is always in a hurry, tailgating, or has any inkling of road rage. Driving is a point of anxiety for me, having been in quite a few car accidents as a passenger. In my twenties, my friends often made fun of me when I complained about their driving habits. "Put Grandma in the back seat," they would say.

Fish Creek Park is a thirty-minute drive away, and I feel at ease with Andrew behind the wheel. He is relaxed, drives the speed limit, and leaves plenty of distance between us and other cars. I love his driving; he couldn't be any more perfect at it.

The three of us begin our walk around Fish Creek Provincial Park. I ask Andrew about his upbringing, having no idea I'm about to get an interesting story.

"I was adopted by a Japanese family when I was little," Andrew explains.

"You don't hear that every day," I respond. "How did that happen?"

"My mom broke up with a Japanese man around the time she got pregnant with me, then she dated another man briefly. When she was pregnant, no one knew who the father was," Andrew begins his story as I listen intently.

"The day I was born, my mom's ex-boyfriend and his Japanese family were waiting at the hospital, hoping I'd come out Japanese. I would be their first and only grandson, and they were really excited. Even though I came out with blonde hair and blue eyes, they still babysat me a lot and treated me as their own," Andrew continues.

"That's adorable," I chime in.

"Yeah, they really spoiled me, and I loved being at their place. I had four adults just showering me with attention and presents. When I was three years old, I threw my wagon at my mom and told her I wanted to go live with them, and she let me. She was struggling to take care of me; she didn't have any family to help her."

"Wow, that was brave of her. Did she stay in your life?" I ask.

"Yup. She was around on holidays, and we would talk on the phone," Andrew answers.

"At Christmas time, there would be an entire living room full of presents around the tree, and they were almost all for me," Andrew continues.

"Ha, that's hilarious," I interject. "My life was the opposite of that. I was raised a Jehovah's Witness, so my family didn't celebrate holidays. I left home at fifteen because my dad and brother are alcoholics, and I was most definitely not spoiled."

"OMG, you didn't get Christmas?" Andrew asks in a surprised tone. "That's so sad."

"That's all I knew, so it didn't seem like a big deal, really," I respond. "We never had holidays or birthdays. I was used to it."

Conversation easily flows back and forth between us while Baxter leads the way on the trail. Andrew expresses how much he hated school and what led him to choose his HVAC trade. I explain how I left home at fifteen, ended up working in cosmetology, and a little bit about my job in the education system. We walk for a couple of hours and embrace Mother Nature.

Andrew's random knowledge of birds and plants impresses me as he points things out I would never notice. We discuss how much he loves powerlifting and my love of martial arts. We end up climbing a tree and sitting in it for a while to give our legs a break. It's refreshing to sit amongst the branches and enjoy the view. We manage to carry Baxter up there with us, making it even more enjoyable. It's been many years since I climbed a tree. Something about Andrew brings out the child in me.

Opening up to Andrew feels effortless. He feels like such a safe space. I do tend to be an oversharer when it comes to my life, but not usually with men, and never this quickly after meeting them. Something about Andrew feels different, nonthreatening. My inability to read him makes it easy to open up without feeling the judgment of his reactions.

The fact that I don't have a crush on him and that we don't know any of the same people are also factors. Telling Andrew the facts of my past comes naturally, even the traumatic parts, because I don't overanalyze anything for once. I'm more myself with him than I am even with my psychologist, and I've been talking to him for years.

One of the more refreshing aspects about Andrew is that he doesn't seem to gossip or complain about other people. He tells me the facts of his story as they happened, without any interpretation of how he wished it had been. Without making judgments on the actions of others.

Patterns like this tell you a lot about a person. People who place blame away from themselves as they tell stories or make a point to make others look lesser-than are not my type of people. They lack the self-awareness needed to see their part in the negative aspects of their life. I can easily feel when people are trying to get me on their side, as they need the support to feel validated. It's an instant red flag for me not to get close to that person.

Even as we speak briefly of his past relationship, Andrew doesn't feel the need to vent or convince me he was wronged in any way. He tells me the details in such a way that I feel zero resentment toward his ex-fiancée.

"We dated for nine years, we were engaged for four, but never did get married. We broke up briefly in 2009 but got back together after a month and a half. Our final breakup was ten months ago, and we are selling the acreage that we own together to split the profits. It just wasn't working out for many reasons."

Andrew never makes a single comment to allude to her character or place any blame on her end. I am intrigued as it is nearly impossible to find a man who exudes this quality. In my many years of online dating, I have only come across a select few, and they have all been older than me, much older.

On our drive home from Fish Creek Park, Andrew asks, "Do you want to work out and play squash at the leisure center again next week? It has a gym upstairs with a heavy bag, so you can get your workout in."

"Sure, sounds great," I reply. "How's Thursday?"

"Thursday it is," Andrew answers. "I'll book us a court."

When Thursday rolls around, we meet at the leisure center as planned. After Andrew kicks my butt at squash, we head upstairs to the gym. I show Andrew how to throw some combos with the boxing mitts, and he puts me through a core workout. Andrew has a little bit of boxing experience, so it is fun to hold pads for him and show him some new tricks. I've always hated core workouts and have no problem verbally expressing this while I'm holding a bridge pose or any other core exercises. Andrew is amused by my obvious disgust for what he is making me do, but through my complaining, I reiterate that I know I need to do it.

We enjoy pleasant conversations and laugh much like the first time we met. My squash skills are improving a little each game, so our rallies are getting more competitive and enjoyable.

As we leave the leisure center, Andrew turns to me and says, "I'm having a bunch of friends over for a bonfire next Saturday because I finally sold my acreage. You should come."

"I'll swing by as long as my fight camp is going well and my weight keeps dropping," I answer back as I get in my car.

Bonfire at Andrew's Acreage

When the day of the bonfire rolls around, I am still not sure if I am going to bother making the thirty-minute drive out to Andrew's acreage. I have plans to go for a bike ride that afternoon, so I am going to see how tired I am afterward.

Mary, my bike-ride companion, and I met on Kijiji when she applied to be my roommate. We had only hung out twice before. She ended up getting her own place but asked me to hang out as she was new to the city. We enjoy our afternoon bike ride as we explore downtown Calgary. We stumble upon a new rooftop venue that has tables available, so we decide to go for lunch.

Over our lunch, Mary tells me all about a guy she just started dating, and I tell her about my various past heartbreaks and online dating adventures.

"I've been hanging out with this guy named Andrew. He's fun to do stuff with, but it's not romantic," I explain. "He's having a bonfire tonight. Do you want to come with me? I'll drive if you want to have a few drinks."

"Why would you bother hanging out with a guy you don't plan on dating?" Mary asks.

"When you've been single as long as I have, it's not always about a relationship," I answer. "Good company is hard to come by, especially for activities that don't involve booze or food."

"It just seems so weird to me. I would never waste time with guys I won't date," Mary replies.

"I suppose a little part of me is open to a romantic possibility with Andrew, but I don't think it's likely," I continue. "If he made a move, I'd feel it out, but I don't think he ever will. There's just something about him. I like spending time with him."

"Is it a large party?" Mary asks.

"I don't think so, but I'm not sure. I've never met any of his friends," I reply. "I'm just going to go for a couple of hours. I want to be in bed by eleven."

"Sure, I'm in," Mary says with enthusiasm.

I text Andrew: *Hey, I am going to come tonight with a friend. Do you need us to grab anything on our way?*

Yeah, if you could get the stuff to make Old Fashioneds, that would be great, Andrew replies.

Ok, do we need to bring snacks? I ask.

No, there is lots of food, Andrew replies.

I look at Mary. "Do you know how to make an Old Fashioned?"

"No," she replies as she grabs her phone, "but I can figure it out."

Once we finish lunch, we hop on our bikes and head back to my place to shower.

As it turns out, Old Fashioneds are not an easy drink to make. There are several ingredients, two of which we have never heard of. Mary and I end up having to go to three stores to find everything we need, and I spend seventy bucks.

As we drive out to Andrew's acreage, I'm aggravated that he asked me to get something so complicated and expensive.

We are the first to arrive for the bonfire. As we pull up, Andrew is outside in his garage. He's dirty and has obviously been working on some project in there.

Andrew greets us and shows us inside to the kitchen. It's a beautiful home that is obviously staged to be sold.

"Here's the stuff for Old Fashioneds you asked for," I say as I hand him the bag. "We had to go to three places to find everything. It's not a simple drink to make," I continue, wanting validation for the hard work we put in.

"Thanks," Andrew says as he grabs the bag out of my hand and places it on his counter.

He doesn't ask if he owes me anything, which nails the coffin even more shut on any romance possibility. I'm not sure if I would have taken the money, but it still bothers me that he doesn't offer it.

Andrew is nowhere near ready to host by the time everyone starts showing up. I'm taken aback by it. He is flustered as he gives Mary and me a brief tour of the acreage. The house is clean and has obviously been well kept.

Within the hour, there are fifteen people outside, most of whom are from Andrew's work. Andrew greets everyone as they arrive, but he hasn't even started putting out any of the food or snacks. It is well past dark by the time anyone is eating, and I am starving as we wait.

Many of us sit around the fire exchanging stories. It's a pleasant evening aside from me being out seventy bucks and being hungry. Andrew is busy in the kitchen and giving tours for the first couple of hours. Most of my time is spent outside enjoying the company of Andrew's friends and their wives. Mary spends most of the evening inside, but she comes out to the fire once the food is ready.

Once Andrew comes out to the fire, I notice something worse than that hideous, almost orange T-shirt he had worn on our hike. Having this thought is going to make me seem like even more of a vanity monster, but I'm going to tell you anyway.

When he sits down at the fire, his chair is slightly in front of mine, and he looks sideways to talk to his friend, and that's when I see it. Andrew...is missing...teeth. He has a hole in the side of his smile, a big hole.

It's the first time I've looked at him from this side angle, so I haven't noticed it before.

Instantly, I'm bothered by it. I'm thinking, *Why does this guy have a giant hole in his smile? Did he get in a fight? Did teeth rot out of his mouth? Why wouldn't he get that fixed? He has a decent job; I'm sure he would be able to get that fixed. We live in Canada... Doesn't he have health coverage for that? How long has it been there? That finalizes it. There's no way I could ever date this guy.*

Yup, I judged him. I judged him hard. I've managed to forgive myself, so I hope you do as well.

And yes, I realize the paradox of me saying I only saw Andrew as a friend, but then also having thoughts of, *Okay, that settles it. There's no way I could date him.* All I can say is, those were my thoughts. Thoughts don't always make sense or make you look good.

After we finally get some food in us, Mary and I stick around for another hour and then leave by 10:30 p.m. as planned. Mary is extremely quiet on the way home, saying nothing about the party or what she thought about anyone.

The following day, there is a funny turn of events. Mary sends me a text asking for Andrew's phone number, but she does it in the strangest way possible. Her text reads, *I really enjoyed being out at Andrew's place. It was quiet and peaceful. I feel like I could get a lot of reading and reflection done there. Is there any reason you wouldn't want to share his number with me so I can visit again?*

It is one of the weirdest text messages I have ever received. I find it to be so strange that I start laughing, and yes, I, of course, take a screenshot of it.

"What's going on?" Gabriel hears me laughing from the kitchen.

While still laughing, I hand him my phone so he can read it. Gabriel reads it to himself and then asks, "What is this?"

"I don't really know, but isn't it strange? Mary sent me that now, after coming out to Andrew's bonfire last night," I answer while gesturing for my phone back.

Gabriel does not hand me my phone. Instead, he brings it close to his face. "Hold on, hold on," he says. "I'm not done with this."

Gabriel now begins reading the text message out loud really slowly. "I really enjoyed being out at Andrew's place... It was quiet and peaceful... I feel like I could get a lot of reading and reflection done there... Is there any reason you wouldn't want to share his number with me so I can visit again?" We are both laughing hysterically as he keeps repeating it.

"Wait. Is there any chance she actually just wants to go read books at his house? Could that be a thing?" he says through his laughter as he finally hands me my phone back.

I explain to him that it doesn't make sense for many reasons.

1. Being that Andrew's acreage had just been sold. She knew that as it was the point of the entire evening.
2. Mary is dating someone who she was quite excited about yesterday.
3. If she thought Andrew was cute and wanted his number, she could have just said that. It would have been much less embarrassing.
4. Calgary is full of beautiful quiet parks that she could read in, and they are much closer than the forty-five-minute drive out to Andrew's acreage.

Other than to assume that she has a crush on him, I don't know what to make of it.

"I don't give out people's phone numbers without their permission, but I'll ask him next time I see him," I respond. This entire situation feels weird.

The next time I talk to Andrew on the phone, I say, "Mary asked me for your phone number, and she really liked your acreage."

"Oh, she sent me a strange message on Facebook, but I never answered her," Andrew replies.

"You didn't want to answer her?" I ask.

"Well, she asked me a really weird question about her air conditioner, and it didn't make sense. I just ignored it because I didn't know how to answer her," he explains.

"Yeah, her text message didn't really make sense either. I think she might have a little crush on you," I chuckle.

"Oh, I hadn't thought of that," Andrew replies.

I only hang out with Mary a couple more times after that bonfire. I never bring it up with her, but I assume she is not bothered by the giant hole in Andrew's smile like I am.

That bonfire is the last normal weekend I will have for a long time. My life is about to change drastically.

ANDREW'S TAKE

The ugly T-shirt Michelle was talking about is an old powerlifting T-shirt that I had from my twenties. It fit really well, so I kept it around long past its expiration date. The logo said *INZER*.

After our first date, we made plans to play squash biweekly. Michelle was very busy training for an upcoming fight, but she still wanted to play. Knowing that she wanted to hang out more and be friends made me so happy. During our first date, I knew having Michelle as a friend would be a blessing.

I, on the other hand, took her advice. She told me that I should stay single, travel, and get experience. So that's what I did. I kept dating and talking to women to learn more about who I was and what I wanted.

Random knowledge seems to be something that I have a lot of. It's just hours and hours of interesting YouTube video-watching and Wikipedia reading. Going down a fun rabbit hole on YouTube about black holes or learning about the Cuban missile crisis on Wikipedia is so much fun. It's nice to hear Michelle appreciated some of my fun facts.

I do tend to speak in a matter-of-fact kind of way rather than gossip. There are times when Michelle thinks I'm being ridiculous and I don't think so. I'm just trying to express to the person behind the counter how the menu on their television is changing too often. It should only display one screen; that's it. No flipping between three different screens plus a commercial. Hmm, maybe I am goofy and I don't know it.

When Michelle and I were doing the core workout, I was surprised that she was complaining about how much it hurt. It felt off with how well she was kicking and punching the crap out of the heavy bag. This and other incidents I've had while training with people have shown me that I can deal with pain while working out better than most. Such as the kind of pain you get after holding a plank for four minutes. The weird thing about plank pain is that once you realize you're in pain, it starts to level out after about a minute and a half. You can usually hold it for another one or two minutes. The pain doesn't increase in a linear fashion.

After reading this bonfire story, I realized that I did not give Michelle any money for the drink ingredients she picked up for me. If she had asked me for money, I would have gladly given it to her. If someone doesn't mention an issue they have and I don't realize that it is an issue, then I assume everything is great.

Having Michelle and other friends over that night was really special. It felt like I was surrounded by awesome people.

On the upper left side of my mouth, I have a missing tooth. It's the first bicuspid. When the baby tooth fell out around the age of twelve, there was no adult tooth beneath it. After all these years, I was used to having the missing tooth and never really thought much of it. Fun fact, I have two more baby teeth with no adult teeth beneath them. Both second bicuspids on my lower jaw are baby teeth, and I plan to keep them 'til I die. Wish me luck!

If Mary did like me, she should have just asked me out on a date. In my mind, since she said her intention was to come and read a book out in the country on a quiet acreage, then that's what she wanted. Life is far, FAR too confusing when you have to decipher what people's true intentions are.

* * *

Photos for Chapter 3
Bellamimalifestyles.com/bookphotos

4
THE FRIENDSHIP CONTINUES

Depression has settled over me like a thick fog.
It's June, and I've been busy hiding out. That big change I alluded to in the previous chapter? Yep, I got yet another concussion that caused me to call off my fight, leaving me devastated. No one has heard from me in weeks other than receiving a text message saying that the fight is off. It feels as though everything I love most about my life has come to an end, and like I let everyone down. I miss martial arts and my training partners. The only time I'm able to feel any sort of peace is on my yoga mat when I feel well enough to make it to my new studio.

I'm sitting up in bed watching mindless TV. My phone is ringing. I look down to see that it's Andrew. I haven't spoken to him since the exchange after the bonfire.

"Hello," I answer.

"Hey, how are you?" Andrew asks.

"Oh, I've been better," I answer. "I've been pretty depressed lately. I've hardly left the house aside from going to work and yoga."

"Why aren't you leaving the house?" Andrew asks.

"I just don't want to run into anyone I know or have to explain calling off the fight," I explain. "I've never had to call off a fight before, and it feels terrible."

"Do you want to come to play dodgeball tomorrow?" Andrew asks. "You don't know anyone there, and it'll get you out of the house."

I think about it for a while before responding. I don't really feel like doing anything. It's much easier to stay home feeling sorry for myself. But Gabriel has been getting worried about me, and I probably should make an effort to do something.

"Okay," I reply. "Send me the details and I'll meet you there."

THE DODGEBALL GAME

As I walk into the school gymnasium to meet Andrew, one of his teammates is quick to grab me.

"Hi Michelle, I'm Janet. A pleasure to meet you. Have you ever played dodgeball before?" she asks.

"Not since elementary school," I reply. "If that even counts."

Janet suddenly starts talking as if she had just downed three shots of espresso, explaining all of the rules to me within a span of a few minutes.

"So the blue line is the out-of-bounds line. When the game starts, you can run up to the red line to grab a ball. People use different strategies to start off the game. You can run up and try to beat someone to a ball or hang back. But these guys are pretty good; it's a risk to hang back," she explains.

My eyes begin to glaze over. She is talking so fast, hardly pausing to take a breath, and it's a lot for my bruised brain to take in.

"Now, I'm not sure if Andrew told you, but we play multiple games. I have you starting in the second game so that you can watch one first to get the hang of things. Then you'll play in another two games after that. There are no headshots allowed, but of course, accidents happen, so be careful. Now, once you're out, you have to go stand behind the green line. You're only allowed to come back in if someone catches a ball, but you have to pay attention to the order that you were eliminated…"

Janet does not stop talking, and I can hardly take in half of what she's saying. It takes all of my willpower not to tell her to shut up. All I can do is smile and nod as I become completely overstimulated.

I begin walking toward Andrew, hoping she will get the hint that I've had enough.

Nope, doesn't work. She's still talking.

My anxiety rises.

Not wanting to be rude, I stand silently as she finishes what feels like a complete orientation on the game of dodgeball.

Andrew takes over and introduces me to the rest of his team.

After saying a brief hello to everyone, I walk over to the bench to sit and watch them warm up.

As I rest and take a look around the gymnasium, I begin to realize how serious my concussion is.

Janet really overwhelmed me, more so than my entire classroom of teenagers. My healthy brain pre-concussion rarely panicked or felt overwhelmed, and now all it takes is a fast talker to send me into a panic state?

This realization causes more panic and vibration inside my brain, and everything begins to feel scary. It's as if my brain is not capable of taking in new information or these new surroundings.

In an attempt to calm myself, I begin taking deep breaths.

For the past few weeks, I have been by myself doing things that were familiar. I didn't know how much a new setting would aggravate my concussion.

The deep breaths help to calm me down, but the calmness only lasts until the game starts.

Now, I'm panicking for an entirely different reason.

Boy, when I'm wrong…I'm wrong. Dodgeball is nothing like I thought it would be. When Andrew said the word dodgeball, I pictured those soft bright-colored balls that we played with at school. The ones that would hardly hurt even if someone stood right in front of you and whipped it at your face. WRONG. These were not the same at all.

These were big rubber balls that were being launched full speed by grown-ass men and athletic women. These players are hardcore. I had no idea how intense adult dodgeball would be. I suddenly understood Andrew's safety goggles, high socks, and knee pads. It is a war zone out there.

Panic takes over as I realize that I have no safety equipment, and even if I did, if one of these balls hits me in the head, I'm SCREWED.

I may as well have just done my kickboxing fight if I was going to be THIS stupid.

I start taking deeper breaths, but it doesn't seem to be helping.

Why did I agree to this? Why did I leave the house? I just want to be in bed snuggled up with Baxter. I don't want to go out there. Deep breaths, Michelle... Deep breaths.

As their game wraps up, everyone returns to the bench. Immediately, I try to get out of playing. "You know what, guys, I'm good. I don't need to play. That looks intense," I say.

Janet was the first one to chime in. "Oh no, you have to play. You came all the way down here. Play just one game, Michelle. You can watch the rest."

Everyone else followed, saying more of the same. "Give it a shot, it's fun. Just one game."

"Okay, I'll play one game," I say as I stand up and stretch a little, "but I'm not going to play all three."

As I walk onto the court, I'm thinking to myself, *Just stay at the back, move around a little, and keep your hands up until a ball hits you in the body. Then it'll all be over. You can handle this.*

WRONG AGAIN. I cannot "handle this."

I'm hardly on the court two minutes before a dodgeball whizzes by my head and launches me into a full-blown panic attack. There is no breathing my way out of this one. My entire body is shaking. I feel more scared on this dodgeball court than I do in the ring.

How can anyone in their right mind think this is fun? There are giant rubber balls flying all over the place at full speed. No thank you.

Before a ball even hits me, I run off the court mid-game. I grab my stuff and bolt to my car as tears fill up my face. I'm so fast that I manage to do all of this without anyone saying a word to me. Thankfully my legs are still in shape from my fight camp.

Once I reach my car, I feel a certain amount of relief, but I am still sobbing. My plan is to start screaming, "Leave me alone!" if anyone comes near my car.

No one follows me outside to see if I'm okay. For this, I am grateful.

As my panic slows down, I begin to process what just happened. My brain is much more damaged than I thought. I have been feeling foggy and tired, but I assumed that it was mostly caused by my depression and loneliness.

This feels different from any other times I've been told I had a concussion. This level of panic is much higher. So much so that it's scary. It feels like my entire brain is vibrating. It's obvious to me that depression has no role in this turn of events. What is happening is 100 percent concussion. There is no more denying it.

It takes thirty minutes before I am able to calm down enough to begin my drive home. I contemplate calling an Uber, but I figure the night is young so I may as well just sit and wait for my brain to stop vibrating.

I only make it halfway home before I have to pull over to calm my brain down again. Oh, why did you ask me to play dodgeball, Andrew? And why did I agree to it?

As soon as I get home, I grab Baxter, turn off my lights, and crawl into bed. The darkness and silence of my bedroom eventually help to calm me down completely.

As I lay with my thoughts, my "wake-up call" sinks in.

My martial arts career is over. I have been forced to accept that. But it has not dawned on me that all areas of my life will be affected by my concussions. Maybe I have to give up all sports? The thought of panicking in front of my baseball team makes me send a text to my team captain: *Sorry, I can't play baseball this year, I have a head injury.* My eyes fill up with tears as I push send. Wow, what am I going to do all summer? I can't believe I'm unable to play baseball.

I pull the covers over me, snuggle with Baxter, and wallow in my sadness.

Andrew calls as soon as he gets home.

As I pick up the phone, I immediately apologize. "Hi, I'm so sorry I ran out... Janet talked so fast—"

"Are you okay?" Andrew interrupts me.

"What?" I ask

"Are you okay?" Andrew asks again.

"Yes," I reply.

"That's all that matters," Andrew responds.

Andrew says it in such a way that I no longer feel the need to apologize or explain myself. It's a nice feeling and one that I am not used to.

"Clearly, sports and social situations are a no-no for me. If we're going to hang out, we have to do something mellow. Maybe out in Mother Nature, away from people," I explain.

"Yeah, we can do that," Andrew answers.

"We need to make sure I don't run into any more fast talkers or big rubber balls," I say in an attempt to lighten the mood.

"Okay," Andrew chuckles.

As I drift off to sleep, the entire evening feels somewhat like a dream.

Backcountry Camping

The next time Andrew and I speak, he offers to take me backcountry camping.

"Sure, that sounds fun," I answer. "I've never been backcountry camping."

"Great, I'll look at my schedule, and we can pick a weekend," Andrew says.

"Are you sure? Because I have no equipment or any idea how to survive in the wilderness," I reply.

"That's okay, I can teach you. I've done it before, so I have most of what we need already," Andrew explains.

"Sounds great. You can decide where we are going," I reply.

I feel terrible admitting this, but after we make the plan, one of my first thoughts is *Perfect, I'll go with Andrew my first time so that when I go with someone I have a crush on, I'll know what I'm doing and won't embarrass myself too badly.*

Yup, in my mind, Andrew was my practice guy. I guess the joke's on me.

We plan to spend two nights in the backcountry. It feels refreshing to be trying something new after all the loss I have been experiencing. The evening before the big adventure, we are texting each other to confirm we have everything we need. We are both excited.

I'm all packed. I text Andrew a selfie wearing my backpack. *But I don't have a sleeping mat to put underneath my sleeping bag.*

That's ok, I have an extra one. I'll bring it for you, Andrew answers, also texting a selfie of his backpack.

Andrew bought us our freeze-dried meals for the weekend, so I grabbed the snacks. A friend gave me some weed brownies to help with my concussion, so I packed a couple of those along with some beef jerky, trail mix, and protein bars.

It's now Friday, and Andrew is an hour late to pick me up. I hate waiting, especially when it means we will be stuck in Friday rush hour traffic.

As soon as he pulls up, I grab Baxter and hop in his truck. "So where are we going?" I ask.

"Mosquito Creek, near Lake Louise," Andrew answers. "I have a book called *Don't Waste Your Time in the Canadian Rockies*, and it helped me decide where we should go," Andrew says as he pulls out of my parking lot.

We have a two-and-a-half-hour drive, followed by a five-kilometer hike up to our camp.

Because Andrew is late, we end up fighting daylight as we hike up to our camp.

"Andrew, how close are we?" I ask. I'm getting nervous because it's getting tough to spot Baxter on the trail.

"Oh, we're fine," Andrew says, remaining calm. "It shouldn't be much further."

The last thing I need is for Baxter to go taking off after a squirrel in the dark, so I pick him up and carry him. As the sun continues to get lower, my anxiety rises.

"Hey, I think we need to start walking faster or just pick a spot to put this tent up," I say.

"We are almost there, and there's an outhouse. We are okay. I have a lantern," Andrew says, still remaining calm.

Once we reach our camp, we need all of our lights and phones on to set up the tent. My anxiety reaches its max as we walk around trying to find a flat spot to put the tent. I feel a panic attack coming on, but I keep it together. I'm telling myself that having a meltdown in the dark on the side of a mountain isn't going to help get our tent set up.

"Yeah, I guess this is pretty bad." Andrew finally realizes the problem I've seen coming for hours.

We find the flat spot, and Andrew brings out the lantern. Thankfully, Andrew has set his tent up many times, so he doesn't struggle to set it up quickly. I hold a flashlight and watch him in silence while taking deep breaths, trying not to let my anxiety completely overwhelm me.

By the time he is nailing the tent pegs in the ground, I am holding up both flashlights so he can see where to aim the hammer. Without these flashlights, he can hardly see his hand in front of his face.

I don't like this. I don't like this one bit. I'm resenting him for being late. *"Don't worry, we're fine" MY ASS* are my thoughts as I crawl into the tent in complete darkness.

Mental note number one: Always make sure you have enough daylight to reach your destination. It makes me uneasy that I didn't get a chance to become familiar with the campsite in the daylight. We could be sleeping on top of an anthill, near a hornet's nest, or close to some bear cubs, for all we know. It seems highly unlikely, but it is still possible.

"Oh man, I was nervous setting that tent up," Andrew admits as he crawls into the tent with Baxter.

Once we are all inside and we pull all of our stuff in, I feel extreme relief. It's amazing how safe a tent can make you feel in the middle of the wilderness. It's just a piece of fabric and, in many instances, can do very little to keep you safe. And yet, it is everything. *Ahhh, comfort at last,* I think to myself.

"Hey, can I have my mat?" I ask Andrew as we begin to set up our beds. In the glow of the flashlight, I see a look of terror on his face. "Oh, shhhhhhit" is all he manages to mumble as he realizes that my mat is in his truck at the bottom of the mountain.

"Are you serious, Andrew? You forgot my mat?" I ask, hoping he's joking.

"I remembered to bring it, but it's in the truck," he explains.

Mental note number two: Always pack your own sleep gear. We both chuckle, all the while knowing that it really isn't funny. It gets extremely cold at night in the Rockies. Nervous laughter seems to be the only appropriate response. Andrew feels terrible, but it is not like there is anything we can do about it.

"Well, I suppose I can just lay all my clothes underneath me," I say.

The weekend is really off to a fantastic start.

Yes, that was sarcasm.

This trip is supposed to be mellow, and I am anything but mellow.

Andrew sleeps soundly as I lay awake cold all night. His snoring is enough to keep the bears away. The ground is freezing, and there is a breeze coming in through the door right next to me. Laying on top of my clothes helps a little, but they keep moving out from underneath me. The only warm spot on my entire body is on my right side near my armpit, where Baxter is snuggled up inside my sleeping bag. At least he is warm.

I've been awake for hours, trying to think of anything to distract me from my misery, but nothing is working. I consider waking Andrew, but I figure at least one of us should get a decent sleep.

Thankfully, once the sun starts coming up, I get just warm enough to get a few solid hours in.

The following morning, we wake up, eat breakfast, and pack up our camp.

"How'd you sleep?" Andrew asks.

I don't spare any details. "Well, between your snoring, being uncomfortably cold, having to let Baxter out to pee, the breeze getting in the door, and my clothes sliding out from under me, I think I got a solid two hours."

"Oh, man. I feel so bad," Andrew says for the third or fourth time.

"Don't worry about it," I say. "I'm used to not sleeping anyways. I've struggled with insomnia since I was a kid."

We both chuckle, all the while knowing that it isn't really all that funny. Nervous laughter seems to be the theme of the weekend.

After we pack up camp, we spend the entire afternoon hiking up to the higher camping spot Andrew has on his map. The more elevation we gain, the more snow there is on the trail. Andrew has to get out his hiking poles. I don't have hiking poles, so he gives me one of his. Mental note number three: buy hiking poles.

It slowly begins to get tougher and tougher for Baxter to keep going. He's just a little Yorkshire terrier, so he doesn't do well in snow. I keep picking him up to carry him, to give his little paws a chance to warm up. When we get to larger snow patches, Andrew is blowing through them to make a path for me. He then reaches his pole back so I can grab it and walk through. It's cute.

As we near the summit, it's evident that we are not going to find the camp. The snow is getting much too deep to continue, and my feet are soaking wet. Mental note number four: Always wear boots in the Rocky Mountains, even when it's summer.

"Andrew, I think we should just go back down. We aren't going to find it," I say. "We can just camp where we were last night."

"Yeah, you're probably right, but let me just go see if it's over that ridge. You can wait here," Andrew says as he reaches for my pole. He's going to need both of them to make it through those snow piles.

As I sit with Baxter, I enjoy the beautiful views and have a snack. Once I finish my snack, I look off in the distance to see that Andrew has gone much further than I anticipated. I do not like this because I can hardly see him. I'm not sure he will even hear me if I were to scream.

My stomach begins to sink once he is so far ahead that I can no longer see him at all, and so begins mini panic attack number two. I quickly find myself realizing that if he were to fall and hurt himself or not make it back for any reason, I have no idea how I will make it all the way down this mountain to get help. Especially since he has the truck keys. I do not like this. I want Andrew back here with me. I feel much too vulnerable without him.

Mental note number five: Never separate in unfavorable weather conditions in the Rocky Mountains. But if you do…both people should have keys to the vehicle.

Andrew is gone for what feels like an hour. I start screaming, "Andrew, come back! AAANDREW!!! Come back now!" He does not hear me. My screams are scaring the crap out of poor Baxter, so I stop.

Eventually, Andrew reappears and is making his way back toward us. Cue sigh of relief. There are spots where the snow is up to his waist, and I can see him struggling to get through. At this pace, it's going to be half an hour before he makes it back over to me. But I don't mind waiting now that I can see him.

Once Andrew returns, I'm anxious to get moving again to warm up. "Can we go back down now? Jeez, you took forever."

"Yeah, I couldn't find it. I wanted to see if it was over that ridge, but there's too much snow," Andrew responds.

"Can we just head back down now?" I ask. "I want to camp where we did last night."

"Sure," Andrew replies. "We can do that. Just let me take a quick break first."

"Of course," I say as I hand him some snack options.

We make it back to our original campsite in record time. We walk fast as we are excited to light a fire and have some dinner. Once Andrew gets the fire going, I immediately take off my shoes and wet socks. Mental note number six: Make sure the hiking boots you buy are waterproof.

Andrew shows me how to use a jet boil to boil water. Once the water is boiled, all we have to do is add it to the meals he brought for us, close the bag and let it sit until the noodles get soft. Mental note number seven: buy a jet boil. It feels nice to sit around the fire and eat a hot meal after spending most of the day in the snow.

As we sit around the fire, Andrew gets out his copy of *Don't Waste Your Time in the Canadian Rockies* book to see why it was so difficult to find our next camp. "OOOOH," he says after reading a couple of pages. "This hike is not recommended this time of year. No wonder it's covered in snow. We're a month early."

"You know, Andrew," I say in a sarcastic tone, "you really should be fired considering you messed up where we should camp even though you have that ultimate guidebook you keep bragging about. And you forgot my sleeping mat."

"Yeah, I'd likely fire myself given the circumstances of the last twenty-four hours," Andrew chuckles.

"But I'm going to let it slide because I'm sitting around a warm fire with a belly full of delicious food," I say jokingly.

Once we are fully rested, we set up our tent. It feels fast and effortless, given the fact that we have daylight on our side.

We return to the fire to have some snacks and enjoy the sunset.

"So, I'm not sure if you're into this sorta thing, but I brought us each a weed brownie. They're medicinal, so they should be pretty mild," I explain.

"Weed brownies? I haven't had one of those in years. Sure, I'm in," Andrew replies.

"Yeah, it's been a while for me as well. Weed isn't normally my thing, but I'm not supposed to have alcohol with my head injury," I explain. "It usually just makes me paranoid, but I don't mind the medicinal stuff."

"Cool, sounds fun," Andrew replies.

"Let's wait to have them until we are comfy in our tent and ready for bed. There's nothing worse than having a weed brownie kick in when you still have to brush your teeth and clean up," I say with a chuckle.

"Yeah, that makes sense. We will get comfortable first, and I'll hang all the food in the bear bag up in a tree," Andrew agrees.

"Awesome! I downloaded some movies on my tablet," I reply.

After a few laughs around the fire, we retire to the tent to eat our weed brownies.

"OMG, look at this," Andrew says as he slides my tablet into a slot at the top of the tent. "HAHA, awesome. This is supposed to dry socks, but your tablet fits perfectly."

"Awesome," I say ecstatically. "I hate having to hold it."

Our weed brownies kick in just as we start watching Micheal Moore's *Where to Invade Next*. It's a documentary where Micheal Moore visits multiple countries to ask about the health care and education systems. We hardly pay attention to the movie because we cannot stop laughing and making stupid comments.

A breeze blows in the tent, and it's absolutely freezing.

"Can we use something to cover the door?" I ask Andrew. "I froze last night every time a breeze blew in."

Andrew looks at me and says in a Yoda voice, "How about Andrew. Andrew can cover the door, yes," and then he steamrolls over the top of me while murmuring, "Steeeaamroller." I cannot stop laughing.

Andrew's sleeping bag has his mat attached to it, so he gets stuck mid-roll. Poor Baxter yelps as he is nearly squished to death by Andrew's rolling body. Tears are streaming down my face because I'm laughing so hard. It takes minutes for us to calm down.

After I gain my composure, I scoot over to the opposite side of the tent. I'm instantly warmer, a lot warmer. "I can't believe you made me sleep by the cold door," I say as I slap his sleeping bag. "Especially since I'm laying on the cold ground."

"Yeah, I didn't think of that. I can be a real jerk sometimes," Andrew laughs. "Will you be warmer now?"

"Ah, yeah. It's so much warmer on this side," I yelp in a mocking tone.

Mental note number eight: Do not sleep by the cold door, or make sure you completely block the door, especially when you don't have a sleeping mat underneath you.

We laugh late into the night before peacefully drifting off to sleep. I sleep much better as I am not nearly as cold. The weed brownie also helps.

The following day we pack up the tent and relax until midafternoon before we head down the mountain. We still have quite a bit of food to eat, so we are not in a rush to get home. The scenery is gorgeous. We have a panoramic view of alpine trees covered in snow and mountain peaks.

On our hike back down, I notice a beautiful spot.

"Andrew, stop!" I yell from a few meters back. "Let me take a few pictures for your online dating profile."

"I have pictures for my online profile," Andrew replies in confusion.

"You need better ones," I say with conviction.

Andrew stands still while I take a few photos. "Strike a pose, don't just stand there," I say.

Andrew points up toward the trees, and I snap the last photo.

"There," I say. "Now you have a couple of new ones, so you can take down the ones in your hideous 90s Oakleys."

Andrew just laughs. He loves his sunglasses, regardless of how many times I make fun of them.

Overall, it is a successful trip. We all get out without a scratch, including Baxter. I'm not sure if I'd call it mellow, but it certainly distracted me from missing martial arts.

Oddly enough, after this trip, Andrew and I don't see each other for months.

* * *

ANDREW'S TAKE

When Michelle said she left the dodgeball court mid-game without anyone noticing, she wasn't kidding. I remember once the game was over, I looked around, and Michelle was gone without a trace. My mind thought she was probably fine and for some reason just had to leave.

Before the game, when Janet was overwhelming Michelle, I couldn't tell at all that Michelle was in a bad state. She seemed fine and hid it well. If that were me having a panic attack, I would have left mid-sentence while talking to Janet.

Adult recreation league dodgeball is super fun. I would recommend it to anyone who wants to exercise and socialize more.

I never knew how Michelle felt about that backcountry camping trip until I read this chapter.

"I resented him for being late. *'Don't worry, we're fine'* MY ASS are my thoughts as I crawl into the tent in complete darkness."

She didn't let on that this is how she felt while we were setting up the tent on that first night. She seemed like she was enjoying herself.

During this time, Michelle didn't speak much about her concussion. It wasn't until much later that she told me more details. After hearing about her recovery, I don't want her to suffer a concussion ever again. Spending time with Michelle was something I enjoyed very much, even if only as friends. We had a great weekend camping together as friends.

After this backpacking trip, Michelle and I didn't speak for several months. During this time, I met another woman on Bumble, and we began to spend a lot of time together. Michelle was right when she suggested I take some time to be single, but that doesn't mean I listened. Apparently, I still had some hard lessons to learn.

* * *

Photos for Chapter 4
Bellamimalifestyles.com/bookphotos

5
THE SHIFT TO ROMANCE

You know those rom-coms when the two main characters start off as friends, and within an hour, you're almost screaming at the screen for one of them to make a move already? Our shift to romance was more like a multi-season TV series with a slow burn, except one of us didn't even realize it was happening.

SQUASH BUDDIES REUNITE

It's December, and for the first time in months, Andrew reaches out to play squash.

"Sure," I respond. "But I may have to dust off my squash racket." I've hardly seen him since our backcountry camping trip in July, and it's nice to hear from him.

For the first time since we began playing squash, I'm finally able to win a few games in a row. I have just returned home from a trip to Nepal, and my legs are in fantastic shape from all the hiking I did in the Himalayas.

My victory is bittersweet. Andrew doesn't seem like his usual peppy self, and he is pretty slow with his racket. I assume things aren't going well in his personal life, but I don't ask. We mostly talk about our trips. I tell him about Nepal, and he tells me about a trip he took to Italy. It feels nice to reconnect.

A few weeks go by, and I begin hearing from Andrew more regularly because he moved into a basement suite near my condo. It isn't long before we start hanging out once a week since he lives so close. We will usually go play virtual reality or Super Nintendo at my place.

"I learned how to make a great spaghetti in Italy," Andrew says as we say goodbye one night. "Do you want to make spaghetti next week?"

"Sure," I reply, "sounds fun."

Next week arrives.

It's spaghetti night, and I'm watching TV, waiting for Andrew.

"So he's just coming over to make dinner?" Gabriel teases from the kitchen.

"Yeah, he has some special spaghetti he wants to make," I say. "He'll be here any minute."

Gabriel smirks as he says, "But dinner is a change for you guys."

"Yeah, yeah. Whatever," I reply.

Gabriel and I live to tease each other.

Andrew buzzes my code and walks in with a large black bag he can hardly carry.

"That's a huge bag," I comment.

"This is everything we need to make the perfect spaghetti," Andrew says as he kneels down to open the bag.

Gabriel is in the kitchen, raising his eyebrows while nodding his head. As if to say, "See?"

Andrew's excitement is infectious as he pulls things out of the bag and shows them to us. Gabriel and I are laughing because we've never seen anyone this excited about spaghetti before.

Andrew and I head to the kitchen to make this perfect spaghetti. Mostly, all I do is stand there as he narrates.

"You can't use packaged tomato sauce. You have to learn how to make your own tomato sauce," he says as he opens up containers.

"You've gotta use real tomatoes, tomato paste, and light tomato sauce. It's the only way to make spaghetti," Andrew continues.

He doesn't seem to need my help, so I just sit back and enjoy the show. "You're really talking a big game, Andrew, so this better be good spaghetti," I tease.

Once dinner is ready, we sit down to enjoy what is indeed fabulous spaghetti.

"Okay, you weren't lying," I say as I go for another bite. "This is delicious."

"See, it's the only way to make spaghetti," Andrew insists.

"Now we just have to clean up this mess," I say as I clear the dishes. "I'm pretty sure you've used every pot I own."

Andrew comes into the kitchen to help me. He passes me a few dishes, and I put them in the dishwasher and close the door. "It's full. I'll just do a second load later," I say.

"Oh no, this machine can handle more than that," Andrew says as he moves me out of the way. "What year is it from?"

"I bought it a few years ago," I reply. "It's pretty new."

"Oh, it's a Miele," Andrew says as he sticks his head inside. "We can load this thing right up. Is the rack adjustable?"

"I don't know. I don't usually use all of my pots for one meal," I answer.

Andrew slides the top rack out and easily lowers it. "Oh yeah, look at this. We can throw all of these pots in." Andrew starts piling dishes on top of each other as I laugh hysterically.

Gabriel comes out of his room to see what the commotion is about. "What are you guys doing?" he asks.

"Oh, just loading up the dishwasher," I answer. "Apparently it can hold ALL the dishes."

Andrew somehow manages to fit all of the pots in the dishwasher and close the door.

"There's no way those are going to be clean," I say.

"Oh, they'll be clean," Andrew says. "We just have to pick the right setting."

Gabriel and I are chuckling as Andrew begins to play with the settings. His energy is unusually intense, and we are enjoying it.

"Oh, here we go… Large load, extra rinse, hot. Yup, they'll be clean," he says with confidence.

"It has all those settings?" I say in amazement. "I just always hit the *Normal* button."

Gabriel remains in the kitchen as Andrew packs up his bag and heads for the door.

"Well, that was fun," I say as I follow to see him out. "Thanks for the spaghetti."

"You're welcome," Andrew says as he walks out the door.

As I close the door, Gabriel is standing in the kitchen with a confused look on his face.

"What?" I ask, expecting to be teased some more.

"I feel like he's missing something," Gabriel says. "There's just something different about him. What's he missing?"

"Yeah, I know what you mean," I reply. "But I really don't know what it is."

To my surprise, every single dish in my dishwasher was clean when I woke up. Andrew wasn't lying.

BUILDING A FORT

What are you up to this weekend? Andrew texts.

Mostly staying home. I'm watching my sister's dog Sparky, and he annoys my neighbors when I leave, I text back. *And there's supposed to be a snowstorm.*

"I'm on call. How about I come over and we play some Super Nintendo?" Andrew replies.

"Sure, sounds perfect," I answer.

Within a few hours, Andrew is over with his on-call suitcase.

"Are we going to build a fort to play video games in?" Andrew asks.

"Obviously," I say as I head to my bedroom to get some blankets.

"No, no. We've gotta get the mattress first," Andrew says once I return with the blankets.

Before I even have a chance to answer him, he calls out from the bedroom, "Come help me with the mattress!"

After we lay the mattress down, we grab shelves to make walls around it and place a bedsheet across the top. The shelves aren't quite high enough, so we use a mop and broomstick to prop it up. Andrew places anchors on top of the sheet so it won't fall down.

"Sweet, I think it's ready," I say as Andrew places the final anchor.

"No, no. We need more pillows," he says as he heads to my room.

"Grab all the pillows!" I yell as I crawl into the fort. Both dogs follow me. Sparky is Baxter's older brother, so he is also a Yorkie. He is a few years older than Baxter and much smaller. When the two of them get together, they tend to fight for attention.

"This is by far the coolest fort I have ever made," Andrew announces as he crawls into the fort. "These walls are solid, and we have a full mattress."

"Yup," I agree. "It's pretty awesome."

We hang out in the fort and play *Donkey Kong Country* until we pass out.

In the morning, I get up to make myself a coffee while Andrew sleeps.

"Have you noticed if coffee calms you down?" Andrew asks me when he wakes up.

"I haven't really thought about it," I answer, "but now that you say that, I suppose it makes sense."

"Yeah, I just noticed that you seem relaxed when you drink coffee," Andrew says. "So maybe stimulants calm you down."

"Maybe. I've never felt like coffee wakes me up. I just enjoy drinking it," I reply.

After Andrew eats some breakfast, we play another solid hour of *Donkey Kong* before cleaning up the fort.

"I think I've been depressed lately," Andrew says while taking down the top sheet.

"Why do you say that?" I ask.

"I've just been spending a lot of time by myself, and I don't think it's good," Andrew replies. "I need to get out more."

"Okay, I'll let you know the next time I'm heading out to do something fun," I say.

"Thanks, that'd be great," Andrew replies.

The Escape Room - Andrew Meets Jackson & Caleb

The following weekend, Jackson and Caleb invite me to try an escape room with them and their roommate. An escape room is when a group of people figure out clues to unlock the door.

"Sure," I reply. "I've never tried one before."

"Us neither, so it's everyone's first time," Jackson says.

"I'm going to see if my friend Andrew wants to come," I say.

"Okay," Jackson replies. "Meet you there at three."

Hey, what are you up to today? I text Andrew. *Do you want to come try an escape room? We are going at 3.*

Sure, sounds fun, Andrew replies. *I've never tried one before.*

Great, it's the first time for all of us. Do you mind picking me up at 2:30? The roads are getting bad, I text back. *We should definitely take your truck.*

Sure, I'll see you soon, Andrew says.

Andrew picks me up as planned. When we arrive, I quickly introduce him to everyone, and we head right into the room.

The escape room is full of jail cells and zombies. None of us can figure out a single clue because we don't know what we are looking for. After twenty minutes, we hit the button to get a clue from a staff member. Even with the clue, we can't figure anything out.

Shortly after our time runs out, a staff member comes in to explain everything that we missed.

Oh, I'm thinking to myself. *Well, how in the heck were we supposed to know that?*

As we are going to leave, we are all feeling defeated. We hardly made it through half the game before we ran out of time. It mostly feels like we wasted our money.

"We have to do another room," Andrew says. "If we go home bummed out like this, the afternoon is a wash."

"Another room?" I say unenthusiastically.

"Yes," Andrew continues. "I think we can nail the next room. We know what to look for now."

"Yeah, let's do another one," Jackson chimes in. "I don't want to go home like this."

As we all pay for our second round, Andrew says, "I'm really hungry so I'm going to run to McDonald's quickly." And then he takes off out the door. He does not ask me if I want anything, and I'm left feeling disappointed. It's cold, and I really could use a coffee. I wish he would think to ask me if I want anything, but he never does.

Andrew returns ten minutes later with a full tummy, and we are ready to make another attempt at an escape room.

Our second room is a success. It's more of a Sherlock Holmes-style room that seems to be inside someone's house. There are so many fun artifacts to play with. We each come up with silly ideas for what might unlock a door, and some of them work. We are all laughing and having an absolute blast.

Without needing any clues, we complete the game with time to spare. We are all in good spirits as we say goodbye and head for home.

The roads have gotten worse as the snow hasn't let up all afternoon. The main highway through Calgary is closed, and there are 238 collisions reported. Thankfully, there is a somewhat busy side road that we can take instead, and Andrew's truck has four-by-four.

We are less than three minutes from my condo when we nearly get in an accident. We are stopped at a red light, and a truck starts sliding sideways toward us. Andrew stays calm and drives up onto the median so we don't get T-boned. It's impressive, and I'm happy Andrew is behind the wheel. I likely would have frozen in shock while the truck slid right into us.

Once I get home, I notice a text from Jackson. It reads, *Who was that guy???*

That was the squash guy with the terrible sunglasses I matched with in Mexico, I write back. *We hang out from time to time, remember?*

Oh yeah I remember those sunglasses, Jackson replies. *Well, we love him. He's like a giant kid. He would be great for you. You should start inviting him out more.*

This text comes as a huge surprise to me. Jackson has never sent me a follow-up text about a guy I bring around…not ever.

This causes me to sit and ponder for a minute if there is any chance I could fall for Andrew romantically. Then I remember how he went to McDonald's to get food without asking me if I wanted anything, and it's a hard no. Of course, his fashion choices do not help things.

I text back, *Definitely not romantic, but he's fun to hang out with for sure. I'll start inviting him out more.*

THE NEW FOURSOME

After the escape room, I start inviting Andrew every time I hang out with Jackson and Caleb, which is basically every weekend. We do several more escape rooms and introduce them to going to play virtual reality games. Jackson and Caleb repeatedly express how much they adore Andrew and his childlike antics. When he is in a good mood, it's as if we are all infected with a childlike sense of wonder.

One Saturday night, Jackson and Caleb suggest we go out dancing. This makes me nervous, as I am worried my concussion symptoms will flare up. Ultimately, I decide that in the worst case, I can just hop in a cab and go home. Me, Jackson, and Caleb light up the dance floor all night when we go clubbing, so I am curious if Andrew will try to keep up with us or stay on the sidelines. Gabriel also joins.

Andrew not only keeps up with us, but he busts out some awesome moves of his own. This is pleasantly surprising. The night ends up being a success in all areas. My head doesn't act up, and we all have a blast. It is also fun to have Gabriel join our dance circle for a few songs when he isn't busy talking to the ladies.

I'm having a blast with Andrew. More fun than I usually have, but I am still taken aback by his clothes. He wears a long-sleeve light gray T-shirt that doesn't fit him properly. It is too short in length and slightly too tight across his muscular chest. After five minutes on the dance floor, it has obvious sweat stains on it that remain there for the entire evening. Why, *why* would he wear light gray to go clubbing? And why do his shirts never fit properly?

For the first time on that dance floor, I look at Andrew and think to myself, *I really wish I liked him* as he is smiling at me while busting a move.

After I have a few drinks in me, I voice this out loud to Caleb. "Man, I wish I liked him. We have so much fun. There are just no romantic feelings there."

"Well, don't force it," Caleb responds. "But it is rare to find a straight guy that will keep up with us on the dance floor."

Caleb is right. I can't force it.

"I'm hungry," Andrew says as we leave the bar.

We decide to walk and get a gourmet poutine at the Big Cheese before splitting a cab home.

"Oh my God, this is the best poutine I've ever tasted," I say, licking my fingers. We debate ordering a second one but manage to stop ourselves.

This is the first time Andrew and I have been drunk together. A part of me wonders if we will feel a drunken attraction on the cab ride home, but it is the same as always. No sparks or flirtations. We say goodnight and go our separate ways after a fun evening. We are content with a belly full of poutine.

The Bond Grows

Andrew and I begin texting more over the following weeks. I take a job as a nanny three days a week because I need a way to make money. My brain is able to handle more stimuli, so I think I am capable of handling a part-time job. This job leaves me with much to complain about. The parents have not been forthcoming about their oldest son's behavior issues, and I hate being on a nanny cam all day. Texting Andrew is helping me vent about how much I hate it.

The family is very nice, but I find it hard to relax while working. I begin making simple mistakes while cooking or trying to figure out the vacuum. The job proves to be too much for me to handle. It is tough for me to admit, but I still am not capable of working. Andrew is a supportive ear to talk to through this process, and our texting banter delivers the giggles that help get me through the day. After only three weeks, I end up quitting.

In March, my yoga studio suddenly announces that it is closing. This upsets me terribly as we only get three days' notice. My yoga studio has been my second home and savior after having to give up martial arts. The staff all feel like friends, and they have been patient and kind to me throughout my healing journey. As I walk out after the last class, I cannot contain my tears. It marks the end of an era.

Andrew knows how much I love my yoga studio and how upset I am that it is closing. It's tough to find a good studio, and I crave a social atmosphere with positive energy. Solo workouts have never been something I enjoy, so I am nervous about filling the void.

The morning after my yoga studio closes, I wake up to the most adorable text message from Andrew.

Do you want me to come over so we can do yoga in your living room after work? I have some good Rodney Yee videos.

The biggest smile lights up my face as I read it. Naturally, I agree. Andrew texts similar messages several times that week. Every other day I get a text asking me if I want to do yoga. Andrew has single-handedly filled the void.

Easter Dinner

It's Easter Sunday, one year to the day since Andrew and I matched on Bumble.

It's 3 p.m., and Andrew walks in with his yoga mat.

"How's it going?" I ask.

"Good. Let's do some yoga," Andrew says while hardly looking at me. His energy seems somewhat frantic.

I lay my yoga mat down as Andrew goes through his phone to pick a video. "I can only do a forty-five-minute class today because I have dinner at five," Andrew says.

"Okay, that works," I say as I begin to stretch.

"You okay with Rodney Yee again? I like his videos," Andrew asks.

"Sure, that works," I answer as Andrew hits play.

During our yoga session, Andrew keeps checking his phone and is obviously distracted. One of my favorite things about Andrew is how little he checks his phone, so it feels odd that he keeps looking at it so much.

Once our yoga video is finished, I go to the kitchen to get us some water. Andrew follows me into the kitchen while looking at his phone. What happens next is tattooed in my brain, as it feels so strange.

Andrew checks his phone again, puts it back in his pocket, looks at the wall—yes, the wall—and says, "I'm going to Easter dinner at my uncle's place at five, and you're invited. You should get ready because we need to go soon." Then, without glancing in my direction, he grabs his suitcase and heads toward my spare bathroom.

I stand there frozen for a while, trying to process.

I'm confused for a few reasons:

1. Why did he look at the wall?
2. Is he seriously inviting me to meet his family on Easter?
3. Will they think I'm his girlfriend?

Andrew comes back into the kitchen. "Get in the shower; we need to leave soon," he insists.

He does not look at me or give me a chance to respond.

There are two full bathrooms on opposite sides of my condo. We both can easily shower at the same time. I stand there for another few minutes trying to decipher what Andrew is thinking. Then I get in the shower.

The water washes over me. It feels like I am living in the twilight zone. Excitement is in the air. Yet I'm mostly confused about what just happened. Easter dinner is happening at Andrew's family's place in an hour. It feels as though we just skipped five steps. We haven't kissed. We haven't held hands. We haven't done anything slightly romantic.

Does Andrew have a crush on me?

I don't think he has a crush on me. At no point this entire year have I felt an awkward moment where I thought he might have a crush on me. He never lingers. Never leans in. Never texts small talk. Never says goodnight. All things I would expect from someone who has a crush on me.

Now, he is asking me to have Easter dinner at his family's house. It causes me to question everything. Jackson would find this hilarious.

I wish I had time to call him and laugh about it before we head out the door.

Andrew's uncle's house is half an hour's drive away from my place. Andrew is on call, so he has to go in his work van. As I follow his van outside of Calgary, I think about how our friendship is shifting. Something is about to change. I have no idea if it will end up being for better or for worse. But a change is happening.

When we get to Andrew's uncle's place, I meet his aunt and uncle, his cousin, her husband, and their two sons. They instantly make me feel welcome. They are easily likable, and the conversation flows nicely as we enjoy a delicious meal. No one asks how Andrew and I met or anything about the status of our relationship.

After dinner, we retire to the game room in the basement. The game room has a pool table and an old-school Galaga arcade game. It is in this game room that Andrew gives me that tingly feeling for the first time. You know, the butterflies.

He is playing pool with his cousin while I play solitaire at the table. In the middle of the game, Andrew suddenly goes upstairs and doesn't bother to tell anyone where he is going. After fifteen minutes, his cousin jokes, "Is Andrew taking a shit? I want to finish this pool game." We all laugh.

Minutes later, Andrew returns with a coffee for me. He walks up and puts it right in front of me on a coaster and says, "I thought you might like a coffee." It's adorable, and my body tingles all over. It is the first time Andrew has ever brought me something. The cherry on top is that I didn't even ask for it.

"What took you so long?" Andrew's cousin asks as she swirls her pool cue. "Oh, sorry, I had to fix something in the coffee machine. It wasn't working," Andrew explains.

As Andrew finishes his pool game, I begin to look at him differently. For the first time, I feel attracted to him. After a couple more games of pool, we decide to call it a night and head home.

We walk outside to a bit of a snowstorm. Through the growing blizzard, Andrew drives right behind me the entire way home. He never says anything, but it feels as though he is making sure I get home safely. He follows me all the way to my condo entrance, which is blocks out of his way. My heart feels happy as I turn into my parking lot. It feels nice to be protected.

As I walk in my door, I'm greeted by Baxter, who is anxious to see me. After petting Baxter, I put on some comfy clothes and crawl into bed. As I plug my phone in, I notice a text from Andrew. *Goodnight. Thanks for coming to dinner.*

As I read it, I crack a smile. It is our first goodnight text.

Goodnight, I text back. *Thanks for inviting me.*

I fall asleep feeling as if a major shift has happened between us. I like it.

Awkwardness Sets In

The week following Easter dinner feels extremely awkward. At least it does for me. Not so much for Andrew. To me, it feels as though things have shifted between us. Andrew keeps on acting as if everything's the same. As if it isn't super weird that he invited me to a holiday family dinner when we aren't dating. Guy friends don't do that. At least not any guy friends I've ever had.

In my eyes, we've left the friend zone, but it seems as though Andrew hasn't gotten that memo.

Andrew texts the following day. *Do you want to do yoga when I'm done with work?*

Sure, see you then, I text back.

I'm assuming things are going to feel different between us when Andrew comes over today. Things have obviously shifted.

Wrong.

Andrew acts the same as always. He comes over. We do yoga. He says goodbye. He leaves. The only thing that has changed is we are now hanging out daily, and he is texting me to say goodnight.

This pattern repeats itself for two more days.

I am frustrated.

The attraction I felt after Andrew got me the coffee has lingered slightly, but it isn't enough for me to know if I like him or not. It feels as though we are living in a gray area. No longer in the friend zone, but not moving forward. Being in limbo is not somewhere I like to be. This feels a little like torture.

On Thursday, Andrew asks if I want to hang out on the weekend.

"Sure, but let's do something different," I say.

I think to myself, *I've got to get him out of this condo, so I can see if we have more chemistry.*

"Okay," Andrew replies, "but I'm still on call, so I have to bring the van."

I pull out my phone to google events in Calgary. There is an improv comedy festival happening all weekend. "Are you up for some improv comedy?" I ask. "It's just over in Inglewood."

"Sure," Andrew replies. "Just let me know what time, and I'll meet you there."

We meet at the improv theater just in time to get the last couple of tickets. Andrew smells good, and I love the leather jacket he is wearing. Because it's a sold-out show, they pack extra chairs in the theater. The chairs are nearly on top of each other. Just by sitting down, Andrew and I are basically cuddling.

It feels nice to be leaning against his shoulder. My attraction is growing. It peeped its head out after Easter dinner, tucked itself away again for a few friendly yoga sessions, then reappeared at the improv comedy show.

The show is outrageously funny. The entire theater is belly laughing for a solid hour.

"This is the best improv I have ever seen," I whisper to Andrew.

"Yeah, me too," he agrees. "This is hilarious."

As I watch the show, Andrew's strong shoulders become one of my favorite things about him, how he smells coming in at a close second.

After the show, people are still laughing as we walk to our vehicles. My car is parked much closer than Andrew's, so we stop to say goodbye.

"Well, that was fun," I say.

"Yeah, it really was. What are you up to tomorrow?" Andrew asks.

"I'm going to go try a new yoga studio at 9 a.m., then probably take Baxter to the dog park."

"Cool, I'm still on call. So I probably won't do much," Andrew replies.

"Ok, see ya," I say as I walk closer to my vehicle.

"Goodbye," Andrew says, and then he continues to stand there.

For the first time in our entire friendship, he lingers. He stands there and stares at me for what feels like a full minute as I think to myself, *Is he going to kiss me?*

Wrong, he does not try to kiss me. It's a long awkward pause with no finale. He does not lean or attempt to say anything. He is frozen.

I'm no stranger to having awkward goodbyes with men, but I've never had one like this. It's usually obvious if a guy wants to kiss me or say something. With Andrew, there is nothing. He is like a statue. He doesn't even attempt to lean in to see if I would follow suit. I have no idea what he is thinking as he stands there and looks at me blankly. This is a behavior I've never seen him do before.

Eventually, I turn around and get in my car. Andrew doesn't flinch as he watches me drive away.

As I crawl into bed, I get a text from Andrew.

Goodnight, tonight was a lot of fun.

Indeed it was, goodnight, I text back.

Let me know if you want company for yoga tomorrow morning. I'll meet you, Andrew continues.

Now, I am getting fed up. Like, what is happening? Make a move already! This is killing me. Aaaaaargh! Like, this is more than friends. Friends don't text you to say goodnight and hang out every single day. At least not in my world.

Aren't you still on call? I ask. *You can't bring your phone in the yoga studio.*

Oh yeah, Andrew says. *Well give me a call if you want to hang out afterward.*

Ok, goodnight for reals, I reply.

I fall asleep. I am most definitely living in the twilight zone.

MICHELLE AND ANDREW PRESTON

* * *

ANDREW'S TAKE

As Michelle read me this chapter, I was confused by many of her statements. It felt as though she were reading fiction. She noticed many things between us that I was not paying attention to.

I'm very grateful for Jackson and Caleb. They are super fun to be around, and I'm glad the feeling is mutual. I had such a fun night clubbing with Michelle, Jackson, and Caleb. I felt like I was hanging out with three new awesome friends. I was very much hoping they would invite me out again.

After Michelle and I ate some yummy poutine, we shared a cab home. During the cab ride, my mind was not thinking that there would be any romance. She already put me in the friend zone. I was happy to be there as long as we were all having fun.

We started hanging out more. We went to a few yoga sessions, played Super Nintendo games, and built a fort in her living room (which was so much fun). After a month or so, I invited her over to my uncle's house for Easter dinner. She didn't have any plans, so I figured it was a nice friendly thing to do.

Turns out this kind of behavior will make the opposite sex think you like them. Especially when you wait on them intently during Easter dinner. The reason I brought her coffee was that I thought she needed to relax and calm down. I was surprised to read that it meant so much to her. In my mind, I was just taking care of a friend.

I remember when we were standing outside a comedy club on the east side of the building after the improv show ended. Just before we parted ways, there was a long awkward silence.

Turns out, in Michelle's mind, she was wondering, *Is he going to kiss me?*

No, he's not. He knows he's in the friend zone and was thinking, *I'm so happy to have Michelle as a friend. I hope we can do yoga tomorrow.*

It's something else to realize how we have gone so far and have miscommunicated so much. In my mind, Michelle had told me, a long time ago, when we first met, that we were just friends. This was the context in which I was operating. Turns out, I wasn't, and sending "goodnight texts" makes the female think you're interested in them. Even though the male was explicitly told that he was just a friend.

This is stranger than fiction. I do not understand this thought process. I have no idea what Michelle means by goodnight text. I don't know what a goodnight text is. She said that this is the last text that you send to someone before you go to bed. It means you're thinking about them before bed.

This is news to me.

Only Michelle realized a change was happening between us. I noticed nothing at the time. I was sending her a goodnight text frequently, and I didn't even know that that was a thing. I know I'm repeating myself. It's just so confusing.

I was so grateful that Michelle and I were doing yoga together and hanging out. I always felt good when I was with Michelle. I didn't think that I had a crush on her because I knew that I was in the friend zone. I never thought to myself that as we were spending more time together anything was changing between us. In my mind, we were good friends who hung out multiple times a week.

The truth is, most of the time I'm oblivious to how I feel and how to handle those feelings. I don't notice the "unspoken" language between people, so I have no idea what she is talking about.

* * *

Photos for Chapter 5
Bellamimalifestyles.com/bookphotos

6
OUR FIRST REAL DATE

Everything feels awkward, and I can't live like this any longer. Something has to happen to tip us in either direction. Kissing Andrew could amplify our chemistry or make it fizzle out completely. Either way, I have to know.

It's more of a turn-on for me if the guy makes the first move, but Andrew isn't leaving me much choice. It has to be me. A part of me is nervous about it, but living in this limbo of the in-between stage is driving me crazy. Everything feels awkward.

I know, I think to myself. *I'll give him one more yoga session to see if he makes a move. Then, if he doesn't, I'll just ask him out.*

Another yoga session comes and goes. Andrew makes no move.

I'm left with no choice but to ask him out myself. I don't make a plan of how I'm going to do it, I just promise myself that I'm taking the next opportunity that presents itself.

Andrew texts, *Hey, do you want to do yoga on Wednesday this week? I have something on Tuesday.*

How about instead of yoga, we just don't see each other all week, and then this weekend, you take me on a real date? I ask with boldness.

Oh boy, a real date! Where would you like to go? Andrew answers.

I'll leave that up to you. You can pick me up Saturday night, I reply.

Sounds good, Andrew says.

We leave it at that.

The Waiting Game

As the big date approaches, I'm feeling more confused about my romantic feelings for Andrew. I thought having a few days away from him might help give me some clarity. It has helped nothing.

On Friday, I call my best girls over, the ones who really know me. It's been a while since I've had a girls' night, and it's imperative I discuss my situation with a few girlfriends over wine. None of them have heard much about Andrew, so I know this is going to be fun.

Over the years, I've enjoyed many wine nights with my girls to discuss whoever I was dating or crushing on. There has never been a conversation quite like this. They are used to me talking about all of the exciting reasons I thought a guy was potentially "the one." With Andrew, I have many reasons as to why I don't think he is the one. It feels good to be breaking my usual pattern and keeping the promise I made to myself about switching things up.

The girls are excited and entertained to be hearing a new type of story. The fact that I have many examples of thinking Andrew is cute, followed by many examples of "There's no way I can date this guy," is amusing to all of us. The more wine I drink, the more I begin to make fun of myself.

How can I not know if I want to date him for real? I am so back and forth about it, and I am never back and forth about anything. Making decisions and executing them is my forte. Wishy-washy has never been my style. We laugh as I talk about how he is the guy that I never try to impress, and yet he likes me anyway. We go around the circle debating if it's "true love" to end up with a guy like that or if it's considered settling. No one knows.

By the end of the evening, we conclude that the only way to know is by actually dating him. It all boils down to attraction and how things feel romantically. No amount of talking can help me figure out how that will go down.

On their way out the door, the ladies joke that the date is either going to be "extremely awkward" or "super fantastic." There doesn't seem to be much room for a middle ground as the stakes are too high.

"We better be the first people you call after this date!" they yell from down the hallway.

"Don't worry, I'll let you all know how it goes!" I yell back.

THE BIG DAY

Saturday rolls around, and I receive a text from Andrew. *Can I pick you up at 5:30?*

It has been five days since we've spoken, so I figure I'll play a little joke on him. *For what?* I text back.

I'm giggling as I feel his panic through my phone.

After a few minutes, I follow up with, *Just kidding. See you at 5:30. Oh wow, you really got me good on that one,* Andrew replies.

Wanting to make sure I'm not overstimulated for our date, I spend the afternoon laying in bed listening to podcasts. Having all that wine last night wasn't the wisest decision, so I drink lots of water.

Andrew is right on time at 5:30. He comes into the building and buzzes my unit number, as opposed to texting when he pulls up like he usually does.

As I turn the corner to walk toward the lobby, I can see that he is dressed well, and his hair is spiked up in the messy way I like. As I open the door to the lobby, I notice that he also smells good. Andrew usually smells good, but it has more of an impact when his outfit also looks nice.

He is wearing a long-sleeve button-up blue shirt and jeans. The shirt is a little large on him, as opposed to most of his T-shirts which were often too short. His jeans fit well, and he is wearing the leather jacket I love. Andrew opens the exit door for me while we leave, and I smile as I walk past him.

"I'm not telling you where we are going; it's a surprise," Andrew says as we hop in his truck.

"Okay, I can live with that," I say as I smile at him. The date is off to a good start.

I'm able to guess where Andrew is taking me when we are five minutes away. I know the city well, and it seems to be the only place he could possibly be taking me in this area.

"You're taking me to Stage West, aren't you?" I ask while we are stopped at a red light.

"What makes you say that?" Andrew asks.

"Well, it's either that or you are taking me to the casino, and you know I hate casinos," I answer.

"Yes, we are going to Stage West. Is that okay?" Andrew asks.

Stage West is a dinner theater that serves an all-you-can-eat buffet. It's well known for having a wide variety of excellent foods and desserts.

"Of course it's okay," I answer. "I've only been there once with a roommate. We saw an 80s musical and had a blast."

"Great. The show starts at 6:30, so we should have plenty of time to eat first," Andrew says.

"Perfect," I reply.

As we walk into Stage West, there is a lineup to hand in your tickets.

"The only way I could get seats up close is by sitting us across from another couple at a table for four," Andrew turns to me and says. "I thought you might like that because I know you like talking to strangers."

"Yes, that sounds fun," I reply.

"The play is Sherlock Holmes. I thought it was the best one because a musical might be too much for your head," Andrew explains.

"Sherlock Holmes is perfect," I reply.

He has clearly put a lot of thought into this evening, and I appreciate it. I'm surprised he sprung for the good seats. When I came with my roommate, we bought the cheapest seats at the back, and even those were expensive.

As we move our way up the line, I express my appreciation to Andrew.

"You really couldn't have picked a better place to bring me," I say. "I've always enjoyed plays, but I rarely make the effort to go see them."

Andrew seems relieved as he cracks a big smile. "Oh good, I was really hoping you would like it," he says as he hands the teller our tickets.

We find our table, leave our coats on the chairs, and make our way toward the buffet area. The play is set to start in forty minutes, which gives us plenty of time to eat.

As we approach the buffet, I turn to Andrew. "Let's just separate and meet back at the table," I say. "This buffet is huge, and I have no idea what I want."

"Sounds good," Andrew replies as he hands me a plate.

The buffet area has every kind of food you could imagine yourself craving. There are so many tables with trays of food that I hardly know where to start. After circling the choices a few times, I decide to try a little bit of everything.

After filling my plate with copious amounts of food, I return to the table. Andrew follows closely behind me, also with a heaping plate.

A couple is sitting across from us, enjoying their food. We introduce ourselves, and they respond with head nods and smiles. It's apparent that they are not in the mood to be talkative…with each other…or with us. Andrew and I don't mind that at all. The four of us sit and enjoy our meals without much interaction.

A waitress comes around to offer drinks. I wasn't planning on ordering anything until Andrew looks at me and says, "Do you want a fruity cocktail? Let's get fruity cocktails."

"Sure," I reply. His enthusiasm is impossible to resist.

"I'll have a sangria," I say to the waitress as Andrew looks at the drink menu.

"I'll have a Long Island iced tea," Andrew says.

The waitress heads off to get our drinks.

"Shall we make one more round at the buffet before the play starts?" Andrew says as we finish our first plates.

"Obviously," I reply, already standing up out of my chair. "I know what the best stuff is now, and I want more of it."

"Oh yeah, that ribeye was to die for," Andrew replies. "I want another slice. And more sushi."

Between the two of us, we easily eat enough to feed a family of four. It's tough not to overdo it at a buffet offering a culinary tour of the best world cuisine.

As the play starts, we push our plates away and turn our chairs to face the stage. Our table is placed perpendicular to the stage, so I am staring past Andrew as I watch the play. We are somewhat beside each other, but because of the size of the chairs and the angle of the table, it is impossible to snuggle up next to him. His chair is slightly in front of mine. He seems a little bit nervous and doesn't make any attempts to hold my hand or put his arm around me.

At intermission, we go get some fruit and dessert. The dessert buffet is just as impressive as the dinner buffet. Intermission is long enough to go to the bathroom and enjoy some dessert, but it isn't long enough to get into much conversation. I go back for more blackberries. They have that just-picked sweetness that is such a treat to find.

After intermission, I decide it's time to make a move. I know I enjoy my time with Andrew; I always have. It's the romantic part we are missing. I need to know what it feels like to snuggle with him.

Given our large chair situation, my only option is to reach out and grab his hand. There's no smooth way to do it. It has to be an obvious reach over his large armrest.

As I reach in, Andrew immediately grabs my hand and cups his other hand over the top. How firmly he squeezes my hand gives me a tingly feeling in my stomach. He doesn't look back at me, but I can tell he is happy. I smile as I sink into my chair a little.

My back is uncomfortable for the remainder of the play as my arm is reached out far away from my body, but it's worth it. It feels wonderful to be holding Andrew's hand.

After the play finishes, we stay at our table to finish our snacks.

"What did you think of the play?" Andrew asks.

"I enjoyed it," I answer. "You can tell that the cast enjoys working together, and I like the good vibes."

"Yeah, it was pretty funny," Andrew replies.

"I think the lead detective girl has a real-life crush on the actor playing Sherlock Holmes. But it's obvious he's into the girl who plays the maid," I continue.

"What?" Andrew says in confusion. "How on earth would you know that?"

"I watched them interacting at intermission, and it was blatantly obvious," I explain. "It makes me sad for her because I've been there."

In my typical fashion, my comment has nothing to do with the play. It has everything to do with the real people who are playing the characters in the play.

"I kept getting distracted by the set," Andrew says as he points to one of the wooden trees. "They used the same cutout for all of these trees."

I turn my attention to the stage and notice the trees for the very first time.

"You see that?" Andrew explains, "They are all perfectly symmetrical. They just flipped some of them so they are backward."

"I see it now," I answer, "but I never noticed them before you said that."

In typical Andrew fashion, his comment had nothing to do with the people or the play and everything to do with the stage setup.

As Andrew finishes his cocktail, I ponder what just occurred. Many people in this world only seem to notice what's happening on a surface level. The ones who are "just watching the play," so to speak. Andrew and I both were watching what was going on behind the scenes, but we were aiming our attention at two completely different areas of interest.

I'm intrigued that Andrew pointed out something I never would've noticed because I've always thought of myself as someone who notices everything.

THE AFTERDATE

"So do you have plans now? Are you going out?" Andrew asks on our drive home.

This shocks me.

"Obviously, I didn't make plans for after our date. I'm not an asshole," I say with a chuckle.

"Well, I wasn't sure," Andrew responds. "Do you want to hang out?"

"Sure," I answer. "Should we just go to my place and watch something?"

"Yeah, that sounds good," Andrew replies. "I just have to go home and get some stuff."

I sit in the truck and wait as Andrew packs his things.

Ten minutes go by.

Twenty minutes go by.

What on earth is he doing? I think to myself. *You'd think he would've prepared a little bit beforehand.*

When we get to my place, we decide to watch some YouTube videos. What we watch is lost on me. What matters is how much I enjoy leaning on Andrew's shoulders for the first time with his arm around me.

Something about laying on Andrew's shoulders makes me feel small and protected. I'm not a small girl by any means, so I am pleasantly surprised. Nothing feels awkward, at least not yet. We watch YouTube videos on the couch for a couple of hours and enjoy the snuggling before heading to bed.

What happens next is certainly not what I expected. We get under the covers, and Andrew spoons me.

It's nice until he starts giggling.

His giggling turns to full-blown laughter.

He begins laughing so hard that it causes me to start laughing along with him. I have no idea what he is laughing about. It's just that infectious.

Eventually, he manages to spit out some words through his laughter. "It's just so weird. I'm in Michelle's bed, and it's weird."

"What?" I ask as I turn to face him. "You've slept over before in the fort; it's not that weird."

"No, no, it's weird. It's not the same." Andrew is still laughing. "Everything is different. I'm in your room. I really like it, but it's weird."

We are laughing so hard that anyone watching us would think we are stoned. Andrew is so giddy and happy. I've never had this effect on a man before.

We lay awake talking and laughing for an hour before drifting off to sleep. The night couldn't have been more perfect.

I have my first glimpse of Andrew's CPAP machine for sleep apnea. It's quite silly seeing him strap that mask on his face before bed, but I appreciate the fact that it stops him from snoring.

I fall asleep feeling peaceful, now realizing that I am falling for Andrew, and I should just stop analyzing it so much. I laugh harder with Andrew than I have with anyone, and that's where I need to turn my focus.

WE'RE IN A RELATIONSHIP NOW

The next time Andrew comes over, he solidifies his boyfriend status. At least, that's how I look at it. We never bother to have an actual conversation about it.

"I bought these for you at the grocery store," Andrew says as he walks into my kitchen. He pulls out some blackberries and puts them on my counter. "I noticed you were enjoying them at the play."

That's it. I'm falling. I can feel stars shooting out of my eyeballs.

No man has ever gotten me blackberries before. Not that I particularly enjoy blackberries. But the thought he has put into them is everything.

For the moment, Andrew has squashed my fear about us not having romantic chemistry. It's one of the sweetest things he could have done.

* * *

ANDREW'S TAKE

When Michelle asked me out on a date, I was puzzled at first because she was the one who friend-zoned me a year earlier. But I knew I couldn't say no because I really liked her.

As soon as Michelle went to hold my hand on our first date, a weight of tension relieved itself as my excitement took over. I wanted to hold her hand in a way to show her how special this night was, so I responded with a double handclasp with intermittent squeezes and hand pets. I liked holding Michelle's hand.

It was fascinating how Michelle noticed personal things about the cast members just by candidly watching them. This kind of awareness is invisible to me.

While I was in Michelle's bed, I would look around the room and think to myself, *I remember looking in this room when I was Michelle's friend. This is Michelle's bedroom, my FRIEND Michelle's bedroom,* which meant I would never go into that room for any reason outside of a friendship. So when I was lying with Michelle in her bed, I was meditating on the idea and feeling the shift. It was a neat experience, and this was why I was giggling before we went to sleep.

A CPAP machine is used to treat sleep apnea. It sends a steady flow of pressurized air into your nose and mouth as you sleep. This keeps your airways open and helps you breathe normally. My sleep apnea is mild, but I always bring my CPAP machine with me to stop my loud snoring.

In my mind, when Michelle held my hand and invited me over, we were boyfriend and girlfriend. No more friend zone. I didn't realize until reading this chapter that Michelle didn't consider us boyfriend and girlfriend until a few days after Stage West. This shocked me a bit. To me, if I'm sleeping in your bed, that means we are boyfriend and girlfriend. No matter if it's the first, second, or fiftieth date.

* * *

Photos for Chapter 6
Bellamimalifestyles.com/bookphotos

LOVE

So now that Andrew and I are in a relationship, life is about to be all sunshine and rainbows, right?

Wrong.

This section is a collection of short stories that all take place in the first year of our relationship, before Andrew's diagnosis. Most of these events unfolded before either of us suspected autism, or understood what the autism spectrum was.

Many people are in somewhat of a honeymoon period during their first year of dating, and it takes a while before the rose-colored glasses fall off. This was not the case for Andrew and me. In fact, we were quite the opposite.

Our first year together was by far our hardest. I struggled to understand him, and he struggled to communicate his feelings. We nearly broke up twice, and I wasn't always sure if we were going to make it.

This was a year full of confusing moments, communication failures, and misunderstandings. As well as magical moments, life realizations, and twists and turns.

Merging any two lives is tough, but when one person is autistic, and you are both unaware of this fact, it can be extra difficult. Andrew was unlike anyone I had ever dated, and there were many things about him that I could not make sense of. I was walking in uncharted territory with no instruction manual, and I definitely stepped on a few landmines. Top that off with my brain injury, substantial weight gain, and depression issues from having to quit martial arts, and it was a year I am thankful I never have to relive.

Sometimes life will have you slog through some pretty negative stuff, but when it's worth it, it's worth it. Looking at it from where we now stand, I am so proud of both of us for learning the lessons.

This section will give much insight into our relationship as we share stories of our many struggles and small victories in our first year together.

If you are looking for a more in-depth analysis of how we worked through these issues and have continued to maintain a successful relationship, we have created a relationship course to support you. It breaks down all of the strategies we've implemented over the years as we've continued to learn more about each other.

This course as well as our other publications can be found here:

Bellamimalifestyles.com

7
THE SMALL STUFF

Love consists of so many things. The small stuff, the romantic stuff, the tough stuff, and everything in between.
We are going to start with the small stuff because it was a slow build to love for Andrew and me.

THE HAMPER

"Why do you keep throwing your clothes on the floor?" I ask. "The hamper is near the door now."

"Yeah, I don't know why I did that," Andrew replies as he picks up his clothes.

Two weeks later, Andrew is still throwing his clothes on the floor where the old hamper used to be.

"Andrew, stop throwing your clothes on the floor. The new hamper is right there (points to hamper)." I begin to get frustrated.

Andrew chuckles. "Sorry, I don't know why I keep doing that."

Anytime I've been in a serious relationship, I'm the one who does the laundry. It gives me a sense of comfort and satisfaction. Cleaning floors, on the other hand, is something I loathe. My boyfriends all got the same speech: "I'll do the laundry if you clean the floors when they get dirty." Most men agreed to this arrangement with a smile. Andrew is no different. When he comes over straight from work, he throws his dirty work clothes in my hamper, knowing they will be clean and folded for him.

This is all working splendidly until I rearrange my bedroom. I buy new teal bedding, curtains, and a hamper to match. After taking out all the furniture, Andrew helps me paint the walls a brighter color. Once we finish painting, I enjoy moving the furniture back into an improved layout. Everything about my new bedroom is enjoyable, but there is one problem. Andrew keeps throwing his dirty clothes on the floor where the old hamper used to be.

For weeks, this pattern repeats itself.

Andrew can't seem to grasp where the new hamper is. After many conversations with him, nothing changes.

Tired of picking his dirty clothes up off the floor, I decide to move the hamper back to where it was in the first place. Surrendering seems easier than trying to get him to grasp where the new hamper is.

I later learn that once Andrew is used to something in a certain place, it's best to leave it there.

* * *

ANDREW'S TAKE

I vaguely remember this. But I do remember the feeling. *Why is the hamper not here?* (don't know). *Where is the hamper?* (don't know) Well, this is where the clothes would go if the hamper were here, so this is where they will go now. Problem solved.

* * *

THE EGGS

I notice that Andrew has an odd way of removing eggs from the egg carton. Personally, I like to remove eggs from front to back while going in order. Not Andrew. He will take one egg from row three, an egg from row six, and then one from the back. There seems to be no rhyme or reason to it, and he doesn't always pick from the same rows.

This random patterning becomes more apparent when I buy a flat of eggs from Costco, as opposed to a carton. The flat of eggs ends up looking like abstract artwork. If Andrew makes three eggs, he will take them from three completely different places. I just don't get it.

One day, I can't take it anymore, so I have to ask him. "Why do you grab your eggs like that? I've never seen anyone grab eggs from random spots out of the carton."

"Oh, I'm just making sure it's balanced," he answers. "So if you have to pull it out of the fridge, it won't topple over."

Of all the things I could've guessed he would say, I never would've thought of that one, and it makes perfect sense. This taught me to always ask why Andrew is doing something I don't understand because his reasons are impressive.

* * *

ANDREW'S TAKE

If you take eggs from one side, eventually, the carton will become unbalanced. Then someone who can't see into the carton will grab the lightweight side, and they could have an "oops." It's like springing a trap on someone. Sometimes that someone is me. To prevent this, you grab eggs from opposite sides and make it balanced. If you grab an egg from the top left, then grab your next egg from the bottom right, and so on. Happy balancing!

* * *

Speed-Reading Course

It's Superbowl Sunday, and I'm visiting a friend for the weekend. I text Andrew at halftime: *Hey, what are you up to?*

He replies with six words. *I'm taking a speed-reading course.*

Immediately, I sit up in my chair to make sure I read that right, nearly spilling my beer.

You're what? I type back.

I'm taking a speed-reading course. I bought a program that includes two sets so you can also take the course if you want. It's pretty interesting. I'm excited to be able to read faster, he replies.

I chuckle as I write, *Thanks, but I think I'm good. Enjoy your speed-reading course.*

It amuses me that while most people are kicked back enjoying junk food, beers, and awesome commercials, Andrew is taking a reading course for fun. Particularly since he has been in school all week. I know he likes to read, but I hadn't realized that it's his favorite weekend activity.

The following week I'm at his place, and I notice he is reading multiple books at once. He reads one for a few pages, puts it down, picks up another book on a completely different topic, and begins reading that one. It's tough to focus on my own book because I become so distracted watching Andrew do this. This is the first time I've witnessed anyone switch books so effortlessly.

I interrupt him by asking, "Do you always read like that? Multiple books at once?"

"Not always. Sometimes I stick to just one," Andrew replies.

"It must be tough to switch between topics like that and remember where you left off," I continue. "I like to stick to one topic at a time."

In the most adorable voice, Andrew answers, "It's not hard. I just use a bookmark."

This showed me how strong Andrew's appetite is for knowledge and also inspired me to keep learning too. I'm certainly not used to dating boys like this, and I like it.

* * *

ANDREW'S TAKE

My interests excite me, and that is what I like to focus on. That speed-reading course had some great insights.

At times I read different topics at once. It feels like, *Well, I've had my fill of that topic for today, now on to something else.*

It feels like I might not be as avid a reader as Michelle portrays me, but I do use YouTube and other media to learn interesting things. It's so FUN.

* * *

The Parking Space

Andrew comes over distraught after work. As he takes his boots off, he says, "I think things might be weird with Chris." Chris is Andrew's friend and coworker.

"What do you mean weird? Did you get into an argument?" I ask.

"No, I'm not sure what happened. I just feel like things are off," Andrew answers.

I prod further. "Well, what happened the last time you guys talked?"

Andrew pauses a moment to think before speaking.

"We had a conference a couple of days ago and Chris sent me a text message that said, 'I saved you a space.' I read it and thought, 'Why would you save me a parking space?' and that was it."

"Did you go sit with Chris when you got to the conference?" I ask.

"No," Andrew replies.

I chuckle as I explain, "He likely meant that he saved you a chair and is probably wondering why you didn't go sit with him."

"Oh, that makes sense. I didn't really know what he meant," Andrew laughs.

Conversations similar to this have become frequent between Andrew and me regarding his work interactions. Minor miscommunications frequently happen in his world. And with each one, we learn a little more. I love being his sounding board.

* * *

ANDREW'S TAKE

Yeah, this was funny.

When someone does something out of their normal habit or routine, I tend to get a little uneasy. Not necessarily a negative uneasiness, more like a strong feeling of, *Something is out of place here. Further investigation needed.* Especially if I've known the person for several years and they say or do something that is unusual for them. This feeling was pronounced on this day, and I couldn't figure it out.

When Chris texted that to me, I was thinking he must mean *parking* space because parking can become crowded, and I've never had a problem with someone saving me a space in the room itself. I know where I typically sit; it varies, but I have a good feeling about how finding a seat in the room goes.

* * *

THE TEXT MESSAGE

I text Andrew, *How's your day going? What are you up to?*

We don't usually small-talk through text messages, but today I'm curious to know what he is doing.

Forty-five minutes later, Andrew responds, *jpeg.*

He sends me a picture with no words to go along with it. It looks like it's the picture of a label on the side of a box, but I can't say for sure. My first thought is that he sent it to the wrong person because it doesn't make any sense to me.

Andrew comes over later that evening.

"Hey, why did you send me this picture?" I ask him. "I don't understand it. Was it meant for someone else?"

"I sent you a picture? I don't remember," Andrew replies.

I pull out my phone and show it to him.

"Oh, that picture. I was trying to tell you that I was steaming something," he explains.

"What?" I ask, still confused.

"I was steaming vegetables. You asked what I was doing, so I was trying to tell you I was steaming something," Andrew explains further.

I start laughing, and it's obvious from the look on Andrew's face that he has no idea why I am laughing so hard.

"Andrew, how on earth would I know you're steaming vegetables from this picture?" I explain, while still chuckling, "All it has is some minutes on it."

Andrew shrugs and says, "Yeah, I do that sometimes. I forget to give context."

This incident taught me to ask follow-up questions anytime Andrew sends me a message I don't understand or seems a little rude. Rather than getting mad or jumping to conclusions, I always ask. This is a good practice for everyone, given the fact that text messages can so easily be misconstrued.

* * *

ANDREW'S TAKE

I have been told this in the past, that I respond with something that makes no sense because I don't give any context. In my mind, I forget that the other person is not with me and that they have no idea aside from this picture what I'm talking about.

* * *

Playing Scrabble

"Can we play a game of Scrabble?" I ask Andrew while we're relaxing at my condo.

"I don't really like Scrabble," Andrew replies.

"I play *Diablo* with you, and it's not my favorite game, so you owe me one. I love Scrabble," I plead.

"Okay, one game," Andrew agrees reluctantly.

We set up the board and each grab our seven tiles.

Placing my tiles horizontally across the center star, I go first.

As Andrew takes his turn, he begins placing the tiles diagonally.

"Andrew, you can only play your tiles horizontally or vertically. You can't put them diagonally like that," I interrupt.

Andrew becomes a little frustrated and needs more time to plan his turn.

He plays a word, and I mark his points down.

Next, I place a word vertically that lands me a double-word score. I talk a little smack. "Yes, double-word score. Eat it."

Andrew takes his next turn, placing his tiles horizontally; this time, he is spelling his word backward.

"Andrew, you can only place your words from left to right or top to bottom," I interrupt again. "You can't spell words backward."

"Arrrgh, that doesn't even make sense." Andrew's frustration increases.

We each take a couple more turns. Andrew is still having difficulty understanding how to place the tiles. It's evident he's not enjoying himself.

Watching him suffer becomes too painful, so I put an end to it by saying, "Okay, Andrew, we never have to play Scrabble again."

Andrew shouts, "Yes!" and begins packing up the game so fast that tiles are nearly flying off the table.

This moment stuck with me because it was so surprising. Andrew can take apart and reassemble pretty much anything with a manual, and yet Scrabble is confusing to him. This taught me that there must be a disconnect somewhere.

ANDREW'S TAKE

Not being able to spell a word diagonally, okay, I get it. But not being able to spell a word backward? Come on. This seemed like one of those moments when you realize how something works, and by extension, it must work this way as well. Right? No.

Turns out, in 2010, Mattel did release a version of Scrabble in the United Kingdom that allowed backward words. So, my assumption wasn't too far from possibility. And clearly, there are others out there that think this should be the case.

I'm sure Scrabble is a fun game, just not logical for me.

* * *

The Blank Stares

There are many times when I say something to Andrew, and he will just stare at me blankly without answering. It feels like he is analyzing what I just said negatively, and I don't like it.

This scenario plays out one afternoon, and I end up snapping at him.

"Why do you just stare at me like that after I say something? It makes me feel like you are judging me."

Andrew is obviously taken aback and surprised by what I said. He doesn't know how to respond, so he says nothing.

We don't talk about it until a week later when Andrew comes over and hands me a piece of paper. It's the first time he gives me a note, and it's written on a cue card in bright blue pen.

I grab the note from him and read, "I'm not judging you. I know exactly what I want to say, but I'm afraid to say it in this moment."

I smile, give him a hug, and thank him for explaining. It's the sweetest note, and I'm happy that he found a way to answer me.

This note lives in my wallet to this day as a reminder to let him pause before he speaks, without assuming he's judging anything. Just because he's being quiet does not mean he's thinking negatively. I stopped taking it personally.

* * *

ANDREW'S TAKE

This happens so often in my life. The thing that I want to say or that makes sense to say goes through a filter that I've created because I've hurt so many people's feelings over the years. And I'm stuck trying to reevaluate what I'm thinking to make it "present-moment friendly."

Often this causes my mind to BSOD. (Blue Screen of Death/Computer Crash). I don't know what to say, so I say nothing. If I were to speak, it would sound odd and uncharacteristic.

* * *

Talking in His Sleep

I wake up startled to Andrew screaming, "I said it was 24, not 27!" over and over.

He keeps repeating himself, "No, no, no. It's 27—27! I said 27, not 24."

Whoever he is mad at is getting an earful. It's quite entertaining.

Andrew talks in his sleep more than anyone I've ever slept beside. It's common for me to wake up in the middle of the night to him having a full-blown conversation. Most times, he is mentioning numbers while laughing or shouting.

My personal favorite is the time I woke up to him petting my stomach with a smile on his face. He was saying, "Oh, it's Michelle. Hi, Michelle." Then he started pinching me (gently) all over my arms with crab knuckles while saying, "Pinchy pinchy pinchy pinchy." Really fast.

I would pay a lot of money to have this on video. It was one of the funniest things I've ever experienced. For weeks I would pinch him with crab knuckles and say, "Pinchy pinchy pinchy." It never gets old.

How much Andrew repeats numbers in his sleep surprised me and solidified my suspicions that his mind works differently than mine. He doesn't wake me up so much anymore. I'm not sure if he's slowed down in the sleep-talking department or if I've just learned to sleep through it.

* * *

ANDREW'S TAKE

Even with my CPAP on, I talk in my sleep. I've only noticed this a few times when I become awake while in the middle of a tirade.

Wish I could tell you more about this. There are lots of funny stories, I'm sure, but I'm asleep, so I don't remember.

But a story I do remember about sleeping is about a lucid dream I had. Lucid dreaming is amazing! Have you ever been aware and in control while you're dreaming? I've only had this experience several times in my life, but one time, in particular, was out of this world.

I woke up in my dream and became conscious while dreaming, so what did I do? At first, I was just shocked that I was fully conscious while dreaming. Then I did the obvious next step: I STARTED TO FLY, of course! Just like Superman, I flew into the clouds, in between buildings, then I landed on abandoned rooftops and started to explore a little bit. Super fun! Highly recommended (10/10 would fly with this airline again)!

* * *

Andrew Loves His Dyson Vacuum

"Man, I love this vacuum. This is such a great vacuum." Andrew picks up the vacuum with amazing gusto.

"The battery on this thing is fantastic." Andrew is simply beaming while he's using the vacuum.

"Dyson makes great vacuums," Andrew repeats two minutes later. His energy is so infectious that you'd think using a Dyson vacuum is better than going to Disneyland.

Three minutes after that, "I'm almost done with the whole living room, and it still hasn't died."

Andrew, as he puts the vacuum away, says, "Have I told you how much I love this vacuum?"

When Andrew enjoys something, he lets you know it. Showing more excitement than anyone I've ever met. His Dyson is the perfect example. Every single time he uses that vacuum, I get a one-man show. His enthusiasm is unmatched.

This also rings true for many of his favorite things. When Andrew likes something, you will hear about it…A LOT.

The most fascinating thing about Andrew, though, and what stood out the most to me, is that his enthusiasm doesn't dwindle as time goes on. The fifth time he says, "I love this vacuum," will be just as enthusiastic as the first time he said it. If you didn't know better, his excitement would have you assume that he just got a brand new vacuum yesterday when in actuality, he's had it for many years. I wish I could keep that amount of enthusiasm for my things.

* * *

ANDREW'S TAKE

Of the several vacuums I've owned in my life, the vast majority are terrible. Absolute waste of money. Once I bought the cordless Dyson vacuum eight years ago, I realized what a good vacuum was. The only thing that has gone wrong with it is the battery started to die shortly after being fully charged. Would you go and buy a new vacuum if this happened to you and spend another $300–$400? NO! I bought a new battery from Amazon and received it in two days. That was three years ago, and it's still going strong, even better than the original battery.

Do you clean your vacuum? Dear god, clean your vacuum. I once walked into a vacuum repair shop and asked the guy if he sold Dyson vacuums. He said no. Then he said, "I don't sell Dyson because most people who own them take care of them, and this is bad for my business."

This makes perfect sense. "I know. It's so easy to clean. The whole thing comes apart. It's great," I responded.

He looked at me and grinned, then chuckled as he said, "You, you're terrible for business because you actually clean your vacuum. Nobody cleans their vacuum." We laughed and chatted for another few moments.

I can't help but praise and smile at any product I buy that keeps showing me how good it is. Every time I use it, this is how I feel: *Hey, it's still working, making me happy, and I don't have to bother trying to find a better vacuum.*

* * *

THE TEMPERATURE PROBE

"How was your night?" I ask Andrew after returning from dinner with a friend.

"Pretty good," Andrew replies with enthusiasm. "I finally figured out the perfect temperature to drink tea. It's 135 degrees F."

I chuckle. "What?"

"I hate drinking hot stuff," Andrew continues. "It burns my tongue, so I used my temperature probe to figure out the point that it's still hot but won't burn my mouth. One hundred thirty-five degrees F is perfect. I won't drink my tea if it's hotter than that."

"That's what you spent your night doing? Tasting multiple tea temperatures?" I ask.

"Yeah, it wasn't hard. I just kept checking it every few minutes until it was the perfect temperature to drink," Andrew replies.

Andrew is an HVAC technician, so I suppose this story is a little more understandable, but I still feel the need to mention how much he uses his temperature probe. He uses it so much that I often refer to it as his best friend.

When he's cooking, he uses his temperature probe to make sure it's cooked just how everyone likes it.

When he's drawing a bath, he uses his infrared temperature gun to make sure his bath water is just right.

When he's bored, he gets out his infrared temperature gun to tell me how hot my arm is.

And now I will never burn my mouth on tea again.

The temperature probe is just one example of how Andrew loves knowing specifics and bonds with his tools.

* * *

ANDREW'S TAKE

The thing about using a poor-quality temp probe for cooking is that it's analog. You know, the ones with a needle that rotates clockwise. You have to sit in front of the thing and stare at it, wondering things like, *Is that 120 degrees F?* If I move my head to the left or the right, the reading changes. Arg! Hence why analog temp probes are antiquated. Okay, what if you have a digital temp probe? That's better, but it's likely a consumer-grade probe which means it doesn't update quickly, and it isn't guaranteed to be calibrated. For me, one update per second minimum; the more, the better.

The temp probe that I used is a *UEI Test Equipment PDT650 Folding Pocket Digital Thermometer*. And the infrared Temp gun that I use is a *Fluke 62 MAX Mini Infrared Thermometer*.

Knowing the moment the middle of the chicken gets to 165°F is amazing. Cooking steak until it's exactly 120°F for rare, 130°F for medium-rare, 140°F for medium, 150°F for medium-well, and 160°F for well done is life-saving. It's hard to mess this up, and now you don't have to worry about over or undercooking meat. You can relax and enjoy cooking more!

Knowing the exact point to turn this steak on the BBQ or the chicken in the oven is worth it.

* * *

Receiving Massages

One of my favorite things to do for boyfriends has always been to give them massages when they're sore or having a rough day. I'm quite good at them, or at least I thought so until Andrew came along.

He complains of a sore back, so I tell him to sit in front of me on the floor. I begin to give him a massage. I find a big knot under his shoulder blade and begin to loosen it up.

After a few minutes, I ask, "How does that feel? A little better now?"

Andrew replies, "Yeah, I guess it's okay."

Confused by his response, I say, "Well, isn't it starting to feel better?"

He replies, "I don't know."

In my many years of giving scalp, hand, feet, and forearm massages in cosmetology, I've never had anyone respond with, "I don't know." This frustrates me, and I take it personally. I up my game a little bit and continue to massage him with all my best moves.

There is zero enthusiasm from Andrew. It seems as though he isn't enjoying himself, and my hands begin getting sore.

Finally, I just give up. "Well, I hope that feels better," I say.

Andrew replies, "Thank you," and gets back on the couch.

It's a while before I give Andrew a massage again, but when I finally do, it's more of the same.

He was still complaining of a sore back weeks later, so I booked him an appointment with my fabulous masseuse.

When I ask him how his massage was, he answers, "It felt like the stuff she was doing should help my back and neck." He never expresses any enjoyment or relief whatsoever, and I find it so strange.

When someone hits a knot in my back, my reaction is instant relief and relaxation as they loosen it up. I love getting massages and enjoy feeling the tension leave my body. Andrew doesn't seem to enjoy them at all. He doesn't complain about them, but he doesn't look forward to them either.

The good news is he doesn't mind giving back rubs, and I often get one to help relax me before bed. I'm not sure I will ever quite understand how Andrew cannot tell if a knot in his back is being loosened.

* * *

ANDREW'S TAKE

I've never been sensitive to massages. I'm not sure what they are supposed to do. I've never had problems with tense muscles. Only recently have I started to use different forms of massage for rehabilitation purposes. It seems to help my neck when I have tense neck muscles.

Someone rubbing me feels…neat? But I don't seek this kind of thing out unless I have a problem that needs to be addressed.

I read an article a few days ago. The title said, "Why does rubbing tired eyes feel so good?" Then I thought to myself, *What on earth is this article talking about?* Followed by *Is this a thing?* Because I've never experienced this phenomenon. Michelle tells me that the feeling you get when you rub tired eyes is a similar feeling of relief that some people experience during massages. Not Me.

* * *

Loud Talker

Andrew turns to me and says, "Yes! OMG, I just got a legendary! Look at my sword!"

"Andrew, stop screaming." I lean hard to the left, moving my ear away. "I'm right beside you."

"Sorry, I'm excited," he apologizes.

Minutes later, the same scenario plays out.

"OMG, look at this sword! It's amazing!" he shouts. "I deal so much damage with it!"

"Andrew, please stop screaming in my ear," I ask as I move my head away.

"Sorry, I just can't believe how awesome this sword is," he apologizes again.

We are playing *Diablo*, one of Andrew's favorite games. I'm getting overstimulated because his excitement causes him to talk loudly. This situation is common for us, as I often have to tell Andrew that we have to stop playing because he is being too loud. It pains me to have to do this because I enjoy playing games with Andrew. But the amount of times I have gone to bed with a headache due to his volume levels has become one too many for me. As someone with a brain injury, I am committed to my health in this regard.

Most days, Andrew seems to have little control over his tone of voice or volume levels. If I lean in to whisper to him, he will usually respond in his full voice. This is known to happen at the worst of times. At the movies, next to a sleeping baby—anywhere we go, really.

Andrew seems incapable of reading the room. When people begin winding down and are clearly tired, Andrew will come in with a loud story out of nowhere. It will often startle me because the room will go from being dead silent to obnoxiously loud without warning.

Andrew's enthusiasm is one of my favorite things about him. When he is having fun, it is infectious to everyone around him, and he absolutely lights up a room with his positivity.

There are moments I just wish it didn't hurt my eardrums.

* * *

ANDREW'S TAKE

This is a work in progress for me. When my mind gets jolted and the excitement ensues, it's hard to be aware of how loud I'm being. When I'm describing things with emotion or intensity, I try to use my volume as a gauge for how intense what I'm describing is. Knowing that my volume level can be so obnoxious, I'm realizing that I should not adjust my volume level to correspond with the intensity of my feelings when I'm talking and use some other verbal or nonverbal cue.

Getting better with this is tough because I get mixed signals from others. Sometimes my loudness and enthusiasm are welcomed very much by those around me. Other times I might be making a fool out of myself or am being obnoxious. Navigating the right and wrong times to be loud can be hard in certain settings. I know not to be loud during certain times, like in a theater, a library, or during a speech. But for the times when there is fun and excitement, or at least *I* think there is fun and excitement abound, I have lots of trouble with my volume.

* * *

THE TRIPLE REPEAT

Andrew bought me a present. I can't remember for the life of me what it was, but for the sake of this story, it doesn't matter. Whatever it was, Andrew could not stop playing with it. He loves his gadgets.

He is playing with it so much that it causes me to say, "Clearly, this is a present for you and not for me."

As I say those words, I hit a trigger. Andrew tilts his head to the side, looks away from me, and says, "I bought it for you, I bought it for you, I bought it for you." Then he walks away.

"Andrew, I'm just teasing. I think it's cute that you're playing with it," I say in an attempt to get him to come back.

"Okay, because people always say that to me, but I really did get this for you," he replies.

"I know you did," I reassure him. "Thank you. I love it."

This moment stuck with me because of the way he repeated himself. It was almost as if he checked out for a moment and didn't realize he was repeating it over and over. His voice stayed monotone and somewhat robotic. I've never heard anyone do that before.

* * *

ANDREW'S TAKE

*Glitching: Stuck in thought while in mid-sentence. This will cause me to have less attention to what I'm saying and can constrain my ability to speak articulately.

When I'm glitching, there is a chance that I will repeat a word over and over. As I thought about what Michelle had just said to me, I was unaware that I was repeating myself.

When I was younger, I would buy presents for people based on what I wanted. What they wanted wouldn't cross my mind at all. It's as if I was mind-blind to the needs of others. During my late teenage years, and early twenties, I learned to buy presents for people based on what would make them happy.

While I was glitching I became overwhelmed with the idea of *Did I buy Michelle something for her?* The extreme urgency that this question demanded caused me to be stuck in my mind until I knew the answer.

* * *

Photos for Chapter 7
Bellamimalifestyles.com/bookphotos

A BONUS STORY BY ANDREW

PRE-CLEAN DISHES? NO WAY!

One thing I found odd about Michelle was that she pre-washed all of her dishes before putting them in the dishwasher. They were almost clean enough to go back on the shelf. Half the reason why I enjoy the dishwasher is the fact that I don't have to clean the dishes at all.

"Worst thing that happens is a dish isn't clean after the cycle, and then we know the limits of this dishwasher. Then we send those dishes through another cycle," I say to Michelle.

"But what about the bits of food on the dishes? Won't they get jammed in the motor and plug it up?" Michelle rebutts.

As soon as her sentence ends, I go straight to the filter under the spray arms at the bottom and remove it to show her. I point to it and say, "This is the filter. It catches things as big as macaroni and as fine as pepper. But if anything does get by, then that thing"—I point to a rotating knife-looking thing in the filter compartment—"chops up any large food pieces."

Michelle has now stopped pre-washing her dishes and knows what level of dirty her dishwasher can handle. I clean the filter every month. Life is good.

* * *

Michelle's Take

Confession time. The man who installed my new dishwasher a couple of years ago actually told me that I'm not supposed to pre-wash the dishes. Apparently, this newer model is made to be run with dishes that are not pre-rinsed. Even still, I feel the need to pre-rinse my dishes. Placing a plate full of sauce in the dishwasher just feels wrong. I'm not used to it. Andrew has become so adamant on the subject that I cave and stop pre-rinsing.

I have to say, he is right on this one. It's less work, and the dishes still get cleaned. I'm not sure I would've thought to clean the filter every month if it was just me, though. I'm thankful Andrew is obsessed with checking filters.

8
SOME LEARNING CURVES

Taking the Game too Seriously

The first time Andrew and I spend an entire weekend together is at my cousin Diane's house in Edmonton. Andrew has been away at school, and meeting in Edmonton means we get to see each other without either of us having to drive more than a couple of hours.

Diane lives with her husband, and they are excited to host us for the weekend. The four of us get tickets for Adventure Hunt, a large scavenger hunt that is taking place all across the city.

We wake early Saturday morning and eat a large breakfast. Then it's off to the scavenger hunt. The four of us will spend the day chasing clues and filming ourselves completing ridiculous tasks to get points.

First, we have to make a slip 'n slide and film ourselves sliding down it. Next, we each have to do some sort of ice bath. We decide to complete this quickly by dumping buckets of ice over our heads. We also have to put two people on a bicycle for a full block. Diane and I manage to pull this one off, even though her bike has flat tires. All of this happens before 11 a.m.

As the hours roll on, the day continues to get more silly. We play suck and blow with a bunch of strangers at a park to get our next clue and then race to the truck. I'm impressed with Andrew's ability to make a fool of himself and partake in all the activities. He offers to be the one to jump in the river while yelling, "I'm a silly salmon!" in order for us to bypass a longer activity. We all laugh at his commitment to his salmon character as he does this.

As the day draws to an end, we are exhausted. We've been running around chasing clues and completing tasks all day. We end up being the twelfth team to finish, which we are happy with, considering there are over a hundred teams registered.

Once we arrive back at Diane's place, we enjoy a nice dinner and play some board games. Diane and I are sharing a bottle of wine, and her husband is enjoying a beer.

We are playing Catan, one of our favorite games. The goal of the game is to reach ten victory points. Players score one point for each settlement they own and two points for each city.

"Can I get you a drink, Andrew?" Diane asks after she takes her turn.

"Sure," Andrew responds. "Can I get a rum and Coke?"

"Coming right up," Diane says as she heads toward the kitchen.

Diane returns with Andrew's drink just in time for her next turn.

"Wow, that's a stiff drink," Andrew says as he takes a sip.

"Oh, I should've warned you," I explain. "Andrew doesn't drink much. A splash of rum would've been enough."

"Do you need me to go add some pop?" Diane asks Andrew.

"No, it's okay," he replies. "I'll just drink it slowly."

As the game nears its end, the pressure rises. Many of us have eight points, and the next person to buy a city will win.

"Can I have a pen and paper?" Andrew asks. "I want to keep track of who needs what."

"Sure," Diane says as she hands him a notepad, having no idea she will quickly regret offering him one.

Andrew begins writing things down as we each take our turn.

In the next round, Andrew gets carried away and starts trying to keep track of every single thing. He's writing down which cards people are looking for and who needs which resources to win. This starts to hold up the game to a point where Diane can't take it anymore.

"Stop writing everything down and just play the game already!" she yells at Andrew as he is lost in his notepad. "What are you doing anyways? Quit holding up the game!"

Andrew stands up and throws his pen with his arms up in the air. "I don't want to play anymore," he says. "I don't understand what's happening."

"Andrew, just play the game," Diane reiterates. "Stop holding up the game. You're ruining the fun."

I should probably explain that my cousin is quite the firecracker. You're never going to wonder what she's thinking because she will just say it right to your face. I'm used to this with my large French family, but poor Andrew is taken aback. The look on his face as she yells at him is something we still joke about years later when we all get together.

"Andrew, we are just trying to have some fun, and you keep getting lost in your notepad," I say. "Just take your turn and hope for the best. Stop worrying so much about a strategy because it's really slowing the game down."

Andrew is hesitant to sit back down next to Diane, but he does so slowly. Things remain awkward until I manage to win the game in the next round, and we all head off to bed.

This incident showed me how seriously Andrew takes his strategies when he's playing games. It was as if he completely disconnected from everyone at the table and entered into his own world on his notepad.

* * *

ANDREW'S TAKE

Even though I'm competitive, I don't take games seriously enough to get visibly upset. While we were playing, I was boasting here and there that the list I made was making me more efficient. I wasn't expecting people to take me seriously because it was such playful, sarcastic trash-talking.

First of all, I wasn't holding up the game that much. It felt like Diane realized I was giving myself an edge with what I was keeping track of, and this motivated her to yell at me. This surprised me because I wasn't really doing anything wrong. In my half-drunken mind, I thought, *Why don't you get your own pen and paper? No? Well then, prepare to lose.'* Because I felt that I wasn't cheating or really holding the game up, I was very upset when Diane came unhinged on me.

The main reason I was writing things down was because I was getting drunk and could feel my IQ points ticking down. So I did what any competitive person would do: I improvised. Rather than having to look at the board every time someone rolled to see how many resources I would collect, I wrote it down. I had a list for 1–12 with what to collect next to it. So awesome! No thinking or looking around every time.

* * *

Magic the Gathering – The Magnitude of the Rabbit Hole

Magic the Gathering is a card game in which wizards cast spells, summon creatures, and exploit magic objects to defeat their opponents. It has more cards and more complex rules than many other card games. Because of this, it is not a game I'm interested in learning. Andrew, on the other hand, loves it. He decides he wants to sign up for a Grand Prix competition that just so happens to be in Calgary. He asks me if I would mind if he competes. I'm surprised he is asking for my permission.

"Of course. Why would I mind?" I say, having no idea that Andrew will quickly become a walking obsession of Magic the Gathering, and our lives will be flipped upside down.

Magic the gathering is all Andrew can talk about for six weeks. He is either practicing, building his card deck, researching, or talking to others online about the game. He is incapable of focusing on anything else. The lengths he goes to building his perfect card deck are as much impressive as they are irritating.

My condo is taken over by his large folding table, printer, and paper cutter. For days he has been printing images of cards and gluing them onto dummy cards so he can practice with multiple variations of his deck. He wants to make sure he ends up with the perfect cards. My entire living room is covered in Magic the Gathering cards, and it's not a small living room.

Andrew's schedule never lets up. He will work all week building his deck; then, on the weekend, he is searching for people to go practice with. This feels like it's never-ending.

This incident teaches me to ask follow-up questions when Andrew comes to me for permission. It's tough for me to keep his attention on anything else. This is my first glimpse into how serious Andrew's obsessions can get. The hyperfocus is real.

* * *

ANDREW'S TAKE

Yes, detailed questions. Michelle asks Andrew, "Is this going to become an obsession for the next six weeks?" Andrew replies, "Yes." I'm not going to lie.

A Grand Prix is a Magic the Gathering tournament that's held up to sixty times a year all around the world. The top eight players get invited to a "Mythic" tournament and also accumulate pro points. About 700 people were playing Magic the Gathering the day I competed. It was awesome to see.

Also, this was not a net deck. I built this deck 100 percent from scratch. I spent $400 to have all the cards I needed delivered to the condo. It would have been nice to win one or two out of the eight matches that I was going to be playing. I won four out of the eight matches. It was the best Magic the Gathering experience ever (from a competitive perspective, of course).

* * *

Talking About Mars

It's a Canada Day long weekend, and we hike up a large mountain to sleep in a cabin next to a glacier for two nights. The cabin sleeps thirty people, and we only know four of them (all of which are female). The weather is quite cold next to that glacier, so we spend most of Saturday inside playing board games.

This is the first time I've brought Andrew to a large social event, and he is clearly uncomfortable. He doesn't talk much and keeps disappearing upstairs to our bunk to lay by himself.

Throughout the afternoon, I feel the need to check on him several times and bring him food. He tells me he is reading, but the stunned look on his face says otherwise. His eyes look as if they are about to jump out of their sockets, and he is only capable of giving me one-word answers.

"Andrew, are you hungry?" I ask.

"YES."

"Andrew, are you okay?"

"YES."

"Andrew, we are going to go for a walk to the glacier."

"OKAY."

I've never seen him like this before, and I'm not sure what to do about it. It doesn't seem like he wants to move, so I decide it's best to leave him alone for a few hours. I go about my afternoon while feeling odd about whatever is going on.

After dinner, we are all playing Yahtzee. Andrew loosens up a little as he enjoys dice games. We make some hot tea and all take turns sharing stories about traveling and our upcoming summers. Andrew seems to get uncomfortable again once the dice games stop, only this time he is far from quiet. He starts talking about Mars in an unusually loud voice, and it's as if he can't stop. The girls humor him for the first five minutes, but it soon becomes obvious that no one is interested in hearing this conversation (including me).

My plan is to wait for an opening and then casually change the subject, but Andrew never gives me an opening. He goes on and on about atmospheric pressure and what life would be like on Mars for what feels like an eternity. It's tough for me to pay attention to anything he is saying because everyone's lack of interest is so blatantly obvious to me. I also can't stand how loud and fast he is talking.

He goes on for so long that I have no choice but to blatantly interrupt him. "Okay, Andrew, enough about Mars. No one wants to hear more about Mars." The girls at the table all start laughing, and I feel the need to apologize. "I'm sorry, Andrew, but I'm so tired of hearing about Mars. Can we please talk about something else?"

Andrew seems stunned. "You girls don't find Mars interesting?" he asks.

The entire table quickly shakes their heads no.

Many people in the cabin begin laughing as they overhear our situation. One man two tables over quickly shouts, "Hey man, I want to hear more about Mars! Come sit over here, buddy. I love talking about space."

Andrew looks at me awkwardly as if he needs my permission to leave the table. I chuckle as I say, "Go talk about Mars with your new friend, Andrew." Andrew is gone from the table before I can even get the sentence out.

This trip taught me that it's more fun when Andrew and I stick to hiking solo or with just a couple of friends. There's no need to book group trips when they cause him so much anxiety.

* * *

ANDREW'S TAKE

When I recall this story in my mind, it doesn't seem the same as how Michelle depicts it. She is likely right with her synopsis, as I've come to realize that I can get excited about certain topics that I find out of this world. Ha.

When I was talking about Mars, it would seem to me that all I have to do is explain a few cool ideas about Mars, and then they will get it and be pulled in by how interesting it is. I've been learning more and more that lots of the subjects that I'm interested in aren't for everyone. Especially several women in a remote hiking lodge in the Rocky Mountains.

While I was in that lodge surrounded by lots of unfamiliar people, I know now that I was feeling overwhelmed and didn't know how to cope. Talking about Mars was a way for me to feel comfortable and social in an unfamiliar setting. Back then, I wasn't as self-aware as I am now.

* * *

Methodical Speed

"Andrew, do you think you could tie your boots in the car?"

I'm anxious because we are twenty minutes late. My mind is working overtime, trying to get us both out the door.

Andrew glares at me like I just kicked a puppy. Next, he slows down. Not because he is trying to, but because I've confused him with the fact that I even dared to ask him that question.

Andrew stays silent as he stops putting his boots on. It seems as though I've scrambled his circuits, and he cannot think straight.

"Tie my boots in the car? Why would I do that? That's not even a thing," he answers minutes later.

I'm frustrated with myself because we are now even more late since I tried to rush him.

After this incident, I never try to rush Andrew again. Asking him to leave the house without him getting to do his routine will completely throw him off for the day. I'm better off standing patiently by the door for twenty minutes without saying a word. That way, I get the best version of Andrew when we do leave, even though we are running late.

This might sound crazy to some of you. You might be thinking that he should meet me halfway. But once you know that it is actually not so simple and make peace with it, life gets better. This can be true of a lot of our partners' deeply ingrained personality traits.

Andrew only has one speed. It does not matter what time it is or how late we are; he is going at "Andrew speed." I envy him, really. I am jealous that he seems completely unaffected by the fact that we are running late.

Regardless of how much time we have, he will do his same routine. He will need to be showered, in fresh clothes, eat, and then he will do a walk around to grab all his things (it throws him off if I grab them for him and bring them to the door). Lastly, he will sit down to tie the shoelaces on his boots so that they have perfectly even tension on both feet.

The same goes for Andrew's nighttime routine. He showers, puts his lotion on, brushes his teeth, mouthwash, and shaves his facial hair if it's a little too long. He cleans his CPAP machine, then puts fresh water in it every single night. All fantastic habits.

There are many nights I am just too exhausted to complete my full bedtime routine, but Andrew never misses a step. His skin needs to feel fresh for the night. I'm not sure it would even be a possibility for him to sleep without doing his routine.

* * *

ANDREW'S TAKE

For context's sake, tying shoes or boots while in the passenger seat of a car is a terrible experience. While someone else is driving, your adjustments to your laces are getting messed up by the jostling of the vehicle left, right, forward, and backward. Plus, you're driving with your head almost touching the surface of the airbag. Bad Idea! In the end, your shoes are now either over-tightened or under-tightened, and you can't just relax into the vehicle comfortably as you always do. All of this is what flashes through my mind the moment Michelle asks, "Can you tie your shoes in the car?" Hence why this isn't a "thing." Okay, I'll stop my rant.

I have found often in life there are moments where everyone has this unconscious automatic response to a change in their surroundings.

For example, when the light turns yellow, many speed up. If your supervisor tells you to go faster, you rush. Sometimes, I agree with changing speeds (like if your life is in danger). But I've found that most of the time, after you assess your situation, you realize there is no good reason to change speed or disposition, except for this vague, ambiguous feeling that you *should.* So don't fret about something that doesn't need to be fretted about.

When there is a rigid time frame, and I know that people will be waiting for me, then I do my best to be there either on time or just before. Magic the Gathering tournaments start at 11 a.m. on Sunday. I can see my teammates in my mind waiting for me leading up to that time. The flip side of this is lots of time frames are loose, and your presence isn't a requisite for the occasion to start. If not being on time will not impact you in any way, then take an extra five, ten, maybe twenty minutes. Don't rush when you don't have to.

* * *

Our First Gift Exchange - The Mug

As our six-month anniversary approaches, I express to Andrew that I want to celebrate. It's been nearly a decade since I've lasted six months in a relationship, so it's a big deal for me. We plan a Saturday full of our favorite activities and decide we will exchange gifts for the first time.

Andrew picks me up for our anniversary date, and as I get in the car, he says, "I have to run home quickly because I forgot something." It's not a big deal since he only lives five minutes away. It's common for Andrew to forget something, so I don't bother asking what it was. We pull up to his place, and he runs in and out quickly before returning to the car.

"Happy anniversary," Andrew says without looking at me as he lobs a mug into my lap. It feels as if it is a hot potato he couldn't wait to get rid of.

I'm left dumbfounded as he continues looking forward and begins driving.

I'm waiting for him to start laughing, say he's kidding, or pull over and kiss me. Nope, he's not joking. This is actually how he's going to deliver my anniversary present.

No kiss, no sentiment, no card, just a hot-potato mug thrown in my lap as he gets in the car without looking at me. Now I'm sitting with a coffee mug on my lap, confused and shell-shocked.

We go to play virtual reality and see a movie. The mug lays heavy on my mind all day, and it puts a dark cloud over an otherwise fantastic afternoon. I wonder if I'll ever be able to use it or like it.

We go back to my place after an afternoon of activities. I give Andrew my gift: a couple of T-shirts, a hat, and a card telling him I'm looking forward to many adventures together. I place the bag in his hand, give him a big kiss, and say, "Happy anniversary."

Andrew thanks me for the gift and then opens it. We share a nice moment as he tries on his gifts and reads his card.

The mug delivery is still bothering me, and I'm hoping to change that. I go to the kitchen, grab the mug, and ask, "Andrew, can you tell me about this mug?"

I'm so glad I ask him this because his explanation is one of the sweetest things he has ever said to me. He doesn't look at me while he says any of it, but this doesn't take away from the sentiment.

"Well, I was trying to find a mug for you," he explains. "But I couldn't decide on one. Then I remembered you like David's Tea. So I decided to go to David's Tea at the mall. I talked to the guy who was working there and asked him to show me their best mugs. I asked if he had a teal one because I know you like teal. He showed me a few mugs. I really wanted to get you one that wouldn't leak, so I asked him to put water in it so I could turn it upside down and make sure it didn't leak. That one was the best one; it didn't leak at all. Most of the others did. You could totally just throw that one in your purse and not worry about it leaking. I also thought you might like that the steeper is at the top because it should give you more flavor as you drink it. So yeah, I really looked around, and that's pretty much the best mug for you."

As he says all of that, I get tingles all over my body. His hot-potato delivery no longer matters. He's put so much thought and effort into getting me a nice gift. It's adorable. With a huge smile on my face, I hug my mug and put it in the cupboard. It remains my favorite mug to this day. Every time I drink from it, I feel happy remembering I have such a thoughtful boyfriend.

This incident taught me never to assume that something was done in an offhanded or uncaring way. Instead of making assumptions, I've learned to ask Andrew what his intentions were, as I am often pleasantly surprised. It's amazing how far asking one little question can take you.

* * *

ANDREW'S TAKE

I'm very glad Michelle asked me about the mug. I might not have told her otherwise. It felt as though she was with me when I bought it. I assumed that she would know that this was the best mug I could find. I wasn't just "buying a mug." This had to be *the* tea mug. The one she wanted, not the one that "works."

Sentimental moments can be overwhelming for me. How Michelle felt when I tossed the mug on her lap was not going through my mind. I wasn't aware of how awkward or unpleasant I was acting. In my mind, to avoid becoming overwhelmed, I made the moment as matter-of-fact as possible.

Since this mug story and many other stories in the past, I've learned that I act this way unconsciously as a defense against becoming overwhelmed. Through inner work and self-care, I've realized that there were many things that I would do without knowing it to avoid overwhelming feelings. Knowing how I avoid certain feelings by acting a certain way in uncomfortable situations has helped me to become aware of these triggers. Now I can heal them.

* * *

Shopping

Andrew only has one pair of shorts that he always wears, and they are terrible. They are brown cargo shorts that are three sizes too big, and they have a dark flower pattern on them that kind of makes them look like an old couch. He has to buckle his belt tight so that they don't fall down. This leaves so much fabric hanging down that the belt is basically just sitting against his stomach while the waistband hangs inches below it.

For months I've made fun of them, but Andrew says they are his favorite. He argues that they are comfortable because they are so big on him. This same argument is used for his t-shirts which are obviously many years old. Any time I bring up the fact that he needs new clothes, his response is, "But these are so comfortable."

After months of pleading my case, Andrew finally caves and agrees to go shopping with me. I'm ecstatic. We walk into a store at the mall that has a summer sale going on, with a wide selection of brands. We grab a few pairs of shorts and shirts from the sale racks and head back to the change rooms. Andrew comes out in his first pair of shorts, and they look great on him.

"They look great," Andrew says as he stretches his legs in the shorts. "But I want to walk around the store for a while to see how they feel. I can't tell if I like them or not."

After trying on a few more pairs and walking around in them, Andrew concludes that he is not sure. We go back and grab a few pairs that are more expensive for him to try on.

"Yeah, I think I like these a little better," he says. "But I need to put the other pair on again to be sure."

I'm developing anxiety as all of this is going on. I am not prepared for this lengthy process. I'm thinking to myself, *They're thirty-dollar shorts, Andrew. Just grab a few pairs so we can get outta here.*

This same pattern continues with shirts. He tries on multiple sizes and styles to be sure he chooses the right ones. There are many shirts that look good on him, but he says, "I don't like how it feels in the shoulders." After trying on over a dozen shirts, he picks only two.

Before this shopping trip, I noticed that Andrew is fussy with his clothes, but I had no idea what the extent of it is. By the time we are nearly finished (or so I think), Andrew begins asking questions about the fabrics and how they wash.

My anxiety keeps rising as the clerks clearly don't understand how to answer Andrew's questions, and yet he keeps asking them. I can sense their obvious frustration. I'm so embarrassed that I walk away and pretend to look at clothes.

After I think we have finally decided on what we are buying, Andrew begins looking through the pile again and says, "Okay, I just want to go try all of these on one more time."

My anxiety hits its limit, and I snap.

"Andrew, we are really bothering all of these salespeople, and you are giving me anxiety."

Andrew replies, "But that's their job?" with a confused look on his face.

"Can't we just get these and go?" I plead. "We've been in this store for over an hour."

Andrew very calmly says, "If I'm giving you anxiety, just go and wait on the bench outside. I'm going to try them on again."

I take his suggestion and immediately walk out of the store. Andrew takes another twenty minutes; this allows me time to calm down on the bench by myself.

We often joke about how I nearly had a panic attack the first time we went shopping together. I tease Andrew that it was his fault because he didn't warn me about what I was in for.

As I write this, I am realizing that I have come a long way with my people-pleasing issues since meeting Andrew, as I've worked on healing much of my childhood trauma. He was right, that is their job, and it's not like he was being rude to them. He was just being high maintenance. So high maintenance that he tried on the same shorts three times to make sure he liked them. It drove me crazy.

I've since learned that how something feels on Andrew's body is extremely important. It needs to be comfortable and efficient. He cares little about how it looks or what it will match with, which is the first thought I have when I am purchasing clothes. If he feels any kind of tugging on his skin from the fabric, or it's not soft enough, it will ruin his day and end up in the garbage. Sensory issues affect so many people. Being aware of this can transform our understanding of those around us.

* * *

ANDREW'S TAKE

As with the spill-proof mug that I bought Michelle for our six-month anniversary, when you buy something, make sure it's the one.

Once I know what I like, then I have a benchmark. But when I don't have a benchmark, I don't know what I like. You might try on clothes and think, *These fit well, but something is off*. The only way to find out what is off is by trying on other clothes and further assessing.

Worrying about upsetting staff will not help you learn what will fit the best and fit just right. It would feel like settling if I were just trying to rush out of the store.

* * *

Learning What Love Is

There is a ten-day period in the middle of summer when my concussion symptoms flare up and become quite serious. It's over a year into my healing journey, but it seems as though I've been sent back to the highly symptomatic early days out of nowhere.

Brain injuries are unpredictable. I will have a week where I feel like myself, followed by a week when I can hardly get out of bed. My head will feel like it's in a vice and I can't think straight. It's terrible, and I never know when it's coming. Nothing but time helps it subside.

When I feel like this, I ask Andrew to rub my forehead to help me relax, and he always does so with a smile on his face. This usually happens every few days or so, but this week it's been constant. All I can do is lay around and ask Andrew to rub my forehead.

Laying in bed, I'm unable to fall asleep. Andrew is beside me reading his book. I'm struggling not to ask him to rub my forehead because he has already done that for most of the afternoon. My head is pounding. But I do my best to fall asleep on my own to give him a break.

I'm thinking to myself, *If I ask him, I'm sure he will sigh or complain about having to stop what he was doing yet again to help me.*

He is obviously enjoying his book, but my head is pounding so badly that I poke him and ask, "Can you rub my forehead so I can fall asleep?"

Andrew smiles and says, "Sure," while he puts his book down and lays on his pillow in front of me.

As he begins rubbing my forehead, he says in the kindest voice, "Just let me know when I can stop."

There is something magical in this moment. He isn't frustrated or tired of helping me at all. He shows me nothing but kindness, and I hardly believe it. He acts as if it is the first time I've ever asked him. This kind of patience is something I've never experienced before. I think to myself, *Oh, so* this *is what love feels like.*

Asking people for help has always been tough for me. In part because of my childhood trauma, but also because I hate feeling their frustrations as they help me. I'd rather do it myself than feel like anyone's burden. Even at my worst, Andrew never makes me feel like a burden.

It's nearly an hour before I can feel myself begin to drift off to sleep.

This entire week, I've felt nothing but high anxiety and panic. But as Andrew rubs my forehead, all my fears drift away. For the first time in my life, I can pinpoint the moment I begin falling in love. I whisper, "Okay, you can stop now. Thank you."

Andrew smiles and says, "You're welcome," and then he kisses my forehead, sits up, and continues reading his book.

* * *

ANDREW'S TAKE

I want to give Michelle what she gives me: loving kindness.

Michelle makes me feel great, and I know this deep inside. To show grief when she needs me, or sigh, for no good reason other than *I don't feel like it* would feel like an inner conflict of epic proportions. It doesn't compute.

* * *

Photos for Chapter 8
Bellamimalifestyles.com/bookphotos

A BONUS STORY BY ANDREW

CONSISTENT RUNNING SPEED

"Michelle, why did you just speed up?" I ask while we pass a couple who were walking on the path.

"I wanted to get around those people," she responds.

While running, I keep a fairly consistent speed. Every third step I exhale, and then every other third step I inhale. This helps me keep my pace and breathing consistent. So it is no surprise when Michelle and I go running together that I notice her speed increasing and decreasing without any obvious reason.

Huh? I wonder to myself. *Get around the couple quickly? Why? This doesn't make sense to me.*

As we're running together, we start a small conversation, and I notice that Michelle starts to slow down. "Yeah, VR arcade sounds like super fun this weekend!" I say as I notice I'm pulling away from Michelle. She realizes that I'm over two meters ahead of her and starts to run faster.

Step, step, step, inhale.

Step, step, step, exhale.

I continue counting my steps and breaths in my mind. All at a fairly consistent pace.

"Hehe. Michelle, you're slowing down," I chuckle. I could have throttled my speed to match hers. But that would require me to become inconsistent and erratic.

Step, step, step, inhale.

Step, step, step, exhale.

I'm really enjoying my pace and speed; it's almost relaxing. Speeding up and slowing down is definitely not relaxing.

"I'm trying to keep pace, but it's really hard," Michelle sighs while panting.

"No worries. You're doing great, Michelle," I respond, trying to show compassion.

I wonder if Michelle realizes how much she speeds up and slows down. Or perhaps I don't realize that I'm being too consistent.

* * *

Michelle's Take

I remember this jog. I was doing my best to get back in shape, and running seemed like the quickest way to do so. Jogging has never been my forte, but I made a goal to be able to make it 5k without stopping.

"That's easy. Just keep it at a 7 km/hr pace the whole time. Don't push it so you don't get tired," Andrew said. "A nice steady, slower pace, and you'll be able to run 5k no problem."

"Can we try that together this weekend?" I asked, surprised that he knows the perfect pace off the top of his head.

"Sure," Andrew answered. "I'll show you. It's easy."

Well, it was not easy. I don't like trailing behind people on a trail if we are going about the same speed. I always feel the need to speed up and go around them. It's also tough to run slow when I get excited, a fact I did not understand about myself until this day.

I did not notice how hard it is for me to keep a consistent speed until Andrew came along. I assume this is because most people mirror me without much thought. Andrew does his own thing regardless of what everyone else is doing. Whenever we are walking or jogging together, he consistently goes at his own speed. If the crosswalk light starts blinking yellow, I naturally tend to speed up. Andrew will just stay behind me unless I stop and wait for him. It's frustrating for Andrew to change speeds; he likes to be consistent. I'm not sure I'll ever be able to be consistent.

9
RANDOMNESS

Abstract Music

"What's that noise?" I ask as I get in Andrew's truck. It sounds like a collection of aggressive sounds that have no melody to them whatsoever. The randomness of it confuses my brain, and it feels overly loud.

"That's my ambient music," Andrew replies. "It helps me focus."

"So, you listen to this to relax?" I ask in a confused tone. "Because it's agitating the hell outta me."

"Yeah, I find it calming," Andrew explains. "This is what I'm usually listening to as I read."

"Well, can we turn it off?" I ask. "Because I can't stand it."

"Yeah, no problem," Andrew says as he turns it off. I feel instant relief.

This stood out to me because I knew that if that kind of music helps him focus, we are most certainly not wired the same. I can't even fathom how music like that could possibly feel relaxing. It made my brain hurt. Having to read while it was playing would feel like torture.

ANDREW'S TAKE

If I listen to music that I'm familiar with, it helps to drown out intrusive sounds that can be overwhelming. I use this strategy when I'm studying or writing.

The song she is talking about is "Too Young for Tragedy" by GRiZ. My strategy since 2016 is to have a list of songs I like and then use the Play Radio feature on a song I'm liking that day. By doing this, you get to find more music that you might like and then add those to your Thumbs-Up playlist. Just keep repeating this cycle, and you will have a never-ending supply of music that you like.

* * *

Disappearing at the Movie Theater

"Can we go see *Deadpool 2*?" Andrew asks for the hundredth time.

I'm nervous about going to the movies. Since my concussion, screens of any kind have the potential to overstimulate me, so a big screen has the potential for disaster. I've told Andrew this several times, so I'm growing annoyed with him asking. But at the same time, I know how badly he wants to see *Deadpool 2*.

"C'mon, please?" Andrew begs. "I want to see it so bad. If your head hurts, we can leave. It's playing tonight at 9:30 p.m."

"Okay, we can go, but I haven't even seen the first one," I answer.

"I don't think it'll matter," Andrew says. "It'll still be hilarious."

Andrew and I walk hand in hand through the movie theater. It's been ages since I've been at the movies with a boyfriend, and it feels good not to be single for once.

"I just have to go to the washroom," Andrew says as he lets go of my hand.

Five minutes go by.

I'm worried he may have fallen in the toilet.

Ten minutes go by.

I don't like standing in the crowded hallway of the theater. All of the noises from the video arcade games are agitating me, and I keep getting in people's way.

Fifteen minutes go by.

I'm fully frustrated and want to go home.

Twenty minutes go by.

Now I'm angry because I'm missing the previews. *If he knew he was going to poop, why didn't he warn me?* I think to myself. *I would have grabbed my ticket or gotten my popcorn and gone to sit in the theater.*

A few minutes later, Andrew comes strolling out of the washroom all nonchalant.

"What the hell took you so long?" I snark. "You need to warn me if you're going to poop."

"Yeah, sorry," Andrew answers. "I didn't know I needed to poop until I got in there."

"We are missing the previews," I say.

"Who cares. We don't need to see the previews," Andrew replies.

"I like the previews. I would've grabbed my ticket and gone to wait for you in the theater if I knew you were going to take forever," I explain. "I was really uncomfortable standing out here because it's so busy. Warn me next time."

"I'll try," Andrew says. "Now let's go get some popcorn."

It's not uncommon for Andrew to disappear for long periods of time without warning me. I've since learned that if he takes a few minutes, I should just go do my own thing and let him find me afterward.

Just in case you're curious, my brain was fine throughout the movie, and I enjoyed the laughs. But the next day I paid a serious price. It's as if my brain shut down in a complete fog. I could hardly function. I took a shower and couldn't even wash all of the conditioner out of my hair. I gave up halfway through to go lay down.

"You still have stuff in your hair," Andrew says when I get out of the shower.

"I don't care. I just need to lay down," I reply. "My head hurts so bad I don't even want to talk."

"I'm so sorry. I feel terrible," Andrew says. "I won't ask to go to any more movies."

"Well, at least now we know I'm not ready for them. You may as well go home and play games," I suggest. "I need to lay in quiet for the next couple of days."

* * *

ANDREW'S TAKE

There are times where plans change, and you don't realize that it's important to let the person who's waiting for you know. Even if you don't think it will be that long, text them and let them know you *might* be twenty minutes.

Yet another thing I work on and have improved very much with. When I realize I might be much longer than was implied, I let the person who's waiting for me know.

* * *

THE HIKING HAT

Andrew and I hiked a lot the first summer we were dating. It's pretty much all we did on weekends. Mother Nature and the Rocky Mountains felt healing for my brain, and hiking was pretty much the only solid exercise I could do.

Andrew wore the same hat every single time we spent the day outside. It was a leather full-brimmed hat with mesh on top, and I hated it. It made him look like a sloppy Indiana Jones because it was quite worn out.

I took it upon myself to buy him a new one while I was out shopping. I bought a blue ball cap in a hiking store that said *Explore More* across the front, and I couldn't wait to give it to Andrew the next time I saw him.

"I saw this hat today when I was shopping for new poles, and I thought it would look great on you," I explain as I toss Andrew the hat.

"Oh, thanks." Andrew looks less than enthused. "I don't usually wear hats like this."

"I know. That's why I want you to try it," I reply. "It's going to look so great on you."

"Okay, I'll wear it on our hike this weekend," Andrew answers.

Andrew wears the hat on our hike, and it looks great. He mentions a couple of times that he doesn't like it, but I don't understand why.

When we get home, it all makes sense when Andrew explains, "I really hate having the sun on my neck. I feel like my neck is burnt even though I put sunscreen on it."

"Oh, is that why you always wear that leather hat?" I ask.

"Yes, I hate ball caps," Andrew replies. "I want my hat to block the sun all the way around. And my leather one has mesh on top, so my head doesn't get sweaty."

"Oh, I get it now," I say as I feel terrible for making him be uncomfortable. "Well, just leave it here then. I'll wear it sometime. Thanks for trying."

This incident taught me that Andrew truly has a reason for everything. I never understood why he only had one hat that he always wore until he explained himself. I looked at his hat differently after this conversation. I was just happy he was comfortable.

* * *

ANDREW'S TAKE

The main reason why I don't like baseball hats is the obstruction of view; a quarter to one-third of your vision is obscured. Not only that, but they do a seriously poor job of being a hat. If I'm going to obscure a third of my view, then the hat better be functional. Your neck and sides of your face are not blocked with a baseball hat. Try wearing a full-brimmed hat for a long day in the sun, and you don't have that blah feeling on your face like the sun just sucked the life out of you.

I've been told "I like your safari hat" by quite a few people.

One thing I've realized that should be obvious but isn't for some reason is that baseball hats are meant for baseball players. It allows them to have peripheral vision and still be able to wear a hat. That's the trade-off to wearing a hat while playing baseball. Why, when you're not playing baseball, would you wear a substandard hat? These are questions that keep me up at night sometimes. Realizing the answer might be fashion is traumatizing.

* * *

Paper Towels

I walk into my kitchen and notice four large balls of bunched-up paper towels on my counter.

"Andrew, why are there always paper towels laying all over the place?" I ask as I pick them up and throw them in the garbage.

"Yeah, I do that a lot," Andrew explains. "And I appreciate that you're not screaming at me about it because it used to drive my ex nuts."

"Why do you leave it laying all over the place?" I ask. "It seems so wasteful."

"I don't really know. I've just always done that." Andrew answers. "I always think I'm going to reuse it later, but then I never do."

"I've just never seen anyone use so much of it," I explain. "I like to be stingy when I use paper towels."

"Yeah, I think it's a comfort thing," Andrew replies. "I hope it doesn't drive you crazy because I'm not sure I'll be able to stop."

"I think I can handle it," I say. "I guess I'll just have to start buying extra."

This stood out to me because it was obvious that Andrew was ashamed of this behavior yet had little hope that he could control it. I decided right then and there that I wasn't going to shame him over this or bring it up again. It seemed as though he was punishing himself enough for the both of us. This is just one of the countless examples of things that couples can decide to either harp on forever or decide to be understanding about and create peace in the relationship.

***

ANDREW'S TAKE

This is something I have been working on. I like to use a new towel to clean my hands frequently. Knowing this, I try to reuse a slightly wet, mostly clean paper towel to conserve paper towels. Then I forget about all of them once I'm done in the kitchen.

My new strategy is to have a clean towel over the oven handle that I use to dry my hands after washing them. This towel is cleaned once every two to four days. Or once it is too saturated with water. Whichever comes first.

Michelle is so accommodating. Maybe too accommodating. She lets me get away with a lot because she wants me to be happy. It's important that I don't take advantage of how nice she can be.

***

Netflix and Chill

Andrew is away at school when he calls me.

"Hello," I answer.

It's apparent from Andrew's breath that he is distraught.

"What's going on?" I ask.

"I don't really know, but I don't feel well," he replies.

"Did something happen at school today?" I prod for a reason.

"Nothing out of the ordinary." Andrew sounds as though he is on the verge of tears. "I just don't feel right."

"How much have you been studying?" I ask.

"Every night I study," he answers.

"Well, it's tough to study every night," I suggest. "Maybe you just need a night off."

Andrew takes a long pause, and it seems as though he is panicking.

"What's your favorite show?" I ask. "What always puts you in a good mood?"

"I like *Rick and Morty*," Andrew answers.

"Okay, turn your phone off and put some comfy clothes on," I say with conviction. "Watch *Rick and Morty* and zone out for the night."

"Okay. I don't usually watch much TV," Andrew replies.

"I know, but you obviously need it," I say. "Don't watch anything educational. Watch something comforting where you can just enjoy it without thinking."

Andrew stays quiet for a little while before he reluctantly agrees.

"Okay, I'll do that, I guess," he says.

"Great, I'll talk to you tomorrow," I answer. "Sleep well."

The following evening I get a text from Andrew. *Watching TV was a great idea, thank you. I feel so much better today.*

I'm glad to hear it, I text back. *You've gotta give yourself a break every now and then.*

Yeah, I just didn't realize how much I needed it, Andrew says.

This was the first time I helped Andrew regulate by insisting he take a break from life. I didn't mind doing it, especially since he sounded so adorable on the other end of the phone. I did, however, wonder why I needed to do it. *Why couldn't he tell he was overloaded and needed a night off?* I thought to myself afterward. *I wonder if this happens to him a lot.* Over time I've learned that this happens to Andrew every two to three months or so. He will become overloaded and will need to shut things down to reboot, but he won't realize it until he crashes.

* * *

ANDREW'S TAKE

Zoning out and watching a show or movie is great to relax. The only problem is that I'm almost always excited to learn something, play something, study something, or work on something. The habit of zoning out and relaxing needs to be strengthened.

* * *

Getting Noticed by the Ladies

Andrew has always been a good-looking guy, but his style most definitely brought him down a point or two. As Andrew's new hairstylist, I encouraged him to grow his hair out and showed him how he could wear it a little messy on top. Caleb and Jackson were always helping by telling Andrew which clothes to get rid of, and they offered to take him shopping.

We discovered that Andrew looks great in Tentree T-shirts, and he also likes the way they fit. This was a huge win. I immediately bought him six more Tentree shirts even though I couldn't afford them. The colors are nice, they are soft, and they are long enough on him.

As we make these minor adjustments, Andrew is becoming increasingly more attractive.

One day, Andrew comes over in a good mood after work and says, "Women seem to be talking to me more."

"What do you mean?" I ask with a chuckle.

"I don't even know, really," Andrew replies. "I just notice that women are talking to me more. People don't usually talk to me, but lately, people are talking to me."

"Well, for one thing, your fashion choices have much improved, so the ladies are going to notice you more," I explain. "But you've also been pretty happy lately, and that'll make you more approachable."

"It will?" Andrew asks with a confused tone. "Why does that happen?"

"People can sense happy people, and you'll come off as being more friendly," I respond. "Pair that with the better clothes, and it's a recipe to get hit on."

"Oh," Andrew says as he looks at the ceiling. "This is new for me. I kinda like it. I like it when people smile at me."

"Eat it up," I say. "In this world, people are nicer to you when you look good. I always got more attention when I was in fighting shape. It's sad in a way, but appearance really affects how people treat you."

The next time we are out with Jackson and Caleb, I immediately bring it up. "So, women seem to be talking to Andrew now, and he's not used to it."

"Oh really," Jackson says as he looks at Andrew side-eyed. "So the new clothes are working then."

"Yes, I guess they are," Andrew chuckles.

I mostly tell you this story to show you how Andrew is evolving through our relationship. But I also found it adorable the way he brought it up in a confused tone by saying, "So, women seem to be talking to me more." His honesty is so refreshing. And don't you worry, bestie. I, of course, have a glow-up of Andrew's fashion evolving in the photo section for you at the end of this chapter.

* * *

ANDREW'S TAKE

This was a big change in a short period of time, so it was very apparent that people were talking to me more and smiling more when interacting with me. Very interesting stuff to experience. Having Michelle, Jackson, and Caleb help me get my fashion game up had some unexpected results.

Not realizing that my being happier would have something to do with more positive attention was very eye-opening, mainly because I had never thought of this before in my life. That my base happiness, my unconscious happiness that I show without knowing it, can have such an effect on my interactions with people. In my mind, I'm always the same. I'm always Andrew. This makes sense because of how poor my ability to know my own emotions can be. Not knowing how I really feel inside means that prior to Michelle, I would have no way of comparing how I feel with how others treat me.

* * *

MICHELLE AND ANDREW PRESTON

NOT BEING ABLE TO LOOK FOR THINGS

Andrew is not a lazy person by any means. He's happy to help me cook, help me clean, or help with pretty much whatever I ask. But when it comes to looking for something he can't find, it's as if he's completely incapable of putting any effort in.

If an object is not in the first place he thinks it should be, he will consider it lost, walk over to me, and ask, "Where's the such and such?" Then he will just stand there until I go find it.

In my fifteen years in the school system, I've encountered many students like this, and I always assumed it was laziness that caused them to not look for things. "Where's the nail polish?" they would ask. I would reply, "It's a giant bin of nail polish. Just walk around the classroom until you find it. Someone must've left it out somewhere." Many students would stand there and wait for me to find it rather than go look, even if it took me ten minutes to finish what I was doing. I never understood why it was so hard for them to go look for it until I started dating Andrew.

Even if I say to him, "It's in one of those drawers," he will just look at me and ask, "Which one?" This is often frustrating, and I'll reply, "There are only six drawers, Andrew. Just open them all and look." He will reply in a confused tone, "But I don't know where it is."

I've learned that if I say, "Check the bedroom or the bathroom counter," he will go look. I have to give him an idea otherwise he will just stare at me.

* * *

ANDREW'S TAKE

It could be anywhere is the feeling I get when I realize that something isn't in the usual place it should be. It's an overwhelming feeling that quickly leads to, *This is going to take forever to find.* I want to make one thing clear: these are not word thoughts. These are the feelings I get; they are not an internal monologue.

The internal monologue I use to calm these feelings is, *Just take your time and start looking in the usual uncommon places*, or *You will find it; it's there.*

I've come a long way from when I was younger. My old employer would get frustrated with me when I would ask where things were all the time. If something isn't where it's supposed to be, I feel anxious because I don't know how long it will take to find it. Could the thing actually not be here? Am I wasting my time? Should I call someone who might have used it last? I don't have time for this.

It's a fast and furious train of overwhelming thoughts that can go along with looking for things that are missing. My truck and all of my tools are laid out very orderly. Everything has a place, and that is its only place. It never DOESN'T go there. Otherwise, I know that I will go through this intense series of feelings and emotions looking for it.

* * *

The Art Gallery

Andrew and I are out on a date night to see *The Book of Mormon* musical. We arrive early to make sure we can find parking. When we walk into the venue, it is quite crowded, as no one is allowed to take their seats yet. To avoid the crowds, we walk down some stairs to look at some artwork.

Andrew walks off on his own and begins to look around. All of the artwork is abstract.

As I stand in front of the many shapes and colors in one painting, I enjoy trying to pick up on the emotion the artist is trying to convey. I do small things like this to train my intuition whenever I can. As I'm standing there I pick up on confusion, and it feels as if an elder female created the painting.

"Awesome, I was right," I say as I read the blurb on a plaque about the artist. This is supposed to represent confusion.

"What are you talking about?" Andrew asks as he walks over to me.

"I like trying to guess who painted the painting and what they were feeling as they painted it," I explain as we walk to the next piece of art.

"Like this one, for example," I say as I attempt to feel the painting energetically. "I think this was made by a younger person, male if I had to guess, and to me, it feels like fear."

I walk up to look at the blurb about the artist. "Oh, I was close," I say. "It was done by a guy in his early thirties, so older than I thought. It's meant to represent frustrations though, not fear."

"How on earth would you be able to guess that?" Andrew asks.

"I can just tell sometimes," I reply. "It's as if their emotion is left on the painting, and I can pick up on it."

As we walk to the next painting, I ask Andrew, "Do you have any guesses?"

"For what?" he replies.

"For who painted it and what they are trying to convey?" I say.

"No. I couldn't even try to guess something like that," he responds. "But look at this one over here." He grabs my hand and leads me to the other side of the room.

"Look at the drip marks on this painting," he says. "The only way they could've possibly done this would be by hanging the painting upside down as it dried. How else would they be able to get it shaped like that?"

"Wow, that's a neat point," I say. "I never think about how the paintings are made, but you're totally right."

"I just can't stop staring at this one," Andrew says. "How would they have done this upside down? I wonder how it was hanging to have them all done so evenly."

In this moment, Andrew seems irresistible to me. I plant a big kiss on him before we walk to our seats.

As we laugh and enjoy the play, I feel a little closer to him. Once again, we were in the same room, looking beyond the surface, but we were paying attention to two completely different areas of interest. I love how his perceptions are so different from mine. His comments open my mind up to understanding parts of this world I've never paid attention to.

FRIENDSHIP LOVE AUTISM

* * *

ANDREW'S TAKE

Since this night, I've gotten better at understanding what Michelle meant when she's trying to see the emotion being felt by the artist when they were creating their art. This took some figuring out on my part. My ability to do this was at a 1/10. It seemed so foreign it must be impossible. Part of the reason for this is because I never ask myself these emotional-type questions while I'm living my day-to-day life. Now that Michelle has shown me this perspective, I've made more attempts to ask these questions in my daily activities.

As of now, I might be a solid 3/10, maybe even a 4/10. It has improved over time by asking the question and then following up with Michelle to see if she would agree. This is a funny concept, the fact that I had the ability to a fractional degree, and once I started to practice it, it grew stronger.

* * *

Photos for Chapter 9
Bellamimalifestyles.com/bookphotos

A BONUS STORY BY ANDREW

THE CAR

The first time I drove Michelle's car, there was a problem—several problems, to be exact.

"How many years have you owned this car?" I ask Michelle as I stare at a rearview mirror blocking a quarter of my view out the front windshield.

"Three years. It's a 2015. Why?" she asks.

"Oh, just wondering," I say, trying to hide my judgment.

This rearview mirror is tilted and articulated as low as it can go, so it is taking up almost a third of the middle of her front windshield. And the seat feels like it's trying to slide you onto the floor beneath the steering wheel.

She's been driving like this for three years?! I think to myself. *I have to help her.*

Once we return from our outing, I decide to stay in the car for a few minutes and make some changes.

"Hey hun, I'll be in in a couple of minutes," I say as I give her a kiss and watch her go inside.

It's going to be exciting to see her reaction once I've made these adjustments.

I articulate the rearview mirror so it is fully in the top shaded part of the front windshield. No more visual obstruction. Okay, now the seat.

The seat takes a few minutes as the eight-direction electric adjustments are difficult to get just right. *No wonder this was wrong to begin with,* I think to myself.

The next day Michelle and I are in the car about to leave the parkade.

"Huuuhhhnnn?" I ask in a cute way to signal something.

"What?" she responds, aloof to what has changed.

"Do you notice anything? Anything different?"

She looks very confused after I say this.

"The mirror is higher. You can see out your front windshield now." As I say this, I can feel that my efforts have been in vain.

I spend the next few minutes trying to explain how much of the windshield was being taken up by the mirror being so low and how her seat was pitched forward like a slide.

"OH! That *is* better!" she exclaims.

A sense of joy finally washes over me as I feel her excitement.

The rearview mirror and driver's seat were never adjusted out of position again.

* * *

Michelle's Take

I remember this well and slightly differently. I remember Andrew yelping as I drove out of the parkade while he said, "You seriously don't notice anything different?"

"No, what's going on?" I asked.

Then Andrew said in a shocked tone, "I changed some things, like a lot of things. How can you not notice?"

I pulled over so he could explain. Once he pointed out that my mirrors were different and the seat and steering wheel was moved, I did notice that I was slightly more comfortable.

In our next book, you will learn more about my history and why I am so used to being uncomfortable. I left home at fifteen and was usually struggling just to keep my head above water. Being comfortable has never been overly important to me, and I'm probably a little too easygoing when it comes to this stuff. I could sit down and see out of all of my mirrors, and that was good enough for me. Making adjustments to improve my comfort never entered my mind.

I think one of the reasons our relationship works so well is because I'm not picky with many of the things Andrew is particular about. He can adjust my vehicle how he likes, and he can also be in charge of which electronics we use. My mind is much more focused on the people we surround ourselves with and how we are getting along to care about mechanical things.

10

MORE LEARNING CURVES

OUR FIRST TRIP TO BROOKS

Andrew asks me to go to Brooks with him for the weekend to meet his friends Gavin and Chelsea. It's the first time I'll be meeting close friends of his, and I'm a little nervous. All he's told me about them is that they are married, have two dogs, and that they all play online video games together.

Andrew picks me up after work on Friday. We joke about how funny it is that we are about to drive to the town I was born in. In all the years I've lived in Calgary, I've never met anyone else that lived in Brooks before. We are enjoying a pleasant drive up while listening to podcasts.

Near the halfway point, Andrew's phone receives a text message from Chelsea.

Andrew turns to me and says, "Can you answer this text? Chelsea probably wants to know our time of arrival."

"Sure," I answer while grabbing Andrew's phone.

Chelsea's text reads, *Do I need to have a bed ready for each of you? I'm not sure what your relationship status is?*

This text makes me giggle. I answer her with a funny-faced selfie and write, *Definitely only need one bed, we've been dating for months.*

Oh, I'm so embarrassed. Andrew never really tells us these things, Chelsea replies.

I take another funny-faced selfie, only this time I'm pretending to choke Andrew. I send her the photo and write, *Don't worry, I'll deal with him. LOL.*

We all have a good laugh over it, and it's a great start to the weekend.

Within minutes of being at Gavin and Chelsea's house, I feel at ease. They are personable, welcoming, and lovely to talk to. Clearly an adorable couple. Gavin was also raised a Jehovah's Witness, which I find interesting. My mother was living in Brooks when someone knocked on her door and converted her to become a Jehovah's Witness. This leaves us much to talk about.

Chelsea is clearly excited to have us and has many delicious snacks waiting. They joke that they have their "Andrew snack cupboard" stocked since he eats during the night. We play board games and enjoy many laughs before heading to bed around midnight.

The following afternoon we are all sitting around the living room chatting, and Andrew seems somewhat nervous. After our delicious pancake breakfast, he immediately puts on his noise-canceling headphones and checks out. He comes to sit in the circle with us, but rather than socializing, he buries himself in his book while listening to ambient music. This goes on for hours.

Andrew has been excited to see Gavin and Chelsea for weeks, so I don't understand why he is spending so many hours buried in his book. It's the longest I've seen anyone sit in a group of people without engaging in the conversation. Gavin and Chelsea don't seem phased by it, so I think maybe this is typical behavior of his, but I haven't noticed it before.

When we play board games he is engaged and chatting, but whenever there are no games being played, it's obvious to me that he is slightly uncomfortable.

By Sunday, Chelsea and I feel like we have known each other for years. We are relaxing on the couch as Andrew packs his things.

I turn to Chelsea and say, "I still can't believe Andrew never mentioned me to you guys. We've been dating since April and were friends for a year before that. I'm surprised my name has never come up."

"No, all he said was, 'I'm bringing Michelle.' Andrew never says much else," Chelsea replies.

"How much did you guys know about Crystal?" I ask.

"Who?" Chelsea asks.

"Crystal, Andrew's girlfriend last year. He lived with her for six months," I explain.

Chelsea chuckles as she says, "I didn't even know he was dating anyone."

"Really?" I say in a shocked tone.

Gavin quickly calls out from the kitchen, "He never told me about her either."

We all have a laugh about it as we say goodbye.

Not knowing what to think, I figure that Andrew maybe isn't as close with them as I originally thought. Andrew rarely talks about other people when he is with me, but these are his longtime friends. He is often out here for entire weekends at a time, and they won't hear one thing about his life? I can't make sense of it.

* * *

ANDREW'S TAKE

To me, not socializing that day seemed normal. It was a chill afternoon, and we were sluggish from the scrumptious breakfast. I didn't get the vibe that heavy socializing was up next.

I do feel close to Gavin and Chelsea, but my relationship with Crystal was one of a dubious nature. I didn't know if I wanted to have Crystal meet them because the relationship was uncertain. I didn't feel a strong need to introduce her, and she didn't seem very keen on going to Brooks. So, I would go alone. It's an interesting thing when you look in the mirror and think, "I'm a little embarrassed to bring her (Crystal) with me because the relationship we're in doesn't feel stable." I was very excited to bring Michelle with me because I felt so good with her, and I knew they would love her.

Sharing things about myself is something I love to do. But with things that I don't feel confident about, I tend to hide them for a while until I've sorted them out and feel better about them.

* * *

The Baxter Incident

Andrew wakes up and says, "We need to get Baxter some training. You need to train him better." He is right, but I'm sick of hearing about it, and I certainly don't want to hear about it first thing in the morning to start my day.

This year Baxter has particularly high anxiety. It's tough for even me to handle. Baxter basically had me home 24/7 during my head injury, and he got used to it. Every time I leave the house now he starts shaking because he doesn't know why I'm leaving him. Baxter has become quite the handful, and it's only gotten worse since Andrew came into the picture. My pup is ten years old, and for nearly his entire life I've been single. He's not used to having someone else around.

The more Andrew stays over, the higher Baxter's anxiety seems to get. He will yelp and whine when Andrew and I are cuddling on the couch because he doesn't have his usual spot. It drives Andrew crazy. With a new routine, I figured Baxter would adjust, but that doesn't seem to be happening. This is not a good situation for any of us, and we need to do something. Andrew wants me to take him to a trainer, and I'm all for it.

This week, Andrew has brought the issue up several mornings in a row. Dog trainers are expensive, and I still haven't been able to resume work since my head injury. So I snap at him, "Okay, I heard you, and I will do something about it. I'm tired of hearing about it every morning. I'm tired of waking up to negative comments. I don't need to hear about this first thing in the morning, Andrew."

It's safe to say I lost my cool and was yelling at him as I said those words. And Andrew was listening to every single one of them.

Months go by, and I'm driving Andrew to get laser eye surgery. It's been a hard day for me. My second attempt to go back to work isn't going well for many reasons. Being in a busy classroom is giving me brain fog and headaches. It's nearly time to admit to myself that I am no longer capable of working in a noisy classroom.

Andrew and I are having a conversation about this when all of a sudden, he goes silent. He clearly has something to say but is reluctant to say it.

Frustrated, I ask him, "Andrew, what are your thoughts on this?"

Andrew looks at his watch and then out the window. Saying nothing.

I repeat myself. "Andrew, I would like to know what you think I should do."

Andrew looks at his watch again and says, "I'll tell you at 3 o'clock."

Confused, I ask, "What do you mean you'll tell me at 3 o'clock? I'm asking you now."

Andrew is clearly frustrated, and yet he stays silent. There really isn't any good news to be said about my work situation, so I know he likely wants to tell me something I don't want to hear.

I persist. "Andrew, you can tell me your thoughts. It's okay, I can take it."

Andrew replies, "I will tell you. I'll tell you at 3 o'clock."

Clearly, we are getting nowhere. So I ask him, "Why 3 o'clock? Why can't you tell me now?"

Andrew replies, "Because if I tell you now, that would be me telling you something bad in the morning, right? I don't know what you consider to be morning, so I figured 3 o'clock is a safe bet."

I remain confused, but we have now arrived at his appointment, so I drop the subject.

As I sit in the clinic waiting for Andrew to come out with a fresh set of eyes, I slowly figure out what I think is happening.

As I remember yelling at him that day about Baxter, I can't help but laugh. Andrew took my words literally when I said, "I don't want to hear about this in the morning." Piecing it together isn't overly hard because it's rare that I yell at Andrew.

It's kind of adorable, really; for months he has been avoiding giving me any sort of bad news before 3 p.m. just to be safe. It's sweet in a way but also concerning to a certain extent. Andrew took my words literally and held on to them for months. I'm really going to have to learn to watch my words, and that's not easy to do when you're upset.

***

ANDREW'S TAKE

I think I used 3 p.m. as an arbitrary time where I don't bring up negative things until after 3 p.m. This is a simple rule in the form of an if/then statement. If/then statements are such easy rules to follow. And at that moment, at 12:30 p.m., my filter caught that I was about to say something negative, and it wasn't 3 p.m. yet.

My mind knew exactly what it wanted to say, but the time made me glitch. I didn't have a backup thing to say, so I told Michelle what was happening in my mind. "Sorry, hun. I can't tell you until 3 p.m."

***

The Night he Checks in all Night

Are you still coming over? I text Andrew. *I'm exhausted, and I want to go to bed.*

It's a Friday night, nearing 11 p.m. I'm waiting to hear from Andrew because he said he would sleep over after he is done playing online games with Gavin and Chelsea. I'm exhausted because I'm on a new medication for my head injury that makes me drowsy. Andrew doesn't have a key, so I have to stay awake to let him into the building.

Andrew replies, *Yes, sorry, leaving in five minutes.*

Forty-five minutes later…still no Andrew.

I text again, *Where are you? I need to go to bed. It's almost midnight.* No response.

Now I'm getting worried because he only lives a few minutes from my place. It doesn't seem likely that he got into a car accident, but it's certainly possible. I'm becoming increasingly frustrated and tired. I really should've just told him to come over in the morning.

Another twenty minutes go by, and still no Andrew. By this time, I'm livid as I consider turning my phone off and going to bed. But I'm too confused about what happened to him to be able to sleep.

At 12:25 a.m., Andrew finally rings my buzz code.

As he walks in, he says, "Hello," casually as if nothing has happened.

"Where were you?" I ask with frustration.

"Oh, I was just sitting outside in my truck talking to my friend Liam. He called on my way over." Andrew is so nonchalant about it. As if it hasn't dawned on him at all that I have been up waiting for him this entire time.

I'm not going to let him off the hook this easily, so I say, "I've been in here waiting for you for over an hour. I'm really tired. You should have checked in with me. I texted you."

"Yeah, sorry, we chatted a long time," Andrew replies. "It's been a while since we last spoke, and it was nice to hear from him."

I snap and give him a big speech because clearly, he doesn't understand what he did. "I'm glad you had a nice chat with an old friend, but you shouldn't have been outside talking for so long without checking in with me. You knew I wanted to go to bed; you should've checked in with me."

"Sorry," Andrew replies. "I didn't realize."

"If you would've just told me, you could've come in and kept talking in the living room while I went to bed, or I could've brought you the key. I was just sitting here for an hour, not knowing what was going on. Check in with me next time," I reiterate.

Andrew still looks confused as to why I'm upset, but I'm in no mood to explain it further. I need to get some sleep.

The following weekend I eat my words.

Andrew goes out with some friends. We have no plans to hang out as he is going to be out late, and I'm in the habit of sleeping as much as possible to heal my brain.

I'm home enjoying Netflix and popcorn when I get a text from Andrew: *Just got to Shanks sports pub with the guys. We are about to order food.*

Great have fun, I reply, thinking I won't be hearing from him for the rest of the evening.

An hour later, I get another text: *Just finished eating, and now we are deciding where to go next.*

I don't really know what to say to that, so I simply type, *Sounds good.*

Half an hour later, I get a selfie picture of Andrew sitting in a virtual reality car along with a text that reads, *We came to the new driving virtual reality place. It's awesome.*

At this point, I'm beginning to question why Andrew is texting me so much, but I'm enjoying it. *Looks cool, glad you're having fun,* I answer.

An hour later, I get a Facebook message request from a name I don't recognize. It reads, *Hi this is Andrew, I'm at a pub. Just wanted to let you know that I forgot my phone at the race car place but I'm going to go back and get it when we leave here.*

I feel myself falling a little more for Andrew as I read the message over and over. It's adorable, but I have no idea why he is checking in so much. We hardly ever check in or text like this, so I think that maybe he is missing me. I go to bed early, grateful for my thoughtful boyfriend.

I wake up to several more text messages.

At 10 p.m., he wrote, *I got my phone back, I'm not sure where we are off to next.*

At midnight he wrote, *I'm eating a pizza and going to catch a cab home soon I think.*

At 1 a.m., he wrote, *I'm in a cab now. Almost home.*

At 1:30 a.m., he wrote, *I'm going to bed, goodnight. I hope you sleep well.*

I smile as I read all his messages, but I am still wondering why he sent so many.

The next time Andrew comes over, I ask him about his night out and he tells me all about it. He doesn't say anything about all the messages, so I mention them.

"I was surprised to wake up to so many text messages. It was cute," I say with a chuckle.

Andrew replies in the most adorable way, "Yes, I was trying to check in like you asked."

I smile, but I'm confused by this. "What?" I ask.

"That night I came over, you got upset and asked me to check in more," he answers.

It suddenly dawns on me that Andrew still has no idea why I was upset with him that night. I do my best to explain it further, but I'm pretty sure I end up leaving him more confused.

"Andrew, I needed you to check in because I was WAITING for you. I was worried because you were on your way, and I waited over an hour. That's why you needed to check in. If I would've known you were going to be talking to Liam for so long, I could've given you the spare key and gone to bed. I don't need you to check in when you are out for the evening and we don't have plans."

Andrew replies in the most confusing way, "But I didn't know how long I was going to talk to Liam when I answered the phone."

At this point I'm dumbfounded, and I just don't care anymore. Andrew still doesn't get what I'm saying, but I don't bother trying to explain it further. I end the conversation by saying, "Thanks for checking in; it was sweet. I know you were trying to do what I asked, and I appreciate it."

For many weeks to come, Andrew will now give me a heads-up every time he calls his friend Liam. It's adorable. He even texts me one night to inform me that he is calling his friend Liam while I'm at home. I laugh as I read, *Hey, I'm calling Liam, probably going to talk for an hour or so.*

Weeks later, we are at his place and I'm reading in his bedroom while Andrew is in the living room on his computer. He comes in to tell me that he is going to go call his friend Liam and that he is going to talk for only twenty minutes because he knows it's getting late.

I crack the biggest smile and say, "Thanks for letting me know. You can talk as long as you want because I can just go to bed if I get tired. Let's just say goodnight now."

Andrew gives me a kiss goodnight and goes to call Liam. I go to sleep with a happy heart because I know I've found my unicorn. It's a unicorn I don't quite understand yet, but I still know how special he is. Shortly after this, I give him my spare key. That way he can just let himself in and I won't have to wait up.

***

ANDREW'S TAKE

While I was talking to Liam, the thought that Michelle was waiting for me and might be upset was not going through my mind. In my mind, I would be thinking I should let Liam go soon, and then he would be saying something super interesting and exciting that I had to respond to. Then after I responded, he would respond to that, followed by me thinking again that I should let Liam go soon and repeat this until I was one and a half hours late.

One thing I have to remember is that the person who wants me to check in is not with me; they don't know what's going on. I have to put myself in their shoes. This isn't difficult exactly, but it is hard to do in real time while you're out having fun, knee-deep troubleshooting an HVAC system, or when I'm spellbound by whatever has my attention at that moment.

***

There's No Right Time

Andrew is known to bring things up at inappropriate times, and I am known to say things that confuse him. Here is an example of this.

Andrew and I are on our way to meet some friends. I'm driving, and he's in the passenger seat.

"Yeah, so I don't really think you should sell your condo," he says to me out of nowhere. "I'm not sure if it'll be worth it."

"Andrew, now is not the time to talk about that," I reply. "Why do you always bring things up in the car? We're almost there."

"Why does everyone always say it's not the right time?" Andrew says as he looks at his watch in frustration. "There is never a right time."

"Andrew, you're bringing up a serious topic when we don't really have time to talk about it," I explain. "My finances are a big stressor for me right now, and I don't want to think about this."

"When is the right time then?" he asks. "I never know when it's the right time, and no one can ever tell me."

"The right time would be when we aren't going anywhere, and you warn me that we need to sit down and have a talk about something important," I explain. "Not when we are about to arrive somewhere and are rushed."

"Okay, so warn you that I want to talk about something. Something heavy?" Andrew repeats my words back.

"Yes," I answer. "Don't bring it up randomly. If we are going to talk numbers and mortgages, I want to be sitting down with a pen and paper while I can actually focus on a budget."

"Okay," Andrew says as we pull up to our destination.

A week goes by.

I'm laying on my bed reading when Andrew comes and grabs my arm. "I need to talk to you. Can we talk?" he says in a serious tone.

"Sure," I say as I get up and follow him into the living room. I have a sinking feeling in my stomach while assuming I am not going to like this conversation.

"So, next weekend, my uncle invited us over for dinner," Andrew says.

I sit and wait for the ball to drop, but there's no ball.

"That's it?" I ask.

"Yes. Can we go?" Andrew replies. "We would need to be there by five."

"Yes, we can go," I answer. "But you had me thinking you needed to have a serious conversation."

"Nope, that was it," Andrew says as he walks back to his computer room.

Andrew repeats this pattern many times over the following weeks. Once again, he is trying to do what I asked but is not exactly understanding what I meant.

ANDREW'S TAKE

This has happened to me countless times in many relationships. I've found that few people are ready to talk about heavy subjects. It's like you take the wind out of them as soon as they clue in to what you want to talk about.

The subject could be "How should we invest our savings?" or "Did you know that a black hole's accretion disk can be over ten million degrees kelvin?" or "Your mom belittled you during your conversation with her, and then you stopped talking. Do you have trauma from past experiences like that?" And any one of these conversation starters could happen at any time.

I've gotten better at this by thinking, *Is this the appropriate time for a subject this heavy and possibly triggering?* If the answer is no, then wait until they are in a happy mood, have just eaten, are well rested, and can handle the subject matter.

* * *

Embarrassing Moments

Andrew and I are at Jackson and Caleb's house for a game night with a few of their friends. We meet Selina, who is a beautiful woman in her late forties who immigrated to Canada from El Salvador.

"How are you liking Canada?" Andrew asks Selina as I take my turn on the game.

"I love Canada," Selina answers. "It's so beautiful here."

"How many years have you been here?" Andrew asks.

"Three years," she answers.

"And what made you move here?" Andrew says.

"Love," Selina answers. "I moved here for love."

"What do you mean love?" Andrew asks.

Selina gets noticeably uncomfortable as she repeats herself. "I moved here for love. Love brought me here."

Andrew still has no idea what she means, so he continues to prod. "What do you mean love? What kind of love?" Another few times.

It's obvious to me that Selina is uncomfortable, as she is clearly talking about a relationship that broke her heart, but Andrew does not pick up on this at all.

English is her second language, so I think she believes Andrew is not understanding her accent.

"I moved here for love," she repeats herself a third time, not offering up any more information.

Andrew goes to ask her more questions, but I stop him. "She moved here for a relationship. That's why she chose Canada," I say as I grab his leg. Then I turn to Selina. "I'm sorry, Andrew takes things literally. Sometimes he needs more explanation."

Things feel awkward for a little while until we each take another turn at the game and forget about it.

On our way home, Andrew asks me in the car, "Why did you tell her I take things literally? I don't understand why you said that."

"It was an awkward moment, and I could tell she was uncomfortable. I just wanted her to know that it wasn't her fault you didn't understand her. She seemed really embarrassed," I explained.

"I just didn't know what was happening or why you said that," Andrew says. "She could've meant love for work or love for the mountains. Moving here for love could mean anything."

"I'm sorry I interrupted," I say with compassion. "It's tough on me to sit there through those awkward moments without saying anything. It felt like you kept asking her a personal question she didn't want to answer."

As the months pass, I get used to having awkward moments like this happen in front of me. I do my best not to interrupt, but on rare occasions, I can't help myself. I make a point to discuss these incidents with Andrew afterward, and he begins to develop more of an understanding of what's happening.

***

ANDREW'S TAKE

After Michelle helped me understand what was happening in the conversation I was having with Selina, I had lots to think about. Everyone felt awkward except for me. I did not know that things were awkward. To me, it felt like Michelle devalued how I felt and apologized for me. This was confusing and didn't make sense.

I realize now, more so than before, that it's safer to assume Selina likely meant a relationship with someone who brought her to Canada. But I'm still going to defend myself. If someone says they "moved for love," my mind struggles to believe that "love" absolutely means a relationship with someone. It doesn't compute in my mind. I felt compelled to confirm that Selina meant a relationship.

When this conversation was happening, my mind was thinking of dozens of things that love could mean. All I wanted to know was what kind of love she meant. Does she have a love of hiking? Skiing? Family? Classic cars?

As everyone else was feeling awkward, I was feeling shame. Like I was stupid for taking things literally.

This story still causes me to feel upset when I think about it. These are the feelings that can sting the deepest. When people look at you like you're so out of touch, yet inside you feel like what you said is valid.

This can be a serious point of anxiety for me. Things that people assume are implied are not implied for me.

When I ask a question, it's often a question that makes me look

A) stupid,
B) like I haven't been listening, or
C) looking like I'm not cut out for the job I'm doing or the game I'm playing.

This is one of the main reasons I get so uncomfortable in social situations. It's a surprise when these moments happen. I don't see them coming, and they make me feel terrible.

***

When Do We Say I Love You?

I'm at Andrew's place, and we've been dating for about seven months. We've just finished discussing some of his struggles at work. I offer a supportive ear while he vents about the many things he doesn't like about his workday.

"So..." Andrew gets awkward and looks at the floor. "When do we say I love you?"

"What?" I ask. "What do you mean 'when do we say it'?"

"Well, I'm sitting here, and I'm feeling very good," Andrew explains. "And I feel like there's something I should say, but I don't know if we are saying that yet."

"Well, you can say it if you want to," I reply. "You can say it whenever, really. I'm not the type of girl that will say it first. I never have anyways."

"Okay." Andrew takes a long pause while looking down at the floor. "I love you."

"I love you too," I reply as I give him a kiss. "Now, let's go to bed."

As we get in bed, I have a smile on my face. Andrew saying I love you was adorable, and I love how he asked it in question form rather than just saying it. Here's the weird thing, though. At this point in our relationship, I, in fact, do not *feel* loved by him. You will understand why when you get to chapters twelve and thirteen, but for now, I will just say that we did not feel like a team.

I appreciated that he said the words, and I was ready to say them back because I was committed to him, but we still had a ways to go before I felt like we were truly in love.

* * *

ANDREW'S TAKE

The memory of this story is foggy for me. The only thing I remember is that there was a strong feeling inside me that needed to be let out. Being conscious of this strong positive feeling is why I brought love up in the way I did.

For me to be aware of my emotions, the feeling has to be very intense. An 8 out of 10 at least. It's sad to read that Michelle did not feel loved by me when I expressed how I felt inside. But it's understandable based on how little I express my emotions.

* * *

Photos for Chapter 10
Bellamimalifestyles.com/bookphotos

A BONUS STORY BY ANDREW

WET SOCKS

I feel an overwhelming feeling of ick when my sock steps into a puddle of water or any liquid. I start to hop like there is a nail through my foot. But really I just dislike the feeling of a wet spot on my sock. This is a common occurrence at Michelle's condo. She will fill her tea cups to the brim, not thinking that this might be a balancing act nightmare once she's done. Hence the many puddles of tea that I have stepped in over the past several months.

"Michelle, why do you fill your tea so close to the brim? It's causing an obscene amount of unnecessary sock laundry," I ask with a grin. Her face is a mixture of being puzzled and stark revelation.

Since this brief intervention, I can say with confidence that our sock laundry has decreased by over 200 percent!

* * *

Michelle's Take

When I make tea, I want to get as much out of my mug as possible. I also do this with my protein shakes. I overfill the glass constantly. Except if I spill a protein shake, I clean it up because it's sticky. I got lazy with my tea because it's only water. After Andrew brought this up a couple of times, I started only pouring to the fill line. I really miss those extra two sips of tea I used to get, but you gotta do what you gotta do for love. Sigh.

11

THE SLIGHTLY TOUGH STUFF

All relationships go through rough patches. You think to yourself that you may actually end up with this person and that some of their traits are not things you want to put up with for the rest of your life. Some big, important arguments will arise. This, of course, happened to us, as well. The fact that Andrew is autistic and that I had absolutely no idea of this crucial fact at this time compounded some of these issues. What we learned, though, is the utmost importance of communication. That's the thing about the tough stuff; it teaches you and helps you evolve as a couple. As unpleasant as it can be, we need the tough stuff to strengthen our understanding of each other.

Andrew Misses Dinner

It's summertime, and Andrew has been working quite a bit of overtime at his HVAC job fixing air conditioners. One night he asks me if I'm getting enough attention because he has been working so much. I tell him it isn't bothering me, and he can continue to work overtime if he wants. After nearly eight years of being single, it's more than enough for me to have a boyfriend that I see a few times a week. Andrew explains that he enjoys working all of the extra hours as he is saving quite a bit of money in the process. We agree that he will continue to do so until he feels overworked or exhausted.

Two weeks go by, and we have plans to have dinner at my sister's house. Andrew will be meeting my nephews for the first time. My nephews are 16 and 18, so it's rare to catch them on an evening when they are both home. Dinner is at six, but my sister's house is a thirty-minute drive outside Calgary. During rush hour, the drive can take an hour. I send Andrew a text to remind him about dinner in the morning. I tell him I'll be ready whenever he is off work. Andrew is usually off from his regular workday anytime between 3:30–4:30 p.m, which will leave us plenty of time to get to dinner.

By the time 4:30 rolls around, I'm getting restless.

I text Andrew, *Where are you? Need to leave soon. Dinner's at 6.*

Andrew replies *I'm still working.*

Wanting to leave, I text back, *How about you just meet me there then?*

Andrew replies, *Yes, that's a better plan. Send me the address.*

Traffic isn't bad, so I get to my sister's shortly after 5:15 p.m. My brother-in-law put racks of ribs on the smoker for all of us, and they smell delicious. My sister has some roasted vegetables and a Greek salad ready.

When 6 o'clock rolls around, I send Andrew another text: *How long are you going to be? We are all waiting for you to eat.*

I'm still working, Andrew replies. *I will come there once I'm done.*

I make the mistake of assuming this means he is nearly done; otherwise, he would've told us to eat without him, or so I think.

At 6:45, I call his phone as everyone is quite hungry and getting impatient.

Andrew picks up.

"Hi, how close are you?" I ask.

Andrew answers with, "I'm at the supplier picking up a part for this job."

"What?!" I yelp. "You still have to go back and finish a job?"

"Yes," he responds.

I feel a shock in my stomach as I realize he is working overtime hours. Rage is now brewing in my belly. I can't believe he took overtime. I had originally thought his last job of the day took longer than expected, but clearly, that was another wrong assumption. I'm frustrated.

"Okay, we are going to go ahead and eat then." I hide my rage.

"Oh yeah, you should eat," Andrew replies in a friendly tone.

Dinner is delicious, but it's tough to enjoy with all the loud thoughts racing through my head. I don't say much to everyone other than, "Sorry guys, he got stuck at work." It's far too early in our relationship to go bashing Andrew to my family, who hardly knows him.

Secretly, I'm thinking, *What in the actual fuck just happened?! He's at the supplier's at 6:45 to buy a part? Like why didn't he just tell me two hours ago he couldn't make it for dinner?*

It would have salvaged the evening to know much earlier on. We waited around for nothing. When I asked him how long he would be, you would think he would've at least given me the heads-up that he was going to be another couple of hours or told us to go ahead and eat without him. What in the hell is going on? Who says, "I'm working, and I'll be there when I'm done"? When they are going to be working for hours to come? Grrrrrrrrrrr.

Long after dinner, I'm sitting on the couch with a belly full of ribs enjoying the company of my nephews. I look down to see a text message from Andrew.

I'm on my way, and google says I'll be there in 24 minutes.

I look at the time; it's 8:40. I'm shocked and confused at the fact that Andrew is still attempting to come so late in the evening on a weeknight.

I call him. "Andrew, turn around. It's too late to come. My nephews have school, and my brother-in-law goes to bed at nine. Just pick up some food on your way home."

Andrew is nonchalant. He just chuckles and says, "Yeah, I guess it is kind of late. I'll just go home then."

I am so confused. How could he have taken overtime work on a night we had dinner plans with my nephews? He knows how important my nephews are to me and how excited I was for him to meet them. When we discussed him taking overtime hours, he must've known it didn't include nights we had important plans. Or did he? I reminded him this morning we had dinner at six. Wasn't that enough?

I drive home in silence to let my thoughts settle. I can't compute what just transpired. I'm upset with Andrew for ruining an evening we had planned for weeks, but at the same time, my instincts are telling me that he didn't do it deliberately. I keep going over the events of the day in my mind, and no matter which way I look at it, it just doesn't make sense. It almost seems like in his head he would just come for dinner when he was done working, but he didn't factor in what time it was. How can that be?

When I ask Andrew these questions later, it doesn't help with my confusion. All he can tell me is that he didn't know how long it was going to take him, and he didn't realize he shouldn't have taken over time (palm to face).

I would later learn about time blindness and how often it affects Andrew. Time blindness involves knowing what time it is now, how much time is left, and how quickly time is passing. It's not uncommon for Andrew to struggle in these areas. I've learned to just go about my day, and he will join in whenever he arrives. There's no need to wait for him to eat. It also helps immensely to ask him more specific questions so I can get more of an idea of how long he will be.

* * *

ANDREW'S TAKE

For context's sake, I would like to explain the following terms.

Service call – Random calls throughout the day from customers regarding their heating/cooling equipment. Anything from simple residential furnaces or air conditioning to massive air conditioning units called chillers on top of condominiums. When it's very hot or very cold, the company might get dozens of calls per day to the point where the company might need technicians to work overtime to clear up all of the service calls.

Service calls are what I have found to be the single best place to learn about your trade/skill/profession. It's super rewarding when you troubleshoot a service call. It feels great to know that you fixed it, and now it's back up and running again.

Rabbit Hole – This is a great metaphor for being willingly lost in the unknown with no idea how long it will take or where it could take me.

Checking in – The simplest way to put it, this is a learned behavior to remember to call, text, email, etc. It is important to check in with someone who would like to hear from you.

When I'm troubleshooting, I don't have anything else going through my mind. I'm 100 percent focused on the task at hand. This particular service call was one that stumped me. I needed time to figure it out and properly diagnose it. It is very hard for me to guess how long it will take; the answer to the service call could present itself at any moment. Plus, the customer was watching me and asking questions. Usually, I don't mind this, but this customer was causing me to lose my train of thought. I was in a rabbit hole, and I forgot to check in. Both Michelle and my office feel frustrated when I cannot give them a rough idea of how long I am going to be. I have this issue often.

* * *

Mr. Long Naps & Sore Tummy

Andrew's sleeping and eating habits are unlike any I've ever seen. If he wants to sleep in the middle of the day, he will just close his eyes and nap for hours. This will completely ruin his chances of sleeping in the evening, and it frustrates me for many reasons.

1. I'm not a napper, so I will be bored while he naps, and then he will want to stay up late and play games.
2. It messes with our routine. Andrew will be up eating a full dinner at midnight while I'm waiting in bed. In the morning, I'll be bored while he sleeps until noon.
3. It doesn't seem to change, no matter how many times we've talked about it. I will attempt to wake him from his long naps, but he will just fall right back asleep.

I will say to him, "Don't come over and nap for three hours. Don't nap for three hours ever. It's a terrible idea. It messes with your nighttime sleep."

Andrew will agree with me but then do it again and again.

The only reason I'm able to handle it is because I'm not working much. I can stay up later with him because I can sleep in. It isn't all the time, but it happens much more than I can handle. He will go to work tired and nap for three hours when he gets home, then be up late and repeat the pattern. It drives me nuts.

Andrew also has a habit of eating until his tummy hurts, forgetting to eat, or waking up to eat full meals at 3 a.m. It's as if he doesn't have a radar detector that warns him when he is full or when he is hungry.

Sometimes, he eats himself sick and then says he is never eating x,y, or z again. Many people eat themselves into a food coma every now and then, but this is different. It happens unexpectedly, and Andrew feels really sick.

I tell him that it's not likely what he's eating but how much he's eating. His portions are often much too large for one sitting, and he doesn't know how to stop when he is full. This frustrates me to no end, but I rarely bring it up because it doesn't seem to be something he can control. When his tummy doesn't feel good, I've learned to just hold my tongue. I'm not sure anything will ever rectify these situations.

* * *

ANDREW'S TAKE

Staying up late, followed by sleeping in with naps mixed in between, has been a bad habit of mine since I was a child. Michelle has helped me realize that napping is more detrimental than it is helpful. Getting a good night's sleep, going to bed, and waking up at the same time every day are so helpful for mental health and an overall sense of well-being.

That being said, I have such a hard time waking up in the morning. There have been times when I was younger when I would hit my five- or ten-minute snooze for two or three hours straight. Sleeping in anywhere from 9 a.m. to 1 p.m. was normal for my younger self. Cultivating discipline when the alarm goes off on a non-workday at times can feel like wishing for a miracle.

I suspect that because of my powerlifting background, I have created an irresponsible relationship with food. I still get the old impulses to overeat when I'm enjoying a delicious meal. From the ages of 23 until 28, I would eat between 3,500 and 6,000 calories daily. Old habits die hard.

* * *

Incident with a Coworker

I go to visit Andrew one weeknight at his place, and he is quite distraught when I get there. I sit down in his brown leather reclining chair and ask him what's going on. Andrew explains that he received a very mean text message from one of his friends at work named Bradley.

Andrew reads the text message to me, and it is quite mean and long-winded. It basically tells Andrew that he is a terrible friend who is always talking down to him and that he is tired of it. It is so full of blame and anger that I would have guessed it came from a teenager rather than a grown man. It reminds me of something one of my students would write because it has high school drama written all over it.

Andrew explains to me that he called Bradley and left him a voicemail asking what upset him so much. Bradley didn't return his phone call. Andrew also reached out in a text message and asked if they could talk about it. Bradley also ignored the text message. Andrew has no idea what he has done to upset Bradley, and it's really bothering him.

"What happened the last time you saw Bradley?" I ask.

"He came over Sunday to pick up his stuff, and then after he left, he sent me that really mean message," Andrew explains.

I chuckle and say, "Andrew, I need more information than that to be able to help you."

Andrew repeats the story nearly word for word. "He came here to get his stuff, and after he left, he sent me that really mean text message."

I get more specific with my question. "What kind of mood was Bradley in when he got here?"

Andrew replies, "He just came in and got his stuff."

I reiterate, "Did he seem upset already when he got here? Or did he become upset in the process?"

Andrew stares at me like I have two heads and yelps, "I don't know."

Having no idea of the barriers I'm up against, I ask him, "Does Bradley regularly get upset with people, or is this outside of his normal behavior?"

Andrew has no response for me other than to say, "I have no idea."

Baffled about what to do next. I start asking more specific questions to see if that will help.

"How long was Bradley here when he picked up his stuff?"

Andrew replies, "About thirty minutes."

"What did you chat about?" I ask.

"Nothing out of the ordinary," Andrew answers.

At this point, I'm wanting to slam my head against a wall, but that would involve me getting out of my comfy chair.

Many things are confusing me. The first being that it's Thursday, and he is only now getting upset about this incident from the weekend. Andrew stayed at my place Sunday evening, and I didn't notice anything off with him. This is surprising from someone who had just received a mean text message from a friend. We also had dinner on Tuesday, and he didn't mention it.

The second is that Andrew can't give me any information about what they talked about that day or describe what kind of person Bradley is in any form. After asking Andrew a half dozen more questions, I learn nothing more about Bradley or why he could possibly be upset with Andrew.

To assist him in this issue, I'll have to take a different approach (puts teacher hat on). I tell Andrew that if he genuinely asked his friend to discuss it with him, and that friend is only saying mean things without being willing to have a further discussion, then it isn't really Andrew's problem to fix. He can't address or fix something he doesn't understand. If Bradley is going to act this immaturely about it, then Andrew shouldn't feel guilty. Bradley might just need a few days to calm down before he calls back. If and when he does call back, Andrew can deal with it then. There is no use stressing out about it in the meantime.

Andrew agrees, then we snuggle up and enjoy a movie.

I never did end up meeting Bradley. I'm sure that was for the best. This incident made me realize how much Andrew struggles with understanding people's individual characteristics. I wasn't sure what to make of it, but it furthered my curiosity to understand what makes him different.

* * *

ANDREW'S TAKE

I appreciated that Michelle helped with this situation. Weeks later, I learned that Bradley was upset because I was late to return some equipment that I had borrowed from him. This was my fault, and I later apologized. I was giving him his equipment back because I was going to school for two months.

I was upset that I hurt a friend and couldn't find out why. He texted me a mean text message, didn't respond to me when I asked what I had done wrong, and didn't answer my phone calls. This bothered me for a few weeks. Another coworker told me not to fret over it too much and that Bradley was in the wrong for not speaking to me directly about what was bothering him.

* * *

Not Having Romantic Moments

In many ways, Andrew treats me the same as he did when we were friends. It bothers me that I don't feel more like a girlfriend and that we don't have romance. Many people dream of falling in love with their best friend, and it's fantastic. It's the most spectacular kind of love, but if you feel too much like friends, it may feel as though something is lacking. At least, that is the case for me. Sometimes, I want to feel more like a girlfriend. Sometimes, I want to be spoiled like it's our first date again.

On my thirty-fourth birthday, we had been dating for six weeks. I was looking forward to a special night out with Andrew, and I even purchased a new dress for the occasion. The night was somewhat of a bust. It was an enjoyable evening (as are most nights with Andrew), but it ended up feeling like every other date we've had. It almost felt like he forgot it was my birthday. We went out for pizza and dancing, but I didn't get a card or a gift. Andrew didn't change anything to mark the occasion. It left me feeling disappointed.

Over time I learned that this is the case for nearly all holidays and occasions. When I bring it up to Andrew, he tells me that he is capable of romance but that he feels like he is "acting." I don't want Andrew to ever feel like he is acting around me, so I tell him to always be himself.

* * *

ANDREW'S TAKE

I've had an experience in my past relationship where I felt like I knew what my girlfriend wanted. I thought I could act in a certain way to give her a great evening out. I tried to be extra nice and extra thoughtful. I avoided doing any of the things I knew she didn't like me to do. And to my surprise, it worked…it worked *too* well. It felt exhausting and weird, but she expressed how great of a night she had and how amazing I was.

Near the end of the night, my mental filter got overloaded. I don't like acting. I will act in certain situations that need it, but in general, I like being me and letting the natural flow take its course. I wanted to tell this girlfriend that I had been acting this entire night. I wanted to be honest with her. After explaining the situation, she didn't quite understand. It was such an odd experience. I felt so bizarre knowing that If I wanted to, I could just act the way that she wanted me to act. She wouldn't know I was acting, and she would thoroughly enjoy it.

Romance is so confusing to me. It feels pretentious. When Michelle told me I didn't have to act around her, I felt happy.

* * *

Really Bad Timing

Months into our relationship, I express to Andrew that I'm wanting him to show more affection. I tell him that I do not like how, in many ways, it still feels like we are just friends, and I'm craving some chivalry and affection. Shortly after having this discussion, we go backcountry camping with Jackson and Caleb for a long weekend. Caleb has planned the hike and booked sites for us, and we are all excited.

Throughout the weekend, there is an obvious difference in Andrew that I much appreciate. He sets up and takes down our campsite while telling me to relax around the fire. He also carries a few of my heavier items on the hike up, which is a first. He is clearly making an effort to do what I've asked of him, and I make sure to let him know how much I appreciate it.

We have a spectacular weekend in the backcountry, one of our best. The weather holds up, and there is a picnic table and firepit where we can easily cook and play Yahtzee.

On Monday, we have a long hike through a valley and down the mountain. It's a beautiful hike with spectacular views, but after three days of being in the bush, it's a rough one. Particularly since we are hungover and the trail is quite crowded.

We reach a log bridge with a breathtaking view of the Rocky Mountains behind us, so we stop to take pictures. I take a few pictures of Jackson and Caleb on my phone, and then Jackson goes to take a picture of Andrew and me on his phone. Many people are waiting on the other side of the bridge for us to pass, so we don't bother exchanging phones in an attempt to keep things moving.

Andrew kisses me on the cheek for the photo, which is cute because he has never done that before. But then he begins kissing the side of my face and hugging me. This goes on for a long time, long after Jackson puts his phone away. Many people are watching us waiting to pass, and Andrew just keeps on kissing and hugging me. He has never kissed me like this in public before, and it gives me anxiety. It makes me uncomfortable that people are watching and waiting for us to move.

I end up making a loud comment to get him to stop. "Sorry, everyone, my boyfriend has decided we are going to hold up the trail," I say as I pull his hands off and ask him to stop kissing me.

People chuckle, and Andrew clearly feels embarrassed. Immediately I feel like a jerk, and I can tell I hurt his feelings.

Andrew walks behind me quietly for half a kilometer past the crowds before I stop to talk to him. Andrew doesn't look me in the eye when I try to apologize. Instead, he looks up and says in a confused tone, "I was showing affection, I was showing affection, I was showing affection," and then he runs past me at full speed.

I do not see Andrew again until I get to the bottom of the mountain. This is extra terrible because he is carrying my water, and we have five kilometers to go. Thankfully Caleb waits for me, so I don't have to do the entire hike down alone. The more I process what happened, the more terrible I feel.

Andrew was doing exactly what I asked of him; he just couldn't have picked a worse time to do it. Public affection wasn't what I was looking for, especially when people are waiting to walk by us. Andrew is always trying to do what I ask. He just doesn't always understand what it is I want.

* * *

ANDREW'S TAKE

In hindsight, I might have overreacted. As with so many other things in life, I'm still working on some of these extreme feelings that can be overwhelming. When I'm told to do something (at a job, in school, or in a relationship), if the person gets mad at me for doing what I feel they expressly told me to do, I get intensely emotional. It's an overwhelming feeling because I'm doing what you told me to do. I want you to be happy, and I've done what I thought makes you happy, but it has made you upset. All I want to do is be away from you and be alone now.

It almost feels like I fell into a trap, and the person who set it on me is a person I care about. I'm still, even to this day, trying to be able to calm myself when these incidents happen.

I would hope that the person who told me what to do before I made a mistake would explain to me what I was doing wrong in a friendly way. At that moment, I'm fragile. I feel bad that I upset you, and getting mad at me makes me feel ten times worse. I wish the other person knew. It matters to me that you're happy.

Life is hard.

* * *

Our Sex Life

It's fair to say that my perceptions of sex were skewed by having many three-month "mini relationships" in the years leading up to dating Andrew. These relationships were mainly based on attraction and started out with high amounts of sexual chemistry. Things would eventually settle down, but I was used to sex starting off with a bang. With Andrew, the sexual chemistry is different. The best way I can describe it is that our sex life started off where I usually ended up with most guys after being together for a while.

We had enough sex, but we were far from ripping each other's clothes off. I had never been in a relationship that wasn't mostly about sex in the beginning, so I thought there was something wrong with us. It seemed as though every time I tried to create some fireworks, my attempts failed miserably, and I didn't understand why. I was often left feeling embarrassed when he didn't realize I was trying to create a romantic moment. That's a terrible feeling. (I give an example of this in the next chapter.)

What was most confusing about Andrew was that our sexiest moments were never when I thought they would be. I would get all dressed up for a date night, and I'd be thinking, *I look hot tonight. He's totally going to be ripping my clothes off the second we get home.* But I would be wrong. That's rarely how it went down. In fact, that is never how it went down.

Andrew doesn't follow societal norms. Dates would be the days he would tell me I look beautiful and then just say goodnight and go home. I didn't know what to make of it. It was new for me to get all dressed up for a date night with a boyfriend, only to end up not having sex at the end of the evening, especially in the early days of a relationship.

Andrew and I did have moments of good sexual chemistry, but they happened randomly. When I planned on creating fireworks, I failed. Then on a weekday in the middle of the afternoon, we'd end up having fantastic sex out of nowhere. Nothing made sense to me.

As I say this, I'm sure it's easy to think, *Well, that doesn't sound so terrible,* and it wasn't. But it sure was confusing. It felt as if we were on different wavelengths. I couldn't tell when Andrew was in the mood or when he wanted me to pounce on him. In all of my previous relationships, I was able to easily tell when my partner was in the mood. With Andrew, I was clueless.

There were times I tried to flirt with him to get him into the bedroom, and he didn't seem to know what I was doing. It made me feel self-conscious. Once I felt self-conscious, I began to overthink before I would initiate sex. I didn't understand why I was questioning everything so much because this was unlike me. There was something that felt different with Andrew, but I didn't understand it. We seemed to live on different channels.

Two months into our relationship, we went on our first weekend getaway together. We rented a room with a beautiful view of the mountains in Salmon Arm, British Columbia. On our first night, I lay awake tossing because we didn't end up having sex. I was bothered that it was our first weekend getaway together, and it didn't feel romantic.

At breakfast the next morning, I express to Andrew how much it's bothering me that we aren't feeling the need to have more sex. I don't feel like we desire each other the way we should on our first weekend getaway. I tell him I feel like we are missing a certain spark.

Andrew replies by saying, "You want fireworks and sparks? Why? We don't want that. I've had that, and it didn't end well. It's not real. It never ends well because it blinds you. What we have is better than that. It's sustainable, and it's real."

He says all of that so calmly while he is making our toast. Andrew is right (as he often is), but it doesn't make me feel much better.

After a little bit of thinking, he follows up with, "I hate to admit that this is a thing, but I think a part of it is that I respect you too much. We know each other too well."

I agree with his statement, but it still feels like something is missing.

It's evident that we have something special because I'm comfortable enough to discuss this topic with him openly, but it still makes me feel sad.

I'm in a constant inner battle with myself. In many ways, I feel the happiest I've ever felt with Andrew, but I miss feeling desired in the ways I've been previously used to. On my emotional days, I worry that we are settling.

Part of the issue was also my insecurity about my weight. I had gained thirty-two pounds since my head injury, and I kept that weight on for the entire first year of our relationship. Looking back, I understand that my weight had no negative effect on our sex life, but it didn't feel that way at the time.

* * *

ANDREW'S TAKE

When Michelle and I first became friends, I was super happy to be friends. Hanging out with Michelle and her friends was always a fun time that I looked forward to. This lasted for a year. Once we went on our first date and then went home and snuggled in bed, it was a huge change. Michelle's bedroom was "my friend Michelle's bedroom." I never saw it as potentially *my* bedroom too. Being in a relationship with Michelle was going to be different than any relationship I had been in before, I knew this.

This is a metaphor that I use to describe a relationship built on lust versus a relationship built on love. A relationship built on love is like a wonderful carnival that has everything, including amazing carnival rides. The carnival grounds are well planned out (maturity). Nice staff (compassionate), and the carnival isn't too expensive (selfless). It's a place that you just love.

A one-night stand or a relationship built on lust is like riding the main attraction over and over again, with no thought given to the rest of the carnival.

No one wants to ride Space Mountain all day long. At some point you gotta get off and check out the rest of the carnival.

After focusing only on the one biggest, most exciting ride at the carnival, you will get bored. You will want to explore the other parts of the carnival. Maybe the one-night stand turns into a relationship, a relationship built on lust. In this carnival, you might find that it isn't laid out very well (immature). You have bad interactions with the staff (fighting often). You don't want to help make their carnival better because you only respect them as long as you can ride the main attraction. And so neither of your carnivals ever improve much.

Knowing all of this, I can say for certain that I love Michelle and will always be here to try to improve both of our carnivals the best I can.

* * *

Photos for Chapter 11
Bellamimalifestyles.com/bookphotos

A BONUS STORY BY ANDREW

MICHELLE'S NON-VISUAL DIRECTIONS

"It's on 36th Street, near 4th Ave.," Michelle says as I begin to cringe.

My mind wants to understand her, but all I see is darkness.

Followed by frustration.

The difference between me learning landmarks by memorization versus visual is huge. It takes me dozens or hundreds of interactions before I connect a visual memory of a landmark with the exact name of its location. I grew up in Thunder Bay, Ontario, and I can walk around 70 percent of the city in my mind, yet I know less than 1 percent of the street names.

When Michelle tries to tell me where we are going, she will tell me the actual location.

"Where is Bankers Hall, hun?" I ask Michelle on our drive.

She responds with "Downtown on 8th Ave." This is no help. She might as well be talking in a foreign language.

"What is near that place, Michelle?" I ask to try to get a visual in my mind. If she can give me a place I know I can then walk, in my mind, to where we are going.

She tells me, "There's a McDonald's and a CIBC." I'm still in the darkness. I've never been to McDonald's or the CIBC downtown. I've never lived downtown. But I do know where the Calgary Tower is, and it's one block east of Bankers Hall. And I kinda know where TD Square Mall is, and that is across the street.

"Can you google map directions to Bankers Hall and put the phone in the cup holder, please?" I ask her politely, not showing that I'm slightly agitated inside. And because Michelle is such an awesome person, she does so without batting an eye or feeling awkward.

Google Maps saves the day again. Relief settles over me.

* * *

Michelle's Take

Ah, yes, giving directions. It's impossible for me to give Andrew directions. It feels as though no matter what I say to him, it doesn't help anything. "It's your third left," I'll say. "Just let me direct you. I'll tell you when to turn."

Andrew always replies, "Nope, I need to see it in my mind."

I do not know how to describe a picture for him of where something is, so I just quit trying. Even if I say, "It's in the same shopping center as the place where we had the good Vietnamese food last week," he still will have no idea which shopping center I'm talking about.

I've noticed other couples argue over directions on many occasions. I now wonder if it's because one person has a visual mind, and the other does not. If this is the case, I feel it's best to let the driver use Google Maps while the other person keeps their mouth closed. Some of these differences are hardwired into our brains, so there's no use fighting over them.

12
THE TOUGH STUFF

The Bigger Issues

The following short stories are about our bigger issues from that first year. The things I didn't understand or know if I could handle. These issues made me question if Andrew and I were meant for each other.

He Knew He Was Happier But Didn't Realize Our Relationship Was The Reason

"People at work are commenting about how happy I seem," Andrew says to me. "I'm having less anxiety and am in a good mood all the time."

"Andrew, do you realize that it's largely because of our relationship and how well we compliment each other?" I ask. "I've also been much happier since we started dating."

Andrew looks at me, puzzled, as if he has never considered that thought.

Within the first six months of our relationship, Andrew's life improved dramatically. He was happier in every way, but he didn't realize that I was a large part of the reason. He acknowledged that he was happier, but he didn't understand why he was happier.

His puzzled expression hurt my ego. I wanted him to turn to me and say, "Of course, it's because of you and our relationship," but he never did.

He couldn't give me any of the credit for his happiness, and I hated it. Admitting to this may not paint me in the best light, bestie, but I'm telling you anyway because it's true. It took him well over a year to be able to give me that validation, and it hurt.

* * *

ANDREW'S TAKE

You can't see what you can't see. I did not see the positive potential of a loving, supportive relationship. It really did take one year before it started to make sense to me.

Noticing that you will feel better naturally when you're in a relationship with a quality person is remarkable, and now I will never forget what I learned. You also realize what was missing in your past relationships. With this new perspective, I started to piece more and more together, also realizing this is the same with family and friends. Surrounding yourself with wonderful people is a great boost to your sense of well-being and to your love tank.

* * *

THE BLUNT COMMENTS & HONESTY

Today is a big deal for me. Andrew's aunt Joanne is in Calgary for an event at the Japanese cultural center. We are watching her dance in the afternoon and then have plans to go to Jackson and Caleb's to play board games afterward. For the first time in a long time, I'm putting effort into my appearance. Post-concussion syndrome only allows for so much brain power in a day, and if I use it up doing my hair and makeup, I usually don't have much left over to socialize.

Andrew's commented a few times that he thinks I look so beautiful when I wear makeup, so I do the full deal. Contouring, eye shadow, fake lashes; I even put lip liner and colored lip gloss on. I wear my bold red dress that has an empire waist. It shows off some cleavage and then flows loosely to my ankles. I'm happy it fits me, given my weight gain. I spend ninety minutes getting ready, and I even curl my hair. I feel pretty and somewhat energized, better than I have felt in months.

When Andrew arrives to pick me up, he tells me I look nice, and we head off to the Japanese cultural center. We arrive early for the show, so we stay outside for a bit to enjoy the beautiful garden.

Everything feels perfect. Until it doesn't.

We are holding hands, enjoying the garden at the Japanese cultural center, when suddenly Andrew becomes engrossed in studying my face.

"How come your lipstick runs over your upper lip ridge?" he asks.

I immediately feel my stomach sink. I'm triggered by the comment. I've never felt good about my lips, which is why I rarely wear any sort of lipstick. My lip line is thin, so it's tough to outline. Lipstick just accentuates this fact.

I must've done a poor job, I'm thinking, feeling completely embarrassed.

I go silent and don't know how to answer.

Abruptly, I get up and head toward the bathroom. Tears of embarrassment run down my cheeks as I make my way there as quickly as possible. Once in the bathroom, I have a solid cry.

Immediately after pulling myself together, I wipe off my lipgloss because I feel stupid for even trying.

For me, this ruins the entire day. Board games at Jackson and Caleb's don't even cheer me up.

Looking back, I realize I was being sensitive that day. But it's tough to hear things like that when you've put in your best effort to look nice. Especially when you're in the middle of enjoying a romantic moment in a garden. Andrew's timing is never his strong suit.

My heart starts pumping a little faster just at the thought of Andrew's blunt comments. If he didn't like my outfit, it was obvious. If I smelled in any way, I heard about it. If I was wrong about anything, I heard about it.

I could give many examples of blunt comments, but I think it's easier to summarize this topic by saying this. Andrew gave me the honesty you often get after years of marriage right from the start of our relationship. There was no buffer period that allowed me to feel comfortable and secure before I got hit with all the absolute truths. When you kiss your husband in the morning and he says, "You didn't brush your teeth," it's not likely to hurt your feelings. When it's your brand-new boyfriend, it's a little tougher to swallow. Andrew's tone is often flat, so it's tough to tell when he's being playful or not. There were many nights I went to bed feeling insecure about myself due to something he said.

* * *

ANDREW'S TAKE

Sometimes when I'm asking questions, I have no idea I'm about to step on a landmine.

When I asked Michelle about her lipstick, I was curious in the same way that you might think to yourself, *Why is the sky blue? Why is green the dominant color in nature?* Or *How come your lipstick runs over your upper lip ridge?* I am genuinely curious and do not mean to hurt her feelings.

* * *

Figuring Out What Andrew Likes

I turn to Andrew. "How did you enjoy dinner?"

"It was okay, I guess," Andrew answers.

This issue plagues us for months, and it makes me feel like he is ungrateful for my efforts.

I've never been much of a cook, and I keep meals simple since it's usually just me. Steamed veggies, chicken, salmon, salads, or omelets are pretty much my go-to.

It's frustrating to know someone is unhappy with what you are serving them, especially when they can't tell you what the issue is. Every time I go grocery shopping I have no idea what to buy. Andrew is very good at telling me what he doesn't like but not so good at telling me what he actually wants. He is well aware of my frustrations on this topic.

One afternoon I get a phone call from Andrew while he is at work.

"Hello," I answer.

"Hun, I figured it out, I figured it out! I'm a dipper," Andrew says with enthusiasm.

"What?" I ask in confusion.

"I'm a dipper. I like to have my food full of sauce, this is why I dip. Dipping a sandwich in cream of broccoli soup is the best thing ever. I want as much sauce and flavor as possible."

"Hallelujah!" I yell, happy to have an answer after weeks of asking him what he wants me to cook. "Cooking sauces is foreign to me; I prefer to use seasonings. But I'm sure I can figure it out."

Shortly after this, I realize that Andrew also lives for carbs; 60 percent of his plate will be carbs, even more so when he is powerlifting. This was another part of our issue. He wanted more rice and potatoes. Once we figured out the issues, Andrew finally enjoyed our meals.

This made me feel better about our relationship. I've often heard that the way to a man's heart is through his stomach, and I'm glad we figured out the missing piece to the puzzle. It did confuse me, though, that it took Andrew so long to be able to tell me how he enjoys his food.

* * *

ANDREW'S TAKE

I don't think I replied with those words exactly, "It was okay, I guess," or "I'm not totally satisfied." But my guess is that my facial expression did all the talking while I said, "Yeah, it was alright." When I try to be nice, I usually fail. I would say something nice in an obviously unenthusiastic way.

Since Michelle started cooking for me, I've realized that I love saucy food. I learned this from a coworker who was watching me dip my sandwiches in soup. He spoke to me in a sarcastic distasteful way, saying, "You're a dipper! Disgusting, haha." He then explained to me what it meant to be a dipper. Someone who dips their food into soup or broth.

For example, East Indian food, where you dip the naan bread into the butter chicken curry, oh my god, life is good. I love pizza, another saucy food. Spaghetti, porridge, cereal, anything where the flavor has a full sauce-like reign over your tastebuds, I'm in!

* * *

Not Realizing How His Friends Affect Him

Who you surround yourself with affects every aspect of your existence, so it's best you be particular by choosing to associate with high-quality people. Andrew was not surrounded by the best crowd when we started dating, and I was surprised by it. I never thought I'd be a girl who would attempt to have much say in who her boyfriend hangs out with, but in Andrew's case, I couldn't keep my mouth shut for long. Within a couple of months, there were many issues I felt the need to point out to him. The first was about his coworker Kyle.

Andrew's friend Kyle would call him often to vent about his life. I met Kyle on a couple of occasions, and he was a nice guy. Easy to like in most regards. The problem was that Kyle's life was in shambles, and he was making zero adjustments to change this fact. He would call Andrew to vent about how hard his marriage was, his work stresses, and various other issues going on in his life. He called Andrew a lot, even during work hours. It was obvious to me that Andrew was not in the best mood whenever they got off the phone, and it began to cut into our alone time.

Andrew mentioned to me a couple of times that he didn't take a lunch break because Kyle had called, and it caused him to fall behind. At first, I didn't think much of it because I just assumed that Kyle was going through a tough time. But it soon became evident that the pattern wasn't changing; if anything, it was getting worse. It's one thing to be at work late because you ended up chatting with a friend who really needed you, but it's another thing when it's a regular pattern.

Andrew's phone rings while we are relaxing at my condo, and it's Kyle.

They talk for half an hour while I watch TV.

"How are you feeling? Did you enjoy your conversation?" I ask after Andrew hangs up the phone.

Andrew shrugs and says, "I don't know."

"Do you feel like he's calling you too much?" I ask.

Andrew pauses to contemplate my question.

"I don't know. I guess he does distract me at work. I don't really like talking on the phone at work," he answers.

"It just seems like he's draining you by complaining about his life. You seem groggy whenever you get off the phone with him," I explain.

"I don't know what to do. He's always thanking me for being such a good listener and telling me how much he enjoys our chats," Andrew replies.

"Pay attention to how you feel when you get off the phone with him from now on. If you feel depleted after talking to him, limit your calls to ten minutes, then tell him you need to get back to work," I suggest.

Andrew sits and thinks about my words as if he has never contemplated that option.

I continue, "You can support your friend, but it's important to maintain your own balance while doing so."

After this conversation, it's only a matter of days before Andrew notices how much Kyle's calls are affecting him.

Andrew comes over after work. "Okay, I am noticing that I am drained after I talk to Kyle. It really messes with my day. I just don't know what to do about it."

I reiterate, "Talk to him for a little while, then tell him you have to get back to work."

"I tried that, but it felt weird. It felt like I was lying, and I don't want to lie to him," Andrew explains.

"It's not lying. You should get back to work," I reply.

"Yes, but I don't really have to. If I really wanted to talk to him, I could," Andrew says.

I get confused and end the conversation by saying, "Well then, find another way to fix the problem."

When people ask Andrew for help, he wants to help them. The problem is he won't notice when giving this help is causing a huge detriment to his own life. Once I told him to focus on how people affect his day, he improved his awareness in this area and began to make changes.

* * *

ANDREW'S TAKE

It's a hard thing to escape when you begin to treat coworkers as friends. It's nice to talk to them while at work; it passes the time in a much more pleasant way. Most of the time I could do my job while talking to them, albeit not quite as fast. I felt bad for wasting time on the phone, and this pattern ruined quite a few days. In hindsight, I used talking to Kyle and others at work as a way to remove oneself from the drudgery of work at times. The truth is we were all guilty of this.

* * *

RUNNING IN THE WRONG CROWD - DUNGEONS AND DRAGONS

Andrew turns to me and says, "Me and some guys from work are going to start playing Dungeons and Dragons on Sundays in September. I'd really like it if you played with us."

"I have no idea what Dungeons and Dragons is," I explain. "As a Jehovah's Witness kid, it was completely forbidden."

"Really?" Andrew laughs. "It's just a fantasy game with storytelling."

"Yes, really," I explain. "To Jehovah's Witnesses, playing that game is as terrible as hanging out with Satan himself. *The Smurfs* and *The Care Bears* were also forbidden because they have to do with magic and spells."

"You've never seen *The Care Bears*?" Andrew chuckles. "That was my favorite show as a kid. Omg, we have to watch it one day. It's so good."

"Sure," I agree. "I'm curious to see what it's like."

"So, will you play? Will you? It would be so amazing if you played." Andrew's voice is now getting fast and loud as if he were giving me a sales pitch. "You can stop playing if you don't like it, but I would really love it if you tried."

"Sure, I'll try it," I say, making Andrew's face light up like a kid on Christmas morning.

"Omg, really? You'll play? Awesome," Andrew replies.

"Sure," I reiterate. "Your enthusiasm is impossible to resist."

"I'm so excited. I totally didn't think you would say yes," Andrew proclaims.

"Well, I don't know what I'm getting myself into, but I'm curious enough to step foot in your fantasy world and take a look around," I answer.

There are eight of us set to start a big game of Dungeons and Dragons that will be held every second Sunday through the fall. I'm the only female in the group, not that it bothers me any. Andrew goes out and purchases the new gamebook and begins studying it for weeks leading up to the start date.

The first Sunday arrives, and I go over to Andrew's place early to help him set up the game and tables. He's put so much time and effort into preparing the game for everyone. He is the Dungeon Master, which I learn is the person in charge of the whole ordeal. The Dungeon Master sets the tone for the game, and Andrew has made sure he is prepared for the job.

The first day is quite fun. We all pick our characters and play long enough to get a feel for the game. I choose to be a barbarian, the same character I always pick when Andrew and I play *Diablo 3*. Barbarians have strength, and I don't have to geek out too much by learning as many spells. Some characters are wizards and are a little more complicated to learn. I never pick those characters; I leave them for the real nerds.

We play for nearly seven hours, which is longer than I expected. I'm okay with it because we have so many snacks. It's neat to see some of the guys commit to their characters, and I'm surprised by how much I enjoy the game.

However, over the following months, I begin to loathe our Dungeons and Dragons Sundays for a few reasons, none of which have anything to do with the actual game. One of the smaller issues is that I've started back at the gym and have finally begun losing the thirty-two pounds I put on since my head injury. Sundays always set me back. I'm going to overeat if I'm surrounded by snacks for hours at a time, and I skip the gym to be there.

A much bigger reason is that I don't enjoy the company. To me, playing games is much more about who's sitting around the table than the game itself. I very much feed off the energy of others. The energy around this table feels like a cesspool of negativity, and I don't like it.

A few of the guys are often late, extremely hungover, or complaining about their significant others. One Sunday it's so bad I nearly leave. The guy beside me can't stop checking his phone, spinning his dice on the table, or complaining about the rules of the game. It takes everything in me not to grab the dice out of his hand and tell him to shut his pie hole. The clanking noise is enough to bother me, but his complaining on top of that sends me over the edge. I can't stand him. I'm thinking to myself, *This is supposed to be fun, dude. If you're not having fun, feel free to leave.*

Two of the guys have obvious substance abuse issues, and none of them seem to be in healthy relationships. I've never met their significant others, but their many comments about hiding things from their partners kind of gives it away.

After a few Sundays, a few things begin to click for me.

Months ago, Andrew had invited me to go to the Calgary Stampede with him and some of the guys, but shortly after, he had to rescind. The guys told him that none of the other wives/girlfriends were invited and that if they found out I was there, they would get mad. They asked him not to bring me along in fear that their significant others would find out.

The Calgary Stampede is a large ten-day rodeo event that is held every July in Calgary. For ten days, the downtown core of the city goes into party mode. Many people wear cowboy hats and take time off work to enjoy the festivities. There's a large carnival with beer gardens and concerts, as well as one of the world's largest rodeos.

Andrew told me it upset him that he couldn't bring me with the guys and offered to take me to the Stampede on a date night instead of going with them.

"It's sweet of you to offer," I said to him. "But I worked it the past three years and am pretty Stampeded out anyways. You go have fun with the guys."

"Okay, but only if you're sure," Andrew replied. "I'll take you if you want to have a date night instead."

"I'm sure. You go have fun," I responded. "I'd rather relax anyway, and you hardly go out with friends."

Andrew went to the Stampede with the guys, and they all ended up at the strip club that night. He was sending me selfies from the strip club with the teddy bear he won at the Stampede. Along with the picture, he wrote, *I feel so awkward here. The guys got a VIP table with bottle service, and are spending copious amounts of money.*

Thinking it was just a rare occurrence of a much-needed guy's night out, I laughed at it all. But as it turns out, this behavior is quite regular for these boys. The same situation happened the next time Andrew went out with them months later and one more time after that.

It seems they live to escape their relationships and go party every chance they get. This is completely their prerogative; it's just quite far removed from the life Andrew lives. It seems as though he and his friends are mismatched and don't really belong together. Once I come to this realization, I stop encouraging Andrew to go out every few months. He doesn't usually have much fun anyway.

My growing dislike for the people sitting around the table causes me to tell Andrew that I no longer want to play Dungeons and Dragons on Sundays. Andrew understands, and it just so happens that a new guy wants to join in, so he can play my character.

Andrew offers to wrap the game up if I want him to, but I don't need him to do that. To me, games are about who I am playing with, but to Andrew, it is really just about the game itself. He really is enjoying being the Dungeon Master, and he is good at it. There is no reason for him to stop playing on my account.

The first Sunday I stop playing, I have some lunch with Jackson. We have a long conversation about how turned off I am by the friends Andrew chooses to keep. Jackson's solution is to hang out with him and Caleb more, which we do. It's a great solution, but I still don't like that I'm dating someone who is surrounded by so many low-quality people. Andrew is one of the most interesting, talented, honest men I've ever met, and yet he is surrounded by quite the opposite. It feels as though he doesn't enjoy the company of his own friends and he doesn't even realize it.

* * *

ANDREW'S TAKE

Remembering that moment when I invited Michelle to the Stampede with "the guys" is triggering.

To me, "the guys" means people who will enjoy each other's company. What it really means is "The guys, without their wives." My friend Chris told me that if Michelle comes, then he can't go because he can't risk his wife finding out and then feeling like she was left out. I was appalled at this idea. This was one of the first times when I was beginning to realize that I'm hanging out with people who aren't really my kind of people.

Months later, another one of my work friends and I were having a conversation. I was going on a rant about philosophy, and he was eagerly listening to me. Once my rant was over, he said, "Andrew, you shouldn't be working here."

He told me that I didn't belong working in the doldrums as an HVAC mechanic. He was trying to express that there was more for me out in the world than this job could ever give me, and I appreciated his honesty. This moment stuck with me and helped me feel more confident. In that moment I realized that only hanging out with people from work was probably not a good idea.

* * *

The Nighty Incident

I'm sitting on my couch anxiously awaiting Andrew's arrival. My condo is spotless, the fireplace is on, and I'm wearing my new silk nighty that leaves little to the imagination. I've never dressed this sexy for Andrew before, and I'm anxious for his reaction. Tonight we have cause for celebration. Andrew has just finished trade school to get his second red seal certificate, and I haven't seen him in two weeks. For the past two months, we've only spent every other weekend together, but this time he is coming back to Calgary for good. Naturally, we will be having sex as soon as he gets here. Or so I think.

My phone rings, and I touch nine to buzz Andrew into my building. Andrew opens the door as I'm walking to my entrance to greet him. He's carrying a duffle bag while pushing a large air conditioner. He gives me a quick kiss on the cheek as he says hello, and then immediately starts pushing the air conditioner toward my bedroom.

Andrew hardly makes eye contact with me and has zero reaction to what I'm wearing. No huge alarm bells are going off in my head quite yet. He's been on the road for two hours, and maybe he just needs a few minutes to settle in.

A few minutes pass, and Andrew has yet to comment or take much notice of what I'm wearing. I'm officially starting to feel self-conscious, but I'm doing my best to be patient and let him get settled.

Then, to my horror, Andrew begins installing the air conditioner. My mouth remains quiet, but my thoughts start shouting at him. *Seriously, dude, you're going to do that now? While I look like this? The air conditioner can wait until tomorrow. It's not even hot in here!*

It feels as though Andrew is not excited to see me at all. I'm hurt, confused, and don't know what to do. He seems uncomfortable and hardly says two words to me. Feeling invisible, I stand there and watch him install the air conditioner.

After spending two weeks apart, I can't get over how unenthused he is to see me. I've never felt this invisible in front of a boyfriend, especially with the way I am dressed. Even if I smelled bad and had just rolled around in dirt, I'd deserve a better greeting than this.

Andrew finishes installing the air conditioner as I sit in silence.

My thoughts turn from anger to self-doubt. *Maybe he's not attracted to me? Maybe he's not happy to be here? Did he even miss me at all? Do I look terrible? He must not like me that much.*

Andrew makes firm eye contact with me for the first time as he says, "I'm tired. Can we go to bed now?"

Dumbfounded, I can only muster up the ability to say one word: "Sure."

My eyes begin to tear up as we get into bed. Andrew gives me a half-hearted kiss goodnight and then quickly turns his back to put his CPAP on. I feel hurt and humiliated. Unbeknownst to him, I lay there and cry as he falls asleep.

Once Andrew is fast asleep, I grab my pajamas and go to my spare bathroom. I wash my makeup off, throw my silk nighty in the garbage, and cover it with toilet paper because I never want to see it again. Tears continue to fall down my cheeks as I return to bed in my comfy jammies. It feels as though I am lying next to a stranger.

Three weeks later, Andrew is driving me to the movies.

He looks at me with a large smile on his face. "I got my test results today, and I passed my apprenticeship. I thought I totally bombed that test. I'm so relieved I passed."

"That's fantastic. I knew you would pass. Why did you think you bombed the test?" I ask.

"I had a really bad couple of days before the final," Andrew explains as he becomes noticeably agitated. "They altered the format in the charting program I use to watch my investments, and it messed with me. I hardly slept the night before the test, and I spent hours on the phone that morning trying to get the old format back."

My face lights up as I realize Andrew's lack of enthusiasm when he returned from school had nothing to do with me or my nighty.

Andrew continues, "After all that time on the phone, they told me the old format was no longer available. I really should've been studying because it was such a waste of time, but I hate the new format."

With a huge smile on my face, I turn to Andrew and say, "That night I was all dolled up, excited for you to get to my place, and you hardly said two words to me… I wish you would've told me that you had a bad day because I ended up crying when you went to sleep. I felt bad about myself, and I didn't think you liked my nighty. It was the first time I dressed up sexy for you, and you didn't even notice."

Andrew looks at me with a puzzled look on his face. "I just remember wanting to install your air conditioner. I wanted you to have a nice air conditioner. I remember thinking you looked nice, but I didn't really think about it. I was just so glad I managed to finish that test; I hardly got through it."

"Well, next time, tell me when you have a bad day so I don't take it personally," I explain. "I felt really down on myself. You didn't seem happy to see me. You hardly looked at me."

"I'll try to remember to tell you next time. Sorry you felt bad," Andrew apologizes.

Attempting to enjoy the movie is a lost cause. My mind can't stop racing as it fills with questions. He didn't complain about his terrible day or even bother to mention it to me for two weeks? He didn't seem worked up when he got home that night, but he was worked up when he told me about it just now. Isn't that backward? Shouldn't he have been more worried and upset about it at that moment? He could hardly finish his test? I didn't even realize he was worried about his test. He seemed fine when I talked to him that day.

This guy is such a mystery, I just can't figure him out. I make a vow to myself right then and there to ask Andrew what his day was like if he ever seems distant like that again and to do my best not to take it personally.

* * *

ANDREW'S TAKE

It wasn't clear to me how overwhelmed I was that night, let alone the need to talk about the cause of my being upset. My mind was focused on getting Michelle's AC installed so she didn't have to suffer in her home anymore. Becoming more self-aware has helped me with poor communication, coupled with Michelle knowing that she should ask me how I'm feeling before she takes it personally. These two skills have helped us avoid many miserable nights, days, and weeks. I can't say this enough as someone who struggles with communication: learning to communicate better as a life skill will save you so much headache and heartache.

* * *

Photos for Chapter 12
Bellamimalifestyles.com/bookphotos

A BONUS STORY BY ANDREW

WE DON'T NEED THAT

Often I tell Michelle that I'm going to buy something new—a TV soundbar, computer, blender, forks, computer chair, automatic can opener, noise-canceling headphones, etc.

She typically looks kind of puzzled because I already have a TV, computer, forks, computer chair… So why would I need or want a new one?

The reason is always simple. I found one with better features or that just plain works better. There would never be a fight, and usually, in the end, she is happy with my purchase.

"Michelle, do you have a blender?" I ask one day.

"Yeah, in the cupboard above the fridge," she replies. I open the cupboard and see this 1980s-era discolored, plastic, basic blender.

Nope! I think to myself. These are terrible. You have to portion food and liquid so the blender won't free spin, or worse, it only liquefies the bottom half of the blender reservoir. *Hard Nope.*

"Michelle, I'm going to Costco," I say as I leave the condominium.

Upon my return we have a new, three horizontal blade blender with all the bells and whistles. At first, Michelle is surprised that I replaced her blender. After two weeks and a few dozen smoothies, she is sold.

This trend happens with several other upgrades over the coming months.

Another thing that I find irksome is using the speakers that the TV comes with for sound. They are so bad and aren't aimed at you, so they sound funny. The next time we went to Costco, I put a Bose soundbar into the cart.

"Andrew, we don't need a speaker for the TV. It has speakers built in," Michelle says in confusion.

"No, no. This is on sale, and I've been wanting to stop using the speakers in the TV. This is no way to live," I reply, knowing that within a month she will appreciate this purchase.

Oh, thank God for soundbars.

* * *

MICHELLE'S TAKE

Oh, there's a lot to unpack with this story. First off, it was awesome when Andrew bought me a blender. The new one really made me realize how terrible my old one was. When you learn about my childhood and the years of abuse I suffered in our next book, you will have a clear understanding of why I never felt as though I deserved nice things. Growing up in an alcoholic family that was in constant financial crisis certainly left its mark on me. Replacing something that was working well enough in my eyes was not something I liked to do due to my childhood trauma.

Andrew and I are complete opposites in this area. I struggle to feel as though I deserve nice things, whereas he always wants the newest and most efficient gadget. He instantly devalues something as soon as he knows there is a better version he can be using. Whereas I'll put something together with duct tape and keep using it until it completely dies.

When I tell him not to upgrade his computer, though, it has little to do with money. When Andrew decides to upgrade something on his computer, it takes over our lives for weeks on end. He will upgrade one thing, then say that his monitor now can't keep up with his graphics card, and this causes a domino effect until he has replaced every single item of his gaming system. It never stops.

Now the soundbar, on the other hand, is a completely different issue. You will learn more about this in the following chapter. But for now, let me just tell you that Andrew was not the one who paid for that soundbar. He put it in the cart, yes, and wanted it for my place, but it was *me* who had to foot the bill, and I didn't even want it. It does sound somewhat nicer than the TV speakers, but to me, it's not worth having the extra remote I have to deal with or the $300 it cost.

Mini spoiler alert. With time Andrew encourages me to raise my standards when it comes to my possessions. He teaches me that I deserve to be happy and to have nice things. You will learn all about this in our next book, as well as the many other ways Andrew saved me and made me a better person.

13

THE TOUGHEST STUFF - WHAT NEARLY BROKE US

I n many ways, Andrew was everything I could ever dream of and more, but in other ways, I couldn't stand him.

As previously mentioned, we nearly broke up twice. Without further ado, here are the reasons why.

MR. CHEAPSKATE

It's Saturday, and Andrew and I are heading to the Rocky Mountains with Jackson and Caleb. The four of us drive out to Canmore, park the truck, and ride our bikes twenty-five kilometers to Banff. We have been wanting to do this for months and are having a stellar afternoon.

Once in Banff, we lock up our bikes and find a restaurant with a patio so we can eat outside. Banff is surrounded by stunning views of the Rocky Mountains, making it a popular tourist attraction. As we all know, tourist attractions aren't cheap.

We eat a delicious lunch while enjoying pleasant conversation. Our waitress is friendly and often sticks around to chat with us. It feels like the perfect day, at least until the bill comes.

Jackson pays the bill for him and Caleb, and the waitress places our bill in front of Andrew.

Andrew picks up our check, looks at it, makes a shocked face with his mouth open, and throws it back on the table. He throws it with gusto as if to say, "No way am I paying that!"

Mortified, I turn to Jackson to see if he noticed. Yup, he noticed. *Everyone* noticed. Jackson rolls his eyes at me as if to say, "What the fuck did he just do?"

Caleb lets out a little chuckle as he sees our reactions, and Andrew just continues to sit nonchalantly.

I know he is cheap, but he has never been this blatant about it.

I think to myself, *Who does that? I think I need to break up with this guy.*

Dumbfounded by what just happened, I grab the check and pay it.

This incident ruins an otherwise beautiful weekend.

To say I was struggling financially the first year I was dating Andrew would be an understatement. My head injury prevented me from working, yet I was denied my disability insurance. My debt was growing every single month, and I was drowning in it. Andrew, on the other hand, was working full time and living in a reasonably priced basement suite. He would brag about how low his rent was and how much money he was saving. Despite this fact, we split nearly every bill in half, even the groceries.

I'm just going to say it: he was a cheapskate. So cheap, in fact, that I nearly left him over it.

To me, there are unspoken rules about money. I bought the movie tickets, so you get the popcorn. If I grabbed the bill last time, then you get it this time. If you are treating me to dinner, maybe don't mention how expensive it is. For me, these rules are a given, and Andrew doesn't follow any of them. He doesn't speak the unspoken language that many of us do, and it drives me crazy.

There were times when we went somewhere, and I had purchased the tickets, so I would be expecting Andrew to pay for the food. When the bill came he would just let it sit there, making zero acknowledgments of it. Eventually, I would grab it and be furious inside.

Andrew also had a tendency to ruin date nights by mentioning the high prices as we ordered or looked at the menu. Talk about a mood killer. When we go out to eat, the last thing I want is to have my date complain about the prices, especially when he's rarely the one who picks up the check.

Approaching someone I'm dating about being cheap is not something I'm familiar with, so I probably took too long to address it. In hindsight, this was not the best play on my part. I was damn near ready to leave him over it by the time I brought it up. Laying out some ground rules earlier would've been the smarter play, but that's tough to do in a new relationship.

There were months when I was spending quite a bit more on our relationship than Andrew was. I never should've let it get that far, especially when I wasn't working. Part of the problem was that I couldn't handle the bill sitting on the table. It drove me crazy how long he could leave a bill sitting there without acknowledging it, so I would grab it before he got a chance to. He didn't seem bothered if the waitress was lurking, whereas I wanted to get it over with. Also, when he mentioned the prices, I would feel like he didn't want to pay, so I would grab it because I felt bad (typical people-pleasing wounded inner child).

This was setting a bad precedent. I wish I would've just said, "Andrew, can you get the bill? It's your turn."

The cheapskate issue bothered me so much, and I thought about it a lot. Since I wasn't bringing it up with Andrew at the time, I had many discussions with Jackson and Caleb about it. They understood my frustrations. They love Andrew, but even they were surprised at how little he picked up the check.

We split the grocery bill in half at the checkout. My stomach is in knots just thinking about it. It used to make me so furious because he ate way more than I did. When he was powerlifting, he usually had two dinners. Eventually, I lost it on him and told him he had to pay 65 percent.

When the cashier would say, "That'll be 173 bucks," I'd be thinking, *Come on, Andrew, pay a hundred, and I'll get the rest.* But Andrew couldn't hear my loud thoughts. He would tell the clerk, "Eighty-six dollars and fifty cents." Yup, he would even say the cents. He couldn't round up to the nearest dollar. Cashiers would look at me with confused looks on their faces, and I would even get the occasional eye roll.

This issue all came to a head when we were planning our one-year anniversary trip. Andrew said he would pay for it after I complained about splitting the grocery bill in half. It was a $2,400 all-inclusive trip to the Dominican Republic, so I was ecstatic when he offered to pay.

After Andrew booked our anniversary trip, I took it upon myself to purchase our $900 flight tickets to Ontario to see his family. I also ordered $500 in the proper currency to use during our trip. Andrew didn't ask me to; that's just what I do naturally. I try to keep things balanced. It was the least I could do since he was paying for the larger trip. Andrew seemed pleased when I told him I had booked our flight for the summer. He spent $2,400, and I spent $1,400. I was happy with that.

The week of our trip, Andrew ends up asking me when I'm going to pay him the $1,200 for my half. I LOSE MY MIND, nearly canceling the trip and ending our relationship.

Andrew didn't make me feel like we were a team or like he wanted to take care of me. A major shift was needed in this area if I was going to stay with him. I expressed that clearly in a letter. It hurt me too badly to continue feeling like a burden to him. I wrote him a two-page letter (front and back) about how I didn't feel he valued my contributions to the relationship and how he made me feel bad whenever he paid for something.

It might've been childish, but I felt the need to point out the many things in our relationship I had paid for in the letter. Laying out all the times he made me feel bad by not treating me like his teammate. It had been bottled up inside of me for too long, and I had to let it all out.

That week was tough on both of us.

Andrew's first response to the letter was to offer me money.

"I'll just give you money. How much do you want?" he said. "I don't care about the money. I'll just give you two thousand dollars."

I was baffled that Andrew thought this would solve the problem. It was very tough for me to explain to him that it wasn't so much about the money. It was about the *way* he was making me feel in our relationship. Like I was a burden and like I owed him something. I needed to feel like we were a team, but I felt like we were two separate entities.

I did things for him because I wanted to. On his end, everything felt transactional.

I wish I could say that this letter solved all of our problems, but that wasn't the case. Not even close. Things improved a little bit after the letter and our trip, but we were far from stable.

It's been a slow climb up a very steep hill, but I'm happy to say that the cheapskate issue has improved significantly.

* * *

ANDREW'S TAKE

Dear God, it's been one heck of a journey.

I'm still working on my issues with money, but I guess I made things worse by trying to make it 50/50 rather than letting the chips fall as they may. Oops.

Context alert: When I offered Michelle $2,000, I wasn't kidding. I meant it as, "Oh dear God, I didn't realize the mistake I made. Please take $2,000, and make it better."

I recognize that I can be selfish, especially with money. As a kid and teenager, I realized that I didn't like being broke. So since I moved out, I made sure to keep my finances in a constant state of never being broke. And so far, it has worked. But little did I know that I would have to adjust this somewhat to have a healthy relationship.

* * *

Not Being Able to Factor Me into His Future

We are set to hike Rawson Lake with Jackson and Caleb. Andrew and I sleep in, but they are kind enough to wait for us on the side of the road for an hour while we catch up. We love hiking with Jackson and Caleb. We crank old tunes and turn the car into a mobile karaoke festival. We are singing along to the Backstreet Boys while head-bobbing. Jackson always has the best playlists that remind me of our junior high days.

It's our first time hiking to Rawson Lake, and it's a struggle for me to keep up with the boys. My concussion symptoms flare up because of how quickly we rushed out the door this morning. My brain is overstimulated, and my head begins to throb. The boys wait for Baxter and me patiently when I need to rest.

Once we reach Rawson Lake, we are blown away by how beautiful it is. It's crystal blue and surrounded by the Rocky Mountains, alpine trees, and clear skies. We sit down and eat lunch while admiring the view. It's breathtaking.

"We are going to hike Tent Ridge next weekend." Jackson turns to us and asks, "You guys in?"

"I wish we could, but we have plans next weekend," Andrew answers.

I turn to Andrew and say, "That's a good hike. We will have to put it on the list for next year."

"How do you do that?" Andrew asks.

"Do what?" I answer with a confused tone.

"How do you know we will be together next year? I have no idea what's going to happen next year." These words hit me like a punch to the heart, and I stop dead in my tracks.

"What did you just say?" I say as my eyes nearly jump out of their sockets.

"Well, so many factors would have to line up in order for that to happen," Andrew replies.

Jackson and Caleb, taking Andrew's words as their cue to leave, get up and continue to hike to the summit. Andrew and I opt to stay by the lake and wait for them.

"Andrew, I would never be in a relationship with anyone if I did not feel that we would be together in a year," I explain.

"I have no idea what is going to happen," Andrew reiterates. "Or if we will still be together."

At this point I'm sick to my stomach thinking, *How can he be saying these words to me?*

"I believe in us," I continue, "and the solid foundation we've built through our friendship. Aren't you optimistic that we will work out since things are going so well?"

"I don't really know," is all Andrew can say to that as he takes another bite of his sandwich.

At this point, I'm speechless and tired of looking at his face.

We sit awkwardly in silence and continue to eat our food. I sit there amongst the most beautiful scenery and lose the ability to enjoy it. I'm numb.

Andrew gets up to go for a swim in the freezing cold lake. Andrew loves to swim, and I usually enjoy watching him, but not this time. This time I turn my back to him to be alone with my thoughts, stewing in my frustrations for far too long.

The boys return to nothing but awkward tension. They begin the descent down the mountain while I walk behind with Baxter. Wanting to be alone, I leave enough space between us so that I can see them but can hardly hear their conversations.

I'm tired of Andrew's inability to tell me that our relationship makes him happy. I'm tired of him not realizing how good we are together. I feel insecure about us and whether or not we will last.

My mind is shouting, *I can't believe he just said that to me! What am I doing putting all this work into a relationship when he has no idea if we will work out or not? How can he not see how good we are together?*

It's a long walk down the mountain, followed by an even longer drive home. Not even car karaoke can lighten my mood.

Once back at my condo, I turn to Andrew and say, "I think you need to go home. I need some time to think and process these emotions."

Andrew hasn't said much since his swim, and he remains quiet as he packs his stuff to go home.

After he leaves, I have a bubble bath and cry. I laugh and enjoy my time with Andrew more so than anyone else, but that doesn't make up for the pain he is causing me. Why is it so hard for him to tell me he hopes we will be together in a year? That's all I need to hear, just a little optimism. Why is it so hard for him to give any kind of optimism?

After a good cry, all I can think about is the obvious signs I have been ignoring, and many red flags begin jumping out at me. He doesn't treat us like a team because we are not a team. He can't factor me into his future because he doesn't plan on having me in it. How could I have been so blind? How can I continue dating someone who doesn't realize how good we are together?

A few hours later, I receive a text from Andrew. It reads, *Alexithymia - The inability to recognize or describe one's own emotions.*

Do you think you have Alexithymia? I text back.

Andrew replies, *I don't know.*

Without giving it much thought, I put my phone away.

Over the next couple of days, I decide I have two choices. I can break up with him, or I can continue dating a guy who doesn't seem to know if I'm the one for him.

Ultimately, I feel too much pride to try to convince Andrew how good we were together or to keep going through this pain. I decide to break up with him, and I feel the need to do it soon.

I crawl onto my bed next to Baxter and hit the call button for Andrew. As his phone rings, I get a sinking feeling in my stomach.

"Hello," Andrew answers, obviously distraught.

"I deserve better than to be with someone who does not know how he feels about me, Andrew," I explain. "This is hurting me."

Andrew is obviously upset, but he doesn't say anything. While holding the phone in silence, I wait for him to fight for me. I'm hoping he will say something along the lines of, "You make me really happy," or "I *do* think we will last the year." But those words never come. All he has for me is tears and silence.

Minutes pass, but still nothing.

"Andrew, you need to say something," I urge.

"I don't know what to say," he answers.

The words, "I need you to bring my key back," keep repeating themselves in my mind, but I'm reluctant to say them out loud. Andrew is too distraught, and it stops me from pulling the trigger.

"Perfect. I guess I may as well hang up then," I say in a snarky tone as I hang up the phone.

My face fills with tears. I do not feel right. Nothing feels right. I do not want to break up with Andrew, but I also can't continue like this. I know there has to be a reason for these things that are hurting me so badly, but I can't make sense of it.

Here is this great guy who clearly cares about me, who hardly has any other priorities. But for some reason, he has a tough time telling me how he feels or factoring me into his future. It's as if his actions don't match his words. This is something I've never encountered before.

I dial Jackson's number because I need backup.

"Hello?"

I'm crying as Jackson picks up the phone.

"I don't want to break up with him, but how can I be with someone who doesn't know if I'm going to be in his future?" I say, hoping for some reassurance.

"I don't think he knows how to factor you in, but I think he just assumes you will be there," Jackson replies.

I'm intrigued.

He goes on. "Andrew is different. I think he just thinks differently. Like he wants you there but doesn't know how to say it. I really do think he wants you there, though. He just doesn't know how to say that he does."

Jackson really hit the hammer on the head with that one. It feels as though he's uncovered an important truth.

I think he just assumes you will be there.

Immediately, I feel better after Jackson says those words. I'm still confused as to where our relationship is going, but I know I want to find out.

I hang up the phone with Jackson and call Andrew. I ask him to come over, not to bring me my key, but to make up.

***

ANDREW'S TAKE

At that moment, just like in the previous story about Michelle's lipstick, I was just making an observation. I really did hope that she would be there, and I didn't think saying something like that, at that time, was as terrible as it sounded.

My memories of this are faint. Months after this happened, I recall talking to Michelle about how she was going to ask for her key back, but she never did. What I felt inside when she told me that she was nearly breaking up with me was intense sadness, despair, and confusion. Knowing that it didn't happen was so relieving, yet knowing how close Michelle was to breaking up with me was scary because I would not have seen it coming at all.

* * *

He Didn't Want to Move In

Gabriel moves out shortly after Andrew and I begin dating. To help me pay my bills for the first few months, I rent out my spare bedroom on Airbnb. An occasional guest here and there helps relieve some of my financial strain. Once winter rolls around, I ask Andrew if he has an idea of when we should move in together.

"Andrew, when do you see us moving in together?" I ask when we've been dating for six months.

"I haven't even thought about it," he replies.

This aggravates me a little bit because it means I have to get a new roommate when Andrew is spending most nights at my condo anyways, but I don't push the subject. I post an ad on Kijiji and end up finding a lovely roommate on a six-month lease. She is going through a divorce and just needs a comfortable place to stay during her transition phase. I figure it's perfect. By the time she'll be moving out, Andrew and I will have been dating for a year, on top of being friends for a year. I assume he'll be ready to move in by then.

I bring the subject up for the second time shortly before my roommate is set to move out. Andrew gives me the same answer: "I haven't thought about it."

I'm baffled and somewhat furious. We are already saying "I love you" and are loosely planning a six-month backpacking trip for next year.

This time I push the subject. "Well I need you to think about it, Andrew. My roommate is moving out, and I'd much rather you move in than find another roommate."

We discuss it a little, but I get nowhere. We basically talk in a giant circle without deciding anything. He mostly dodges the subject. I don't know what to do.

Andrew lives in a basement suite with no bathroom or kitchen. Every time I have to pee in the middle of the night, I have to go up a full flight of steps, and I need to have clothes on. It feels like I'm in my twenties again having to share a bathroom with multiple men. I'm in my thirties, dammit, and if I want to go to the bathroom half-naked in the middle of the night, then that's what I'm going to do.

We rarely get to cook dinner without other people being in the kitchen with us. They are nice people, but I'm over it. Everything about this situation is annoying me. Grocery shopping is frustrating because I don't know how many nights Andrew will be coming over. I'm also spending quite a bit more than I'm used to on food, and I'm still not working. Living together will make everything so much easier. I'm excited to get into a routine with Andrew, to live in one place, and to plan our meals properly.

As my roommate's move-out day draws closer, I become more frustrated with this situation. I was lucky enough to find a decent roommate for six months the first time. What are the chances I'll find another one, and do I even want to? If Andrew still feels unsure about living together at this point, then maybe we aren't supposed to be together. At thirty-four years old, I'm certainly not prepared to keep dating someone who isn't sure if he wants to live with me after knowing me for two years. I'm a proud person, and trying to convince anyone to live with me seems degrading, but I need to bring the subject up again.

The end of the month is approaching, so I need to act fast if Andrew is possibly going to give his notice for next month.

Andrew is on his way over for dinner. I'm making salmon, veggies, and steamed rice. My intuition tells me this isn't going to go well, and I have a heavy feeling in my stomach.

While we are eating, I bring up the subject of moving in together, similar to a way I would in a business meeting.

"So my roommate is moving out in a month, and we need to make a plan for when you're moving in," I say. "If I have to find a new roommate, I need to know for how long."

"Well, I haven't really thought about it," Andrew repeats what he's always said. I want to punch him right in the nose. Dude, think about it already.

"Well, I need you to think about it because I'm not happy that I have to find another roommate when we could easily be living together. I'm tired of going back and forth all the time and always having other people around us," I reply sharply.

"I like my setup there, and it's so cheap," Andrew reiterates as I clench my fists under the table in an attempt to hide my rage. I promised myself that we were not leaving this table without a plan, so my only choice is to keep asking questions. To avoid yelling at him, I channel my frustration into the center of my hands.

"Well, how long do you think we should be living together before we go on our big trip?" I ask.

"I have no problem giving my landlord six months' rent upfront while we go on our trip," he replies.

This comment makes me want to throw him out of my house. My rage reaches a level that is no longer disguisable, and I am now yelling.

"So, you don't plan on moving in with me until after that trip? That's eighteen months away. And you're comfortable helping a *stranger* pay his mortgage while we travel when you could be helping me with my mortgage?"

"I figured we'd move in together if that six-month trip went well," Andrew answers.

"I'm not comfortable planning a six-month backpacking trip with someone I haven't lived with yet!" I shriek. "I don't understand how you can tell me you love me and still be eighteen months away from wanting to move in with me."

Andrew sits in silence, not knowing what to say.

I'm furious inside. This is so much worse than I was anticipating.

"I think you should leave," I declare. "And I need time to calm down before we speak again."

I have little optimism that Andrew and I are going to make it. The next couple of weeks are blurry because I don't handle the stress well, given my head injury.

Again, I write him a letter explaining how much I am hurting and why I am questioning our relationship. I write, *I'm excited to live with you, but I don't want to live with anyone who isn't as excited to live with me.*

As tough as it is to admit that money is a factor in my frustrations, it certainly is. It really hurts me that Andrew is okay with handing his landlord six months' rent in advance when that money could be going to help me with my mortgage while we are traveling together. It makes me feel like we aren't a team and like he can't possibly love me.

Tears land on the page as I fold the letter, finishing it off by telling him that I'm beginning to think that he should be planning the backpacking trip on his own so he can figure out what he wants in life. All my fears and feelings are laid out for him. It feels like I have a man who "kind of" loves me, and to me, that's worse than being alone.

Andrew takes some time with my letter. He explains that he hadn't understood how much living together mattered to me. I don't remember it being a big magical moment, but Andrew tells me he will move in one month later.

A large part of me feels like he is moving in because he doesn't want to lose me, more so than actually wanting to live with me. This doesn't leave me feeling fantastic about our relationship, but we will know soon enough if it's a mistake or not. If Andrew moves in and I don't feel like he is happy, then I'll know we aren't right for each other.

I wish I understood then how hard change is for Andrew. It would've saved me some tears and heartache.

* * *

ANDREW'S TAKE

I really didn't realize how much Michelle was hurting, but I do remember a night shortly before I moved in when it hit me, and I was so scared to lose her. I shifted gears fast and moved in.

There were other reasons why I was hesitant to move in, aside from the fact that I didn't realize the "obvious" reasons. I have allergies to dogs, cats, and many other animals. Michelle had Baxter, and I didn't want to come between her and her dog. I had lived with two dogs in a previous relationship, and I was constantly dealing with allergies. Living without pets and without having to take any medication to keep my asthma in check was so nice. I never wanted to live with pets again.

Baxter was the first dog that I've been around that gave me anxiety. Poor thing would always be at a 9/10 or 10/10 for anxiety, and this gave me anxiety. I was not used to this, and I didn't really like it.

I realize in hindsight the signs that I missed. I really felt bad once it made sense to me. Regardless of Michelle's dog, I was moving in. Michelle is my favorite person, and that will never change. I have more devotion to her than anyone else in my life.

* * *

Photos for Chapter 13
Bellamimalifestyles.com/bookphotos

A BONUS STORY BY ANDREW

DRUNKEN JIUJITSU ATTACKS

Michelle asked me to write about anything I didn't like about her when we were first dating, and only one story comes to mind. There was one night when Michelle drove me crazy—crazy with armbars, leg locks, and chokeholds. She went out for a lady's night and had a bit too much wine to drink. She arrived home late, on a work night, around 11 p.m. I was ready to go to sleep soon, but she wanted to stay up and hang out. This was okay, except it felt weird that she was drunk. She could walk and talk well enough, but it felt odd to me as I was sober. I had slight anxiety about going to sleep soon so I wouldn't be tired for work the next day.

We started to cuddle on the couch while watching some random half-hour show on Netflix. This was followed by her taking my arm from around her shoulder and into an armbar submission. I thought this was cute; a drunk Michelle wants to play fight, okay, game on. So we wrestled for a little bit. Michelle is tougher than I realize every time we play fight, but this can't stop my overpowering strength.

On this night, though, her unyielding urge to submit me began to exhaust me. I would submit her, and she would just go again, and again, and again. I would say, "Okay, that's enough," followed by a chuckle. Nope. Now she wanted to kick and punch. Not hard; she just wanted to add some more intensity to the wrestling. This back and forth went on for another few minutes, and I was getting tired from this drunken jiujitsu at 11:30 p.m. I finally let her know that I was done with play fighting and wanted to go to sleep. And so I began getting ready for bed.

Can you guess what happened once we were both in bed?

"Armbar!" she exclaimed. Another armbar, another round of me overpowering her.

"Leglock!" she hollered. And another round of me overpowering her in play-wrestling fashion.

After another ten minutes of this, I was exhausted and angry. I was very stern with Michelle and told her that she had to stop and we needed to go to sleep. The look in her eye told me that she did not want to stop. But I didn't care; I protested verbally several more times as she tried to wrestle me. Luckily by this time, she was tired, and she passed out. The following day she knew that I was upset with her, and we had a small fight. I told her that I didn't like how she acted. She understood me, but her pride prevented her from totally owning up to it at that moment.

* * *

Michelle's Take

Oh, Drunken Michelle and her arm bars, she really gets out of hand (insert sarcastic tone).

In my eyes, I was flirting with Andrew, but apparently, I was borderline obnoxious.

Seems about right. Sometimes I overdo it on the wine.

14

LIVING TOGETHER

Our Relationship Improves

Once Andrew decided to move in, our relationship improved significantly. That same week he did the most adorable thing. I went to the mailbox and was shocked to see two pieces of mail for Andrew. One was from Shaw, and the other from Telus. It put a smile on my face because he wasn't moving in for another five weeks, and it surprised me that he had changed his address so soon.

Andrew never opened the letters, and I ended up moving them around the condo for weeks.

Finally, I brought them to him and said, "Can you open these already so I can stop looking at them?"

"Oh, those are old," he says. "You can just throw them out."

"What do you mean they're old?" I ask. "They just came in the mail for you."

"I called Shaw and Telus and asked them to send an old bill to this address," he explains.

Still confused, I ask, "Why would you do that?" not expecting the sweetest sentiment that was about to come out of Andrew's mouth.

"I thought if you went to the mailbox and saw my mail, it would make you happy. I wanted you to know I was committed to moving in," Andrew says without looking away from his computer.

"That's so sweet," I reply as I hug the letters.

"It was tough for me to get them to send an old bill," he continues. "But the girl agreed when I told her it was to surprise my girlfriend to show her I changed my address."

That's the thing about Andrew. He will be the most romantic when you least expect it. I'm glad I kept bugging him to open those bills. Otherwise, he would never have thought to tell me he did that for me. I wrote this memory on the back of the Shaw bill and keep it in my filing cabinet so I will always remember this beautiful thing he did.

Once Andrew moves his stuff in weeks later, he begins nesting. Personally, I nest by organizing. I like to have all of my things organized in drawers so I know exactly where I can find them. I enjoy hanging my clothes and unpacking whenever I stay somewhere new. It makes me feel settled. Andrew nests in a completely different way. A way unlike any I've ever seen.

The first thing he does is check all my filters. The one in my washing machine has never been cleaned, so Andrew gives me a speech.

"You know, I swear I only have a job because people never clean their filters," he says as he sits on the floor in my laundry room with a lap full of wet towels. "This filter needs to be cleaned every one to two years. Otherwise it gets really hard on the motor."

Once all of my filters are up to Andrew's standards, he decides I need a new thermostat.

"This thermostat is terrible. I'm going to get you a new one," he says as he inspects it.

"There's nothing wrong with my thermostat!" I yell down the hallway from my living room.

"You can't tell how many degrees it is in here," Andrew replies.

"Who cares?" I yell back. "If it gets too hot in here, I move the knob down a little. If it gets cold, I move it up."

"This is unacceptable," he replies. "I'm buying you a new thermostat, a digital one. I actually think I have one laying around that's much better than this. You can set the temperature with your phone."

"Whatever," I say as I get back to my television show.

The next day Andrew gets home from work late and decides he's going to change my thermostat.

"Don't do that tonight," I protest. "It's late, and you haven't even eaten dinner yet."

"This won't take long," Andrew insists as he begins taking the new one out of the box while he's still in his work clothes. I don't even know why I bother trying. He never listens when I tell him to wait to do something. His compulsion overpowers my words every single time, and yet I constantly feel the need to try.

Andrew installs the new thermostat, but he can't get it to work. He's tripped a breaker, and he goes downstairs to the parking garage to learn that he's unable to get into the mechanical room.

"Ah, I think you have to call your condo company," Andrew says. "They are going to have to handle it because I can't get into the room to fix it."

"Fantastic," I say in a sarcastic tone. "I told you not to touch it. It was fine before."

The following morning I call my condo management company and tell them what had happened. The girl on the other line is not impressed with me.

"You're not supposed to do renovations by yourself," she says in a stern voice. "Your boyfriend tripped a breaker that took out three other units, and now I have to send someone out there to fix it."

"Sorry about that," I say in an attempt to lighten the mood. "He does this for a living, so I didn't think it would be a problem just to change a thermostat."

"Clearly your boyfriend has no idea what he is doing, so I want your word that he will not be trying to fix anything else in your condo," she continues to get more aggressive.

"You have my word," I say.

"I'm going to have our guy call you this afternoon, and I'm going to be billing the invoice to you for whatever time it takes for him to fix this issue," she explains. "His name is George, and you'll need to be home to let him in your unit."

"Yup, I'm home," I say. "He can come anytime."

When George arrives he is much nicer than the woman I dealt with on the phone. "These older condos are tricky," he explains. "There are only two thermostats they are compatible with, and they aren't the most common ones. If your boyfriend isn't used to working on older units, he wouldn't have known that."

"Oh, I'll have to explain that to him," I say with a chuckle. "Because he had no idea why that happened."

"Well, it's all fixed now. Unfortunately, the one I installed isn't much better than your old one," he says. "It's basically the same, just a little newer."

"Fantastic, so it really was a complete waste of time," I reply. "What's this going to cost me?"

"I was in the area anyway, so I'm only going to bill you for the hour and the new thermostat," he says. "It'll be about $160 or so."

"Thank you so much. I appreciate that," I say as I show him to the door.

"You have my number now, so you can always call me if you have any questions. I work on these units all the time," he says as he walks out into the hallway.

Andrew felt bad about the whole thing, but it was a pretty easy fix in the end. No real harm done.

Less than a week later Andrew says to me, "I'm going to install motion-sensing lights in your closet and laundry room."

"Really?" I reply. "Do you think we really need that?"

"Oh, yeah. It's easy, and it'll be so much better," Andrew says. "You don't have to flick the light every time you go in to grab something."

"Okay, just try not to trip any breakers," I joke. "Or I'm going to make you talk to the mean lady on the phone this time."

Andrew has the new lights installed by the weekend, and I have to admit, they are pretty fantastic. I never realized it was annoying to flick the light switch every time I walked into my closet until I didn't have to do it anymore.

For weeks Andrew yells, "Man, I love this motion-sensing light switch!" every time he walks into the laundry room. "Don't you just love these light switches?" he asks.

"Yes, Andrew. I love the light switches," I assure him for the hundredth time. "You were right. They make life easier."

Once Andrew is nested and happy with the new gadgets throughout the condo, he turns to me and says, "This is really fantastic. It's much better than how we were living before. You were right. We really should have done this sooner. I didn't realize how annoying it was to live separately."

"I'm so happy you feel that way because I've been a little worried," I say as I let out a huge sigh. Andrew has finally realized what I've known all along.

"Yes, life is so much better now, and I'm really happy," Andrew reassures me wholeheartedly.

The following Saturday afternoon, Andrew and I run out to get some last-minute groceries.

"We have to hurry back, so let's only get a few groceries," I say. "Because I'm excited for our date night tonight. It's been a while since we've gone out."

"Yeah, we will just go grab a few things for now," Andrew agrees.

While at the grocery store, we are laughing through the aisles. Andrew always has to compare the price per gram to make sure we buy the best deal, and this amuses me. We are joking and laughing as much as ever, and it feels nice to finally be getting into a routine. I've longed for this moment for a while now, and I'm happy that we are buying food for one place.

On our way out to the car, Andrew is racing toward me with the cart while attempting to stand on it. I grab another cart to race him through the parking lot. It feels as if we are two teenagers playing hooky from school, just enjoying the moment and acting like goofballs. There's a rare magic in the air, as many of us adults lose the ability to get lost in the moment like this. Suddenly, my heart feels fulfilled as I'm overwhelmed with a realization.

My relationship with Andrew may not have had the magic I was expecting, but what we have now is so much better than anything I could've imagined. It's taken us a year to get to this point, and it was a bumpy ride, but this is so much more special than anything that can be portrayed in movies.

What we have is magic in our day-to-day life. Trivial things that used to seem mundane are my favorite things to do with Andrew. This is the best kind of magic. He makes the most boring days exciting. We often clean the house while joking around to old '90s tunes. More importantly, Andrew is always cheering me up when I'm sad or compensating by giving me special attention on my toughest days. This is the kind of magic that takes time to build, but it lasts for the long haul.

There was a quote by Monica Drake that hung on the wall at my yoga studio that I've never fully understood until this moment. That quote reads, *"The Buddhists say if you meet someone and your heart pounds, your hands shake, your knees go weak, that's not the one. When you meet your 'soulmate' you'll feel calm. No anxiety. No agitation."*

Every time I read that quote, a part of me always thought, *How can that be true? If I meet my soul mate, I'm going to be so freaking excited and far from calm.*

It took me until the age of thirty-four, but I finally get it now. During my first few months with Andrew, my heart felt so calm it almost felt as though I was settling. But it's slowly grown into the greatest love I've ever known. In all of my past relationships, I somewhat lost myself in the other person, and the beginning was the best part. With Andrew, it feels like we are walking side by side as our own people, and everything just keeps getting better as time goes on. Our love story didn't start off with a bang, but it sure has blossomed into something spectacular. I never miss the beginning. I'm much too busy being excited about where we are headed together.

In this moment, everything about us feels perfect and rock solid. All of the feelings I have about craving more romance melt away as I realize that what we have is better than anything I could've imagined. The friendship and laughter I share with Andrew are better than romance. I wouldn't change a thing about our story or the bumpy road that got us here.

"So, where do you want to go for our date night?" Andrew asks when we get home.

"You know what," I reply. "I don't even feel like I need a date night now."

"Really?" Andrew asks in confusion. "But you were so excited."

"I had so much fun grocery shopping with you that it feels like we've already had a date today," I explain. "Now that we have groceries, we may as well just stay home in our sweats, play *Diablo*, and relax."

"Oh, really?" Andrew says with excitement. "That sounds awesome!"

* * *

ANDREW'S TAKE

It really was eye-opening that Michelle knew how great it would be if I moved in, and I didn't. Contemplating this over the months after I moved in taught me that Michelle can see things that I can't, and I was so happy that I was with someone who was strong where I was weak.

My friend Liam once explained a similar Buddhist quote to the one that Michelle referenced. "Being with someone who makes your heart pound, your hands shake, your knees go weak, is terrible," he explained to me. When Liam told me this, it hit me like a freight train. It made so much sense.

It's like being on fire with excitement and telling friends around you how intense the feelings are. Meanwhile, if they understand this quote, they're looking at you like you're on fire. And rather than celebrating with you, they want to dump a bucket of water on you.

I felt the same way about Michelle when we were dating: calm and relaxed. Being with her was different from my other relationships. Having been friends for a year helped to create a strong foundation. There was more genuine respect.

By the time I said "I love you," I knew that I trusted her. There would always be moments in past relationships when I would notice something that caused me to question trust and integrity. If a girlfriend showed me that they have limited knowledge in, say, used cars but then argued with me that they knew what they were doing, I would feel very worried that the relationship was about to get difficult.

If I know that someone does not have the ability to do something, and my gentle concern is dismissed without consideration, this is a huge red flag for me. I've never felt this way with Michelle.

* * *

The List I Never Read

Weeks later, I'm cleaning Andrew's computer room when I come across some papers. Andrew printed off a feeling wheel (a wheel full of emotion words he was using to help him identify his feelings). At the top of this feeling wheel, he's written the words, *You and Michelle are probably going to break up, and I don't know why.* He also circled the feelings *Sad, Upset, Angry, Confused,* and *Frustrated.*

When I see this, it makes me realize that Andrew hadn't understood what was going on when we nearly broke up. He genuinely had no idea, even though I did my best to explain.

Behind that feeling wheel, there is a beautiful list written down on a lined piece of paper.

It's a list about me, but I've never seen it before. It reads:

Michelle
You're special to me
You make me a better person
The way you handle things (your nephews, me, plans, traveling, awesome adventure ideas, Archery Tag, VR, working out, yoga, hitting pads)
Makes me feel so happy to have you
I love touching you, to remind you, "you're special and right now I'm twitterpated."
How happy you get for our dorky dates
How even though I seem to be having a tough time
You give me space to grow and breathe
I will always try
How strong and independent you can be but are still aware of us.
We can be strong together...We will make a very strong team together.
You're into things I'm so happy that my GF/Wife would be into.
Spirituality, yoga, meditation, UFC, working out, traveling
If we ever got into a fight, we could play fight each other
(Talk about take my breath away)
You're going to be an awesome mother.
Helping me with my family means so much to me
Very calm under pressure

MICHELLE AND ANDREW PRESTON

Likes to hang out and play games with my friends
How you will try things with me that you may not like
You're good at poker (wink face)
I always have fun with you when we go out

The list is so adorable that I read it over and over again. The word "twitterpated" is new to me, so I have to look up what it means. For those of you who are as lost as I am, it means "infatuated, or obsessed." As I read that, I melt into my chair a little. It's the sweetest list anyone has ever written about me, and I know it was written from the heart.

It's everything I needed to hear months ago when I was struggling to understand how Andrew felt about me. I cannot believe he wrote this but did not think to show it to me. It would have helped us by alleviating 99 percent of my insecurities about Andrew's feelings toward me. He's expressed more emotions in this one list than he did the entire first six months of our relationship. It's ironic that by the time I'm reading it, Andrew has moved in and we have said "I love you." It's still fantastic to read, of course, but the time when I needed to hear it most has long passed.

When Andrew gets home from work, I tell him I found the list and that it's really beautiful.

"Andrew, if you would've shown me this list, I never would've even considered breaking up with you," I say. "This list was all I needed from you. The only reason I was thinking about breaking up with you was because you never really told me how you felt about me. This list would've helped everything."

Andrew's response is, "Oh, I thought I showed it to you."

"No, you did not show this to me. If you would have shown this to me, I never would've been so insecure about us. You never said nice things like this to me," I explain. "And I really needed to hear them."

All Andrew has to say is, "Well, I'm glad you found it. I really didn't understand why we were about to break up."

Breaking up with Andrew would've been the biggest mistake of my life. He felt all of the things I hoped he would feel. He just never knew how to express them to me.

* * *

ANDREW'S TAKE

Michelle was the first girlfriend I had who tried to understand me and was good at it. She is very mature, disciplined, and cool under pressure. All the things that a touchy, quick-to-be-overwhelmed anxious guy could ever hope for.

The list was written as a gratitude exercise for myself, and I never really planned on showing Michelle. I must have been confused about thinking that I showed it to her. It never dawned on me how important that list could be to Michelle. To me, the list was to help me become more aware of my feelings and how I feel inside, so I don't forget.

There are so many things like the story of this list where I've learned important ways to be a loving, caring boyfriend or to just be a better person. But I have had to learn them by going right to the edge of almost being dumped and not even knowing that the edge was so close.

It's weeks or months afterward when I'm contemplating what happened, or better yet, when someone helps me understand what happened, like Michelle, that I can learn and do better next time.

My guess is that most people do this instinctively without thinking about it or from learning it subconsciously. Yet, for me, my instincts are almost nonexistent, and I know that the only way for me to improve is through a conscious effort to learn what I did wrong.

* * *

Photos for Chapter 14
Bellamimalifestyles.com/bookphotos

A BONUS STORY BY ANDREW

YOU NEVER KNOW SOMEONE UNTIL YOU LIVE WITH THEM

"Where's my glass?" I ask Michelle as I walk into the kitchen.

"Just grab a new one," she responds. "It's in the dishwasher."

This is a common theme that occurs when you live with Michelle. She likes the kitchen and counters to be clean and free of any dishes and is not discerning in this endeavor. If you leave your cup of tea or cocoa on the table with plans to use it in the next five, maybe fifteen minutes, there is a good chance that it will be in the dishwasher when you return. There is even a chance that by the time you realize it's gone, it's already been cleaned and is back in the cupboard.

I can live with the overcleaned glasses, but are you familiar with the cup cover for a container of laundry detergent? Do you fill the cup to the brim before you start your laundry? If so, you are doing this very wrong, and so was Michelle. It took a few weeks before I saw her in the act.

"What are you doing?!" I say in shock.

"The laundry," Michelle is obviously confused as she replies.

"Why are you filling the cup full of laundry detergent? Do you always do this?!" I ask.

"Yes, Andrew. This is the cup that came with the detergent. This is how much you are supposed to use." As Michelle says this, I'm having to control myself from showing my utter disbelief in what is happening.

"Michelle," I say as I grab the cup from her hands and hold it up to the light. "Do you see the numbers one, two, and three? And below them is a level indicator?" I ask.

This is followed by Michelle realizing she's been doing laundry wrong for years. And by wrong, I mean very, very inefficiently. The clothes themselves were always stain-free and very clean.

"So I use the number three line?" Michelle asks me.

"No, hahaha! The three line is for large, heavily soiled laundry. Like stains and whatnot. You use the number one line the majority of the time unless you need an extra kick. Do you see how this container says it will last forty-eight loads of laundry? That's only if you use the number one line. Hehehe."

We begin to save a lot of money after this intervention.

* * *

Michelle's Take

Yes, I am guilty of overcleaning glasses. My previous roommate used to always say to me, "Where's my water glass?" I clean without thinking about it. It's a habit. If I see an empty glass on the counter, it goes in the dishwasher. It's not so much that the glass is bothering me; it's more like a reflex because it gives me something to do.

Also guilty, I use too much laundry detergent. But you know what really chaps my ass? Andrew uses too much of basically everything else, and I wasn't even going to mention it.

He fills his palm with more of my $45 conditioner than I do, and my hair is halfway down my back. I bought him his own stuff, but he prefers to use mine.

"Andrew, that's my expensive stuff for dry, frizzy hair. Don't use so much of it," I've said to him a hundred times.

Yet he continues to fill his palm.

"But I love this stuff," he replies. "It smells so good."

When he makes protein shakes, he uses two scoops of my expensive green powder when you're only supposed to use one. No matter how many times I've asked him to stop using two scoops, he can't seem to lay off the powder. I stopped buying it because it's too expensive with Andrew around.

So yes, I use too much laundry detergent. Only filling the cup to the first line just feels wrong, but when it comes to wasting products, I maintain that Andrew is the much bigger culprit.

15

THE BEDROOM

There's been debate about whether or not to include this chapter in the book. Some of you may be offended. Yet I know some of you need to hear this. Ultimately, I've concluded that it would be unfair to our story to leave these things out.

Since we are besties sharing some beverages, this is the part where I've completely lost all inhibitions and do some serious oversharing. We've discussed our sex life, but this chapter is specifically about our bedroom activities the first year we were together.

I've made you a promise to divulge all of the juicy details of our relationship, and this is me keeping that promise.

If I had understood some of these things before dating Andrew, it would have saved me some tears. It gives me hope knowing this chapter may help others avoid some of the confusion I suffered through.

My intentions are to be of love and assistance to those of you who need to know you're not alone. If you're offended by talk of sex or are simply not interested in hearing about it, please skip over this chapter and move on to the section on autism. Skipping this will not affect the rest of the book.

THE ACT OF SEX

Sex with Andrew has always been quite different from my previous relationships. How we bonded in the bedroom felt foreign to me.

Sex is often portrayed in movies as one of the key factors in a relationship. Society can make you feel like if you're not having passionate sex, you are with the wrong person, or there's something wrong with your relationship. I'm here to say that it can be quite the opposite, and this isn't a negative thing.

I'd argue that if you're having the best sex of your life, it could mean that you are likely blinded to many of the issues your relationship has. I'm not saying this is always the case, but it's very tough to think straight and look at someone objectively when you're having tons of passionate sex.

With Andrew, there's passion in knowing deep in my soul that I've found my perfect life partner, but there's little to no passion in the sex. We get the job done, and our bodies have needs that we satisfy, but this is not what we excel at together.

I've broken this chapter down into five aspects that affect our sex life the most. For each of these aspects, I'm going to explain the issue to you, give you an example story of how this affected us, and then offer up a solution that has helped me deal with it.

It took the entire first year of our relationship for me to pinpoint what these issues were and to learn to understand them. Originally I thought our sexual chemistry was off because we were friends. But I've learned that my confusion had little to do with so-called sexual chemistry and much more to do with the fact that my brain works differently than Andrew's.

It's tough to merge sexually when you live on different wavelengths.

Aspect #1 - Andrew Doesn't Mirror

I was so used to men mirroring my intensity levels in the bedroom that it never even dawned on me that someone might be incapable of doing that. It took me a while to understand why I felt so powerless when it came to initiating sex with Andrew. Before him, I felt like I had a certain superpower.

I could shoot a look across the room that would tell my boyfriend we'd be all over each other the second we got home. This gave me a certain amount of control over when someone was turned on by me.

I just had to act turned on by them, and they would mirror it back. It had always been simple, and I loved the buildup. The more in the mood I was, the more in the mood they became. I thrived on this.

With Andrew, I will never have that power because he doesn't mirror my intensity. It feels like he's on his own path of pleasure, separate from mine.

It isn't so much the mechanics of sex that turn me on; it's the emotion behind it. I'm very much attracted to feeling someone's attraction toward me escalate as mine escalates. I didn't fully realize this about myself until I started dating Andrew and this aspect was lacking.

STORY - "DON'T SQUEEZE ME"

Andrew drops a bomb while we are discussing sex. "You know how you squeeze me like this…" He reaches out and pinches my arm with his whole hand.

"Yes," I reply.

"I don't really like that. It overwhelms me, and it doesn't feel nice," he says.

"Oh," I say, feeling embarrassed. "I think I'm doing that to try to get some emotion out of you. I'm squeezing you to up the intensity, and I'm letting you know that it feels good."

"Well, that's not what it feels like to me," Andrew explains. "It just feels like squeezes and pinches. It's distracting."

"Okay, I'll try not to do that anymore," I answer. "But can you maybe try to push your body up against mine more often? It will make me feel more connected to you, and then I won't feel the need to squeeze. I like feeling the pressure of having someone on top of me."

"Yeah, I can do that," Andrew replies. "Just let me know when I'm doing it right so I know."

SOLUTION - GO WITHIN OR GO VERBAL

I laugh about this now because I was trying to up the intensity level of our sex by squeezing Andrew when I could've just shouted at him to go faster or harder. It's that simple; it just took me a while to realize this. He doesn't speak body language, so the solution is to use my words.

Another solution is for me to go "within" when we are having sex. Rather than trying to get my emotional fix by feeling Andrew's pleasure, I embrace my own. I'm not always able to do this, but I'm getting used to turning inward as opposed to focusing so much on us as a couple.

* * *

ANDREW'S TAKE

Every partner you have will teach you something new. Adding to the first story about being squeezed, I would hope that talking about sex could happen sooner than later. Once Michelle and I started talking about it, a lot of mysteries were solved. I knew something was off during sex, but I wasn't sure what it was. And rather than ask, I just let it slide and thought up some reason for what was happening. Then Michelle told me to put pressure on her while having sex, and once I did this, I could feel how much more into it she was. *Holy crap, I thought to myself. I wish she had told me this sooner. She's really enjoying this, and I get it now. I know what she wants.*

* * *

ASPECT #2 - HIS EMOTIONS DON'T MATCH HIS FACE

Andrew's facial expressions don't always match his emotions.

There isn't much to explain with this one, but I'll let your imagination sit with it for a minute so you can visualize how awkward this could make things in the bedroom.

...

Got It? Great.

Know that I just chuckled along with you.

This aspect stirred up trouble the first time we were visiting Gavin and Chelsea for the weekend.

I left out an important detail about our first trip to Brooks. But not to worry, bestie. I can't keep things from you for long.

STORY - HOT SEX AND THE PERMA SMILE

We finish playing board games with Gavin and Chelsea and head downstairs to bed.

Andrew and I both have a slight buzz going on, which is a first for us. It's the perfect recipe for hot sex. I'm tipsy enough to pounce on him and rip his clothes off without inhibitions but not so tipsy that I'm sloppy about it. Andrew meets my passion, and we proceed to have the hottest sex we've ever had.

Multiple orgasms hot. Ride him like a cowgirl with my hands in the air, hot.

It feels as though we've completely forgotten we've been friends for so long, and we can finally just embrace our sexuality.

It's a moment I've been hoping for, and it does not disappoint. It's fantastic on every level.

At least that is…until it's over.

Andrew gets quiet and goes to the bathroom.

The expression on his face is blank, and his demeanor shows zero enthusiasm. This quickly kills my euphoria and makes me wonder if he even enjoyed himself. I go from feeling super attracted to him to feeling extremely insecure in a matter of seconds.

When he comes back from the bathroom, he crawls into bed, says goodnight, and turns his back to me.

My mind gets loud: *Seriously? This is the reaction I get? Did he not like that? There's no way he didn't like that. What is happening?*

I lay unable to sleep, and I don't bring it up to Andrew.

A little over a week later, we are playing video games at my condo when suddenly Andrew looks at me side-eyed with a smirk on his face.

"What?" I ask.

"So, that weekend in Brooks, in the basement…" Andrew starts off but then stops himself.

"Yes, go on," I urge, having no idea what he is about to say.

"Yeah, ummm, I really liked that." Andrew is leaning in such a way that shows his embarrassment.

"You liked what?" I ask, still confused about what he's getting at.

"The sex, it was hot," Andrew says as his face lights up with a huge smile.

I pause the game and turn to face him.

"So, you enjoyed yourself?" I ask. "Because afterward you got all quiet and it almost looked like you were angry."

"I really liked it," Andrew says as he rubs my leg and kisses me. He is finally showing the enthusiasm I expected that evening.

"Andrew," I start off in a serious tone, "it's really hard for me to tell when you are enjoying yourself in the bedroom. Your face doesn't show much emotion."

"Really?" Andrew asks in confusion. "I'm always enjoying myself. But that night, I was *really* enjoying myself."

"Well, I can't tell at all, and it's frustrating. It makes me self-conscious," I explain, having no idea that this is going to cause Andrew to overcorrect.

"I don't know what to say other than tell you that I am always enjoying myself," Andrew says as we unpause the game.

Over the following weeks, Andrew begins trying to express how much he is enjoying himself through his facial expressions while we are having sex. I look up at him and he has a "perma smile" screwed on his face. It's really awkward and completely ruins the mood. His mouth isn't moving, and it's so unnatural.

I can't handle it anymore, so I ask, "What are you doing? Why do you keep smiling like that?"

"I'm trying to show you how much I'm enjoying myself," Andrew responds.

"Well, stop it. It's awkward," I say while we are still having sex.

"But how can I show you that I'm enjoying myself?" Andrew asks.

"Just don't worry about it," I reply. "I know now that you're enjoying yourself. Stop trying to show me."

I instantly regret mentioning anything to him because it's only made things worse.

It takes Andrew a while to stop trying so hard, so things continue to be awkward for weeks.

I start going out of my way to make sure we have sex in the dark, and this really helps ease the awkwardness.

SOLUTION - BE NATURAL

First off, maybe don't make the same mistake as me by mentioning it in the first place. Because yeah, I just made things more awkward.

Let your partner express themselves naturally, even if this takes some getting used to. You should also express yourself naturally. That way, no one feels like they are having to pretend on a regular basis.

I learn shortly after this that I enjoy sex with Andrew much more in the dark. Experimenting with blindfolds helps us spice things up. We don't feel so different when I can't see his facial expressions. I'm able to get out of my head and just enjoy our bodies. It seems as though he feels the same, and this helps us initially.

Now that more time has passed, I've learned to just ask him if I'm confused. It wasn't easy at first, but I'm used to it now.

"Do you like this position? Do you want me to move? How does that feel?" These are all easy questions to ask now that we have been together a while.

* * *

ANDREW'S TAKE

Andrew tries to compute how to avoid Michelle thinking that Andrew is not having a great time in bed when he is, in fact, having a great time in bed.

Computing...

If you are enjoying yourself with Michelle in bed, then try to smile or show a happy face.

This is a great if/then statement that helps me remember to show that I'm happy with Michelle in bed. Turns out this is a very strange and creepy thing to do in practice. Well, I guess that's how you learn what works and what doesn't work.

Like with anything in life, once there is attention brought to something, it's hard not to let the attention make it worse than it was beforehand. For example, next time you're walking, just think about walking and try not to walk funny. See?!

* * *

ASPECT #3 - HE NEEDS VERBAL CONFIRMATION / WE TALK TOO MUCH

It's not uncommon for us to be making out, then one of us will say something that has us laughing, and before we know it, the making out stops completely so we can talk. I love this about us now, but in the beginning, I was worried about it. I had never been in a relationship before where we would be nearing sex and then stop to talk. It made me think Andrew wasn't enjoying himself when in actuality, his mind just switches states quite quickly sometimes. It had nothing to do with me or our sex life, but I was unaware of this.

STORY - "CAN WE HAVE SEX NOW?"

Andrew and I are making out on my couch. Things are getting heated and I am loving the buildup.

"Can we go have sex now?" Andrew asks in a somewhat serious tone.

I stop and look at him. "Yes, we can go have sex now."

As we walk to my bedroom, I am left feeling disappointed because this has ruined the mood. I don't want to be asked. I just want to be taken to the bedroom, somewhat forcefully, and thrown on the bed.

Solution - Give it Time

Andrew is one of the kindest, sweetest men I've ever met in my life. He's never going to want to do something that makes me uncomfortable. He's going to ask first. Even though I love this about him, this was a huge turn-off for me in our early bedroom days.

The solution to this one was time mostly. Andrew no longer feels the need to ask me for permission as he's learned what I like and he's now more comfortable. I told him many times, "I'm your girlfriend, and if I'm making out with you, it means I'm up for sex." But it still took Andrew time to get comfortable enough to stop asking.

I've gotten much better at telling Andrew what I want without feeling like it kills the mood. I can get into it now, even when we are talking, but it took some time.

* * *

ANDREW'S TAKE

Because I have trouble reading the emotion of the moment, it's become a bad habit that I ask Michelle's permission or ask if we should or will have sex. This is likely due to us being friends before we started dating. I've been in relationships where sex is more of a spur-of-the-moment thing, but those relationships were based on sex to begin with. Very different precedent.

This is true, I can switch states quickly. There is a part of me that is nervous, and at times I can't help but talk my nerves out. I've learned that this is inappropriate in bed and know when to stop. When I say learned, I mean *learned*. All of this has come with many awkward, funny, and hot sexual encounters.

If something really funny happens during foreplay or sex, letting yourself go and laughing about it isn't all bad. The intense emotions of the moment will make the thing that much funnier, and deep bonding can still occur through the laughter in the awkward moment.

* * *

Aspect #4 - It Feels Somewhat Emotionless

Andrew makes me feel loved and cared for in all the areas no man ever has before, but in the bedroom, everything feels somewhat emotionless. Sex feels more like a workout with a satisfying climax at the end. We keep each other satisfied, but I don't feel like we are bonding while we are having sex. At first, it really bothered me that he wasn't displaying the intense emotions in the bedroom I was craving, and I took this personally.

Story - Cosplay

"Is there anything you want me to dress up as in the bedroom?" I ask Andrew. "What do you think is the sexiest?"

"I like cosplay," Andrew explains.

"Send me some pictures, and I'll see what I can do," I reply.

Throughout the week, Andrew sends me many cosplay pictures. They are mostly of women in short skirts wearing lots of makeup and colorful wigs.

Okay, I think I can manage this, I text him. *I just ordered a pink wig and a long white wig off Amazon.*

Awesome! Andrew replies. *I can't wait.*

A couple of weeks later, I decide to dress up in cosplay for the first time. I do my makeup and put the pink wig on. I'm surprised by how cute I feel. Rather than purchase any clothes, I just wear a silk robe I already have that is quite short and a black lace bra.

I text Andrew a selfie in my wig on his lunch break. *You're in for it when you get here xoxoxo.*

Oh wow, you look fantastic, Andrew replies. *I'll be there right after work.*

Andrew comes over after work, and I pull him into the living room. We have sex, and it's nice, but Andrew feels the same as always. I was expecting to get more emotion out of him by spicing things up, but this isn't the case.

A few days later I ask Andrew, "Did you like it when I wore the pink wig and makeup for you?"

"Yeah, that was hot. I enjoyed that," Andrew replies.

"Okay, I wasn't sure if it was worth the effort because you seemed the same as always," I explain.

"I think it was worth it," he says. "You looked hot."

As I write this, I am having guilt in realizing that I never did this for Andrew again. I've gotten lazy because it mostly felt like regular sex to me, aside from the fact that we did it in the living room. Just because his demeanor seemed the same to me, it doesn't mean he wasn't enjoying himself more than usual. I should go back to putting the effort in every now and again.

Solution - Adjusting Expectations

I've lost the need to feel emotions in the bedroom and have learned that it's not important in the grand scheme of things.

Even when Andrew tells me I look beautiful, I know he means it, but it just doesn't have the same frequency behind it. Things will never feel the same with him as they did in my relationships before him, and that's okay. It's great, in fact.

Andrew still cuddles, holds me, and kisses me like he did that first year we were together, and I love that so much. I would never trade that in for hot sex. I much prefer having that positive reinforcement in my daily life rather than in the bedroom. I feel silly that it used to bother me so much. Not getting what you want is often a blessing because life has better things in store for you.

Now that we've been together a while, I like that we keep emotions out of the bedroom. My favorite thing about sex with Andrew is that if I'm not overly in the mood, I don't feel the need to put on any theatrics. Because he's on his own wavelength, it doesn't seem to bother him much if I'm doing the mechanics of sex without much emotion, and I love that. In my past relationships, I would feel the need to fake enthusiasm to keep the guy in the mood. This isn't the case with Andrew, and it's a relief.

ANDREW'S TAKE

Andrew thinks to himself after reading the above story, *Have women faked enthusiasm to keep me in the mood in my previous relationships?* Andrew thinks about this some more. *Oh god, that must be exhausting. Don't do that.*

Because Michelle doesn't fake enthusiasm to keep me in the mood, it helps me know when we really do have good sex. I would feel so awkward and hurt if years were to go by and then Michelle tells me that she is pretending to keep me in the mood.

* * *

Aspect #5 - Overwhelm States

Andrew gets into overwhelmed states when he is overstimulated or upset.

Story - Michelle Learns the Hard Way - A Blow Job Gone Wrong

I've had a few embarrassing sexual moments in my life, but never one like this. I can't believe I'm about to share this with you, but we've come this far, so I may as well spill all the beans. Welcome to one of the most embarrassing moments of my life.

Andrew is having a rough day, so I decide that I'm going to pull him into the bedroom and cheer him up with a blow job.

This is a first for us. I've never given him a blow job like this before. This is meant to be just for him while he sits on the side of my bed.

Now, one thing you should understand about me is that I'm typically different in the bedroom depending on who I am with. The reason for this is that I largely play off of my partner's reactions. I get turned on most when my partner is turned on. When I can tell they are enjoying something, that's where I will focus my attention. I don't necessarily have a plan that I execute, as I'm mostly letting the guy's reactions run the show. This has always worked well for me in the past.

Andrew makes this tough. He's the first partner that I can't read. As I begin doing "the job," he is not giving me much reaction. He's giving me no reaction, actually. He is hard, but I can feel zero excitement or enjoyment on his part. No sounds, no leaning, nothing for me to go off of. As far as I can tell, he is not enjoying himself at all.

Because of this, I keep trying different things. Hoping that he will give me a hint as to what he wants. I try focusing my attention more so on the head than the shaft by swirling my tongue around. I try some ball play, I slow things down, then speed things up again. After minutes of this, Andrew remains reactionless.

Now one thing you need to understand about Andrew is that when he is in an overwhelmed state, he becomes like a statue. He somewhat freezes on the outside because he is so stuck in his head. Attempting to cheer him up with any kind of sexual favors is basically the worst thing I should be doing right now. I'm unaware of this, so I keep attempting.

As the minutes roll on, nothing changes. I'm getting increasingly embarrassed. He is hard, but he doesn't seem to be overly excited about anything I'm doing. I have no idea what to do next, and it begins to show in my technique.

This all comes to a stop when Andrew looks down at me and asks, "Do you not know what you're doing?"

I'm mortified. And the worst part is that he says it in the kindest voice. As if he wants to teach me.

"You're giving me nothing to go off of," I say in an attempt to salvage what's left of my dignity.

"But do you know where the most sensitive part of the penis is?" he asks as he feels the need to point it out to me. "It's right here." He points to the underside of his penis. "There's not much sensation on the head. The most sensitive part is along the center vein underneath the penis."

"I was trying to build up to something," I say as I give up completely and sit beside him while he pulls up his pants.

"Don't worry about it," he says. "It's not a big deal."

"It *is* a big deal! I'm never this bad at this!" I shriek. "Our chemistry is off. You don't react like I'm used to, and it's confusing. It makes me overthink what I'm doing."

"I'm really in my head right now," he replies. "So I'm not in the mood anyways. Don't take it personally."

"Yeah, right," I say. "As if that's possible. There's nothing more personal than giving your boyfriend a terrible blow job." I walk out of the room and try to distract myself with the television, but it's all I can think about all night.

Andrew comes out of the bedroom and goes to play games in his computer room. He seems quite unaffected by the whole thing.

Yup, that actually happened.

I pretty much died of embarrassment. Particularly because oral is an area in which Andrew excels, and I typically do, or at least I thought I did.

It takes me days to get over how mortified I am. Many weeks pass before I am able to try again.

"You need to verbally tell me when you're liking something," I say before I begin.

Andrew does this, and things go more smoothly.

Andrew hardly even remembers this incident. To him, it wasn't a big deal, but to me, it was the lowest point of our sex life. Thankfully that's all behind us now, not that I'll ever forget the humiliation.

SOLUTION - KNOW WHEN TO AVOID THE BEDROOM

I learned the hard way to avoid the bedroom when Andrew is overwhelmed and have never made that mistake again. Sex is not what he needs when he is upset. He needs time to do nothing with low stimulus to process his thoughts. Do not take this personally.

*　*　*

ANDREW'S TAKE

This is not the first time I've had a woman say they can't "read me" in the bedroom. I remember it like it was yesterday.

"You're the only guy I've ever been with who I can't read," one woman says to me after a long night of multiple rounds of sex. "I have no idea what's going through your mind," she finishes.

My response is a funny face with a big smile as I lean in for another kiss. I didn't know how to properly unpack what this woman told me.

As far as Michelle's advice goes, it is sage wisdom. When I'm in an overwhelmed state, sex is not going to be hot—at all. My mind is very much overstimulated. A calm and relaxing atmosphere is the best thing during these times.

*　*　*

SUMMARY

I've learned to look at sex differently in my years with Andrew. It feels more like a physical activity we do to fulfill our body's desires as opposed to it being an emotional act that validates our relationship.

I'm embarrassed I tried so hard to make our sex life something it wasn't in our first year together. I was attempting to turn it into something I understood rather than just embracing it for what it was. Had I not tried to create moments with "fireworks," I feel things would have gone more smoothly for both of us.

Andrew doesn't do anything society expects of him, and I love him for that. In many ways, it was me who was the problem. Thinking sex should be a certain way instead of just allowing it to unfold for what it was. I was overthinking it.

My magical moments with Andrew are always unpredictable. They don't happen when I expect them to. I've come to love this about our relationship.

I challenge you to look at sex differently. Is it where you need to excel? It's certainly not the case for Andrew and me, yet I've never been happier. The fact that we've had to communicate in this area so much has made us stronger and brought us closer. I hate to think that there might be couples out there who gave up on each other prematurely for not understanding some of these things.

I will say that there is one aspect I miss about my sex life before Andrew. I miss feeling like I'm great at it. Is this important in the big scheme of things? No. It's just one aspect I miss.

Yet my friends who have read this chapter tell me that it's this flexibility and communication that means we are truly great at it. Because true authenticity is missing in so many people's sex lives.

* * *

ANDREW'S TAKE

I've had other relationships based on how good the sex was. If the sex and attraction are out of this world, then I've found this makes the relationship intense. Almost too intense to the point that I'm in a constant overwhelmed state and don't even know it. Before Michelle, I didn't know what a stable, healthy relationship was. To me, the excitement of sex was a large part of what held it together because I had never experienced a healthy, stable, loving relationship.

Having a relationship that isn't so intense allows me to regulate better and not worry so much about frivolous things like *The sex wasn't great. Is this the end? Does she still like me? I hope she still likes me.* Or *Things seem to be slowing down with our sexual chemistry. Do I have to worry about this?*

Being free from these worries allows me to be myself in our relationship. No more do I have to feel like I'm trying to upkeep a relationship to keep the excitement and intensity at a certain level.

* * *

AUTISM

Learning about autism was a gift I didn't expect. It instantly helped me to stop taking so many things in life personally. Not only in my relationship with Andrew but with everyone around me. As humans we tend to make everything about ourselves when in fact, very little has to do with us. We are all wired differently and yet are taught so little about this fact.

This section will take you through our diagnostic process. We share our entire experience with you so that you may learn along with us. As they say, "knowledge is power," and truer words were never spoken. It's unfortunate that so many will never have the luxury of receiving an adult diagnosis, whether it's for autism or some other form of neurodivergence. They can be expensive, and even if you have the means to pay for one, it's not always easy to find a specialist in your area who offers them.

I am forever grateful that we were able to receive an adult diagnosis and go through the sessions together. Getting this diagnosis empowered us to start thinking and relating differently. This was, of course, a process and not always an easy one. I know it's only a small step to rectify the injustice imposed on so many who have lived their entire lives not understanding their differences. But I share the knowledge we learned with you in hopes it will continue to empower others and spread across the globe.

16

NOVEMBER HAS ARRIVED

The day we have been anxiously awaiting has finally arrived. It's time to sign up for the intake session with the ever-so-popular Dr. Baker, who specializes in adult autism diagnosis.

It's 1 a.m., and Andrew and I are waiting to board our flight to Thunder Bay to visit his family.

Dr. Baker's website has been open on my phone since midnight as I await for registration to open. Every time I hit the refresh button, I'm disappointed. Dr. Baker is who we want to perform Andrew's assessment, and I'm feeling relentless.

An announcement comes over the loudspeaker: "Now boarding Zone 3. Zone 3 is now boarding."

Andrew touches my shoulder and says, "That's our zone, hun."

Without looking up from my phone, I answer, "Just let me know when there's no lineup left. We can be the last ones to get on the plane."

Every time I click the refresh button, I feel a glimmer of hope that the sign-up button will be illuminated. Determined as ever, I'm not going to stop clicking it until it does.

Before I know it, Andrew is touching my shoulder again, "Okay, hun, we have to get on the plane now."

Reluctantly, I put my phone in my pocket and board the plane.

We place our bags overhead and take our seats. Once I fasten my seatbelt, I take my phone out to keep trying.

An announcement comes over the loudspeaker: "Please turn off your phones, and stow away all electronics."

Rather than listening, I drape my large coat across my lap in such a way that it disguises my hands.

The safety demonstration begins as I click refresh for the hundredth time. My hope begins to fade as the flight attendants motion to show us where the exits are. The demonstration is nearly over, and still no luck.

Another announcement comes over the loudspeaker: "Flight attendants, please prepare the cabin for departure."

My time is running out, but I keep clicking that refresh button. Finally, I'm able to click the sign-up button. My excitement cannot be contained as I grab Andrew's forearm while yelling, "Yeeeees! Oh my God, it's open for registration!" Andrew shares in my excitement as he shakes my arm.

The sign-up button directs me to an information sheet I need to fill out.

The flight attendant is now walking toward me.

"Ma'am, you're going to need to put your phone away."

"I know," I answer her without looking up. "I'm sorry. I just have to fill out this very important form, and then I'll put it away."

She stands there a minute and reluctantly walks away.

The form asks for Andrew's name, birthday, and address to start. After filling that out, I click *next*. To my horror, there is now a page full of questions. A bead of sweat drips down my forehead as I notice the flight attendant walking back toward me. This time, she doesn't look so patient. Every single question gets a three-word answer. I figure they will get the point.

"Ma'am, you have to put your phone away. We are about to take off."

Andrew interjects on my behalf, "She only has two more questions, and then she's putting it away. Sorry, this is really important; we've been waiting for this sign-up for weeks."

This time she is not moving. She's clearly going to stand there until she sees me put my phone away. The plane is now rolling. After I click *next*, I'm directed to a button that says *submit application*. I click it and wait until it goes through before I turn off my phone and put it away.

Thankfully, the flight attendant doesn't become overly frustrated with me during this process. Andrew's using his charm to help give her a little more patience.

As they dim the lights in the cabin so everyone can sleep, we cannot contain our excitement.

"Omg," Andrew keeps repeating, "did you seriously just register as the plane was taking off? I can't believe that happened. We are so lucky. We are so lucky!"

Relief flows through my body as I pull my coat up as a blanket to get some sleep.

We are officially registered for the intake session in February to receive an adult autism assessment with Dr. Baker (the best guy there is). Now, all we have to do is wait.

Meeting Andrew's Japanese Family - The Iwasas

We are going to Thunder Bay to visit the Iwasa family. The Iwasa family consists of Andrew's nana (who is in her nineties), his aunt Joanne, and her brother Brian (who Andrew considers to be his stepdad). Andrew's papa passed away in 2006.

We arrive in Thunder Bay at 5:30 a.m. We are to be staying at Andrew's aunt's place, and we insist on taking a cab from the airport. There is no need for everyone to lose hours of sleep.

As we arrive, we are greeted by Andrew's aunt Joanne, his stepdad Brian, and Nana. The apartment is warm and welcoming. Pictures of Andrew are everywhere, along with the rest of the family. Everyone is tired, but we agree to sit down and do quick introductions before going to bed.

Joanne asks, "So, how did you guys meet?" as we walk into the living room.

Andrew answers with two words: "On Bumble."

After a brief awkward silence, she then asks, "When did you guys meet?"

"April 2017," Andrew answers, again saying only two words.

This was followed by an even longer awkward silence.

After a few moments of exchanged glances and confusion between them, I feel the need to intervene.

"Hey Andrew, tell them the story about how we started dating," I say with enthusiasm in an attempt to break the awkwardness.

"That's not what she asked, though?" Andrew says with a puzzled look on his face.

"But that's what everyone wants to know," I reply.

His family nods their heads in agreement.

Andrew then went into the detailed story about how we met, were friends for a year, and started dating. Everyone seemed to enjoy the story.

Once he's finished, we say goodnight and head off to bed.

As we crawl under the covers, I say to Andrew, "You can't give two-word answers when they ask about me; that's rude. Tell them a story."

"They didn't ask for a story. If they want a story, they should ask for one," Andrew says in a frustrated tone.

Andrew is clearly tired after the flight, but I still find this interaction to be quite peculiar.

* * *

ANDREW'S TAKE

This is why I love Michelle. She noticed this about me and helped me understand these situations. My family will likely never understand what a difference it makes when you phrase a question differently. I saw this kind of miscommunication as normal behavior. No one had ever explained it to me this way before.

* * *

You Told Them I'm a What?

After a few hours of solid sleep, I wake up and take a shower. Andrew is still asleep, so I get dressed and head out into the living room.

I'm greeted by Andrew's aunt Joanne. "Michelle, I made cucumber water for you," she says.

"Thank you," I reply as she hands me a glass.

"Andrew told me you like cucumber water. I had to google how to make it. I hope it's okay," she explains. I notice the jug on the counter, and it's as fancy as can be. It's filled with at least an entire cucumber chopped up in it, possibly two.

"It's delicious, Joanne," I say while taking a sip. "This is much fancier than I usually make it. I just cut up a couple of slices and drop them in my glass. Thank you."

"Do you eat eggs?" she asks. "I made some eggs for breakfast, but I can make something else. I bought stuff to make a chicken salad for lunch, but I didn't really know what you would want in it."

"Joanne, I'll pretty much eat anything as long as it isn't too spicy. Don't you worry about me. Eggs are great, but chicken salad is also great," I answer, hoping to ease her anxiety.

Joanne looks at me puzzled and says, "But Andrew told us you were a vegetarian. That you only like salads and cucumber water."

"What? Why on earth would he say that?" I'm somewhat laughing but am also extremely confused. "I do like salads and cucumber water, but I also eat pretty much anything else."

"Oh, well, I wish I would've known that because I went to different stores trying to find nice vegetables for you because I'm not used to making salads," she explains.

Feeling terrible that she's been under the impression I'm a picky eater, I head to the bedroom to wake up Andrew.

"Hey, why did you tell your family I'm a vegetarian?" I ask while shaking his arm.

"I didn't tell them you're a vegetarian. I said you like cucumber water and salads," Andrew answers while stretching his arms overhead.

"Well, they think I'm a vegetarian, and they went through all of this trouble. Why did you tell them that?" I snark.

"They kept texting me while I was at work, and I didn't know what to say," Andrew explains.

This situation is particularly disappointing because I'm interested to learn about their traditional Japanese meals, and now we will be eating salads all week.

Anywhere I go, I'm happy to eat whatever is served. It baffles me that Andrew contributed to his family thinking otherwise. The only conclusion I can come up with as to why this happened is that Joanne must've asked him around the same week that I gave Andrew a big speech about wanting to eat better. I lectured him once about how we couldn't keep eating spaghetti and pizza, and I think his brain may have defaulted to that one conversation when he was asked what I liked to eat.

* * *

ANDREW'S TAKE

This is one of the reasons I struggle to talk with certain members of my family. I get the feeling that they're trying to figure something out, but are not asking for exactly what it is that they want. This is very frustrating.

Being aware of this since Michelle brought it to my attention has saved me from getting overwhelmed and frustrated with my family more times than I can count. Prior to realizing this, I would let the frustrating talks with my family get out of hand and turn into a fight.

When Joanne asked me questions about Michelle's palate, I would respond with simple answers. Joanne never asked specific questions or explained what she was trying to figure out. She was just asking questions, and then she stopped. In my mind, I'm thinking, *Joanne is going to have salad and cucumber water. That's a great start.* That's it, nothing more.

* * *

The Trip

We pack a lot into a one-week trip with family. It's nice that Andrew is from Thunder Bay because I have several cousins that live there. After spending a couple of days playing games and visiting with his family, we spent some time with my family.

My cousin Kate and her husband Chris take us to see Kakabeka Falls and a tree farm as a double date. The four of us spend an enjoyable afternoon outside. Kate is ecstatic that I have a new boyfriend, given the fact that I've been single for so many years.

As we leave the tree farm, Kate turns to me in the back seat and whispers, "I like your new boyfriend, and I even thought he was cute until he put those ugly sunglasses on his face. What's with those glasses, eh?"

This is hilarious to me, so I reply in a full voice, "Oh, you don't have to whisper about Andrew's ugly sunglasses. He is well aware that I hate those glasses." I tap Andrew on the shoulder in the front seat, "Andrew, Kate also hates those glasses. Add her to the list."

Andrew turns around and says to Kate, "You don't like my glasses? Man, nobody likes these glasses." At this point, we are all laughing hysterically, including Kate's husband Chris.

"Yeah, it's almost as if you should stop wearing them," I blurt out in my most sarcastic tone.

"No, I love these glasses. I paid $350 for them in 2008, and they are still in perfect condition. I also just got new lenses," Andrew explains.

After our chuckle, we stop to get some Persians. Thunder Bay is known for its Persians. They are kind of like the doughnut version of a cinnamon bun, with strawberry icing on top. Andrew's birth father, Raymond, makes them at one of the local bakeries, and they couldn't be more delicious.

As the boys go in to buy some Persians, I joke with Kate in the back seat. "I've been bugging Andrew about those sunglasses for a year. Many people bug him about those sunglasses. Andrew doesn't care. He loves them."

"Really?" Kate asks in disbelief.

"Yes, really. No amount of comments is going to make Andrew get rid of his glasses. It drives me crazy, but I also kind of love that he's never trying to impress anyone," I reply.

"Yeah, it's cool that he's just himself, but man, those things are ugly," Kate laughs.

It's nice to have Andrew meet some of my extended family, but I'm most curious to meet his birth father, Raymond. As previously mentioned, Andrew seems incapable of describing anyone. All he told me about his birth father was, "Yeah, he's an interesting man, you'll see."

We meet Andrew's birth father briefly at a doughnut shop. He is a kind man with a warm smile. His genuine honesty is apparent in his demeanor, and it reminds me of Andrew. We each order a hot chocolate and a doughnut.

As I watch them interact, it becomes obvious to me that Andrew gets many of his traits from Raymond. And when I say "many of his traits," I mean the autistic ones. The similarities between them are uncanny. They both pay attention to details, share a similar posture, have impressive mechanical skills, and live for a routine. However, I find these traits to be a little milder in Andrew.

Watching them have a conversation amuses me as they are both stubborn in their beliefs and have done their research on the topics they bring up. I tune them out to enjoy my doughnut as they discuss all sorts of things I don't understand. Meeting Raymond has solidified my belief that Andrew is autistic.

THE JOURNEY HOME

Over the course of the trip, I feel myself falling a little more for Andrew. Meeting his family makes me feel more like a girlfriend, and it's been nice to sleep next to him for a week straight.

After spending a few more days with the Iwasa family, Andrew and I begin our journey home. We are excited to go home, knowing that this trip has made us feel closer. We can hardly keep our hands off each other, holding hands for the entire duration of our flight.

During our layover in Winnipeg, we opt for a romantic dinner at an airport lounge. We have survived our first family trip together, and all is well in the world. That warrants having a nice dinner—as nice as you can find at the Winnipeg airport anyway.

While we are waiting to board our second plane, Andrew decides to tell me about a conversation he had with his uncle. Andrew's uncle invites us over for many Sunday dinners, and we enjoy going over there.

"I'm glad my uncle convinced me that I should stay with you. This trip went really well," Andrew says to me as we wait to show our boarding passes.

"Excuse me?!?!" I respond.

It is the weirdest thing because Andrew says it with a smile on his face as if he were giving me a compliment.

"A while back I was telling my uncle about the big trip I wanted to take, and he convinced me that I should probably bring you with me. He told me to stop planning my life without you in it. He told me how special you were. I was surprised because I didn't think it was true." Andrew continues to put his foot in his mouth.

Silent, I stand there, feeling like I want to throw up. It's the worst thing Andrew has ever said to me. I'm thinking to myself, Who says that? *He convinced you to stay with me? You didn't realize I was special?* This is not a fantastic way to end our trip.

As we walk onto the plane, it takes everything in me not to throw him onto the tarmac. All I can manage to say is, "Stop talking to me," as I break eye contact to walk in front of him.

For the next three hours, I don't even glance in Andrew's direction, not even to order snacks on the plane. At this point, I'd rather go hungry than have to interact with him.

It's the first time I've been upset with Andrew to anywhere near this level. Just looking at him makes my blood boil. My mind is screaming at him, *I just spent an entire week getting to know your family, and you needed to be convinced to be with me?*

As we land in Calgary, I still can't bring myself to look at Andrew. My car is parked at the airport, so we need to take a shuttle to get to it. We remain silent on the shuttle and for the entire drive to his place.

Once I pull up in front of Andrew's, I turn to him and say, "I really need a few days to calm down before we talk."

Andrew just says, "Okay, that makes sense," and gets out of my car.

Three days go by before Andrew calls me.

I answer my phone by saying, "Okay, I think I'm ready to talk now. I'm a little less mad at you."

Andrew replies in a shocked tone, "You're *mad* at me? Why? I had no idea you were mad at me?"

I'm baffled, as it is clear he is being honest; Andrew is always honest.

"Of course," I snap back, "I'm mad at you. I even told you I needed a few days before we talked."

"I thought you just needed a break after the trip," he replies.

"But I didn't look at you or acknowledge you the entire second flight home," I argue.

He seems puzzled as he answers, "I just thought you were tired. I had no idea you were mad."

"Oh, just come over," I tell him as I hang up the phone. I am in shock that he hasn't realized I am upset with him. I mean, I practically had a red siren blinking on my forehead telling him to fuck off for three hours on our way home from that trip.

When Andrew gets to my place, I tell him that what he said hurt my feelings. He doesn't remember what he said, so I repeat it to him.

He chuckles in nervousness and says, "That's not what I meant to say at all."

I ask him what he meant to say, and he can't tell me.

"I do this sometimes. I try to say something nice, and it comes out all wrong. I was trying to tell you a good thing," he explains.

"Well, it didn't sound good. It sounded like you had to be convinced to be with me and that you have been planning your life without me in it because you didn't realize I was special," I respond.

Andrew apologizes. "I'm sorry. That's not what I was trying to say at all."

He seems genuine, and we easily put it behind us.

* * *

ANDREW'S TAKE

This might be one of the single hardest things in my life to deal with. I've said so many things that have offended people, and I'm left thinking, *How in the world are they offended?* If there is one thing that causes me the most turmoil, it's being misunderstood, followed by the person thinking I'm being insensitive.

I didn't realize that what I was saying would hurt Michelle. This was an intense experience for me. I don't like hurting anyone's feelings. In hindsight, I could have reworded it rather than saying the "first draft" that came to my mind.

I was happy with what my uncle told me because he helped me realize something that, to most people, might be obvious. I was thrilled that I was with someone so amazing. I told Michelle the context of why I felt this way rather than just expressing how I feel. I see how this is a bad idea.

* * *

NOT BEING ABLE TO EXPRESS HIS FEELINGS

A week after being home from Thunder Bay, Andrew phones me late in the evening.

I answer his call by saying, "Hi, is everything okay?" because it's strange for him to be calling me so late.

He replies, "I'm not sure. I feel like things are weird." Andrew gets quiet for a minute and then reiterates, "Everything is just so weird."

"Andrew, you have to elaborate because I don't know what you mean by weird," I say.

"I just can't sleep. I'm feeling weird," he says, offering me no new information.

I sit on the phone for a minute listening to the silence because I have no idea what to say.

"How was your day? How was work?" I ask, hoping to figure out the culprit of this weird feeling.

"Work was fine," Andrew answers.

"Andrew, I can't help you unless you give me more information," I insist.

"It's just weird. We were on vacation, and you were with me all the time, and now you're not, and I'm feeling weird. It's different that you are not there all the time," Andrew explains.

It is the sweetest thing. After a little chuckle, I ask, "Are you trying to tell me you miss me?"

Andrew takes a long pause to think about it. Complete dead air for a solid minute. Then he replies with, "Yeah, I think I am." It's as if I just listened to him realize what he was feeling.

"Oh, so this is what missing someone feels like? Cool," Andrew says with amazement.

It's absolutely adorable, and my heart melts a little.

The trip was an emotional roller coaster for many reasons. But one thing's for sure: now that it's over, we are closer. *Much* closer.

* * *

ANDREW'S TAKE

This was interesting. I thought I knew what missing someone felt like. Turns out, I wasn't so sure. It's a wild thing to think you know a lot of these base feelings and then to find out you aren't quite there.

* * *

Our First Christmas

Back in September, we had a loose plan to go to New York with Jackson and Caleb for Christmas break. The four of us wanted to ice skate in Central Park and spend New Year's Eve in Times Square.

While we were looking at expensive places to stay for the trip, I said to Andrew, "Well, we just won't do presents this year. New York will be our present."

He replied, "Sounds good."

By the time November rolled around, going to New York was out of the question. My return to work was unsuccessful, and there was no way we could afford it. On top of that, my brain was not healing as I expected, and being in crowded Times Square no longer seemed appealing. Jackson and Caleb also decided the trip was going to be too expensive to make it worth it, so they opted to stay in Calgary.

"Okay, so we will just stay home for Christmas," Andrew says, after I tell him Jackson and Caleb are also rethinking the trip.

"Yes, and we will do presents," I reply. "Do you want to know how much I plan to spend on you for Christmas? Or should we just wing it?"

"I don't need to know," Andrew says. "Don't tell me anything."

"Okay, sounds good," I answer. "It'll be nice to stay home and relax."

Throughout December I buy Andrew many presents. Nothing overly expensive, just some things I think he will like. After wrapping them, I leave them sitting on my desk because we never bother to get a Christmas tree. Andrew's name is written clearly on the large labels on top of the presents, and he's walked by them several times.

It's now Christmas Eve, and Andrew is in the shower with the door open. We are getting ready to go out to meet Jackson and Caleb.

"Andrew!" I yell from the bedroom. "Do you want to open one present tonight, or just open them all in the morning?"

"Ah, what?" he says in a confused tone. "I thought we weren't doing presents."

"Are you joking?" I ask. "You seriously didn't get me anything?"

"Oh, ah, yeah, I'm joking," he says awkwardly. "It's not like we had a conversation about not buying presents or anything."

I walk into the bathroom and open the shower curtain. "Andrew, that conversation was because we were going to New York," I explain. "When our plans changed, we decided to get presents."

Andrew is acting so confusing that I still can't tell if he's joking or not. "Yeah, okay," he says. "I'll figure something out."

I go to the kitchen to make a snack while Andrew gets ready. It isn't long before he calls out from the shower, "So, is there anything you need for the condo?" he asks. "Anything at all?"

"Are you being serious right now?" I ask. "Because it's really hard to tell."

"Maybe," he replies. "Just tell me some things you need around the condo."

"Okay." I begin to look around my kitchen. "I could use a new coffee maker and some folding chairs for our game nights."

"What else?" Andrew asks. "I want as many ideas as you can give me."

"I like scented candles, and I think my body wash is almost empty," I reply.

"Ok, coffee maker, folding chairs, scented candles, body wash," Andrew is repeating everything I said out loud. "I still need more than that."

"Andrew, I can't believe you're serious," I say with frustration. "We are supposed to leave in an hour, and you still need to run out and get me something?"

"I'm just going to run to Walmart. It's still open," Andrew says as he gets dressed. "Just come outside when I get back, and then we will leave right away."

Before I know it, Andrew is out the door.

A part of me is frustrated, but Andrew gets a lot of leeway because I suspect he is autistic. I'm aware enough to realize that this miscommunication likely has something to do with that, even though I don't quite understand why.

I text Jackson, *So Andrew never got me anything for Christmas, so he just ran to Walmart. We might be a little late.*

Jackson texts back, *Of course he didn't, LOL. See you when you get here.*

When Andrew returns, we go spend an enjoyable evening with Jackson and Caleb. We paint wooden ornaments and have many laughs taking photos with some props I bought at Dollarama. It's a lovely Christmas Eve, and it feels amazing not to feel lonely over the holidays for once.

Christmas morning, Andrew wakes me up with excitement. "C'mon, c'mon, it's Christmas!" he says, and he leads the way into the living room.

I walk out of my bedroom to see the most adorable tree and many Christmas presents wrapped underneath it.

"Oh my goodness, you bought a tree?" I say as I place my palms on my cheeks. "I can't believe you got a tree."

"It's kind of a Charlie Brown-looking tree, but it's all they had," Andrew answers. "But I really wanted to give you a real Christmas. I wanted you to wake up with lots of Christmas presents under the tree for you like I did as a kid."

And just like that, Andrew completely redeems himself for all of the other missed holidays.

"Wow, I can't believe you did this all in one day," I say as I give him a kiss. "I love it so much. Thank you."

"You're welcome. I still can't believe you didn't have Christmas as a kid," Andrew says. "Every kid should have Christmas."

Andrew and I sit around the tree and open our presents while Baxter runs around playing with the wrapping paper. It's the most special Christmas I've ever had, and I soak up every minute of it. I feel loved; I feel cared for; it feels like family.

I laugh as I open presents to learn that Andrew bought every single thing I rambled off while he was in the shower. A new coffee maker, body wash, a scented candle, and folding chairs.

"OMG, you seriously just bought the things I said while you were in the shower?" I laugh.

"Yeah, and those folding chairs were really hard to wrap in the middle of the night," Andrew says. "But I really wanted all of your presents to be wrapped."

Wow, am I a lucky girl or what?

ANDREW'S TAKE

From September onward, I was on autopilot, thinking we were not exchanging gifts. The conversation we had in November went in one ear and out the other. I didn't feel the full weight of what was really being said when we changed plans to exchange gifts for Christmas.

My mind thought, *Exchange gifts for Christmas; yeah, sounds good.* Followed by days and weeks of not applying that new precedent over the old one of "not buying each other gifts because we're going to New York." It was stuck firmly in my mind all the way up until Michelle mentioned she couldn't believe I didn't get her anything. Thank God Walmart is open on Christmas Eve.

* * *

Photos for Chapter 16
Bellamimalifestyles.com/bookphotos

17

ROBOT MAN, PERIOD GIRL, AND THEIR LOVE LANGUAGES

ROBOT MAN

Our trip to visit Andrew's family left me emotionally exhausted. Our intake session was months away, and navigating our relationship was becoming increasingly hard. I'd been thrown into the deep end of unknown waters. At times, it felt as though I was drowning. I knew someone was coming to help us eventually, but in the meantime, we had to keep our heads above water.

Professional books written about autism didn't interest me as I find they tend to be quite dry. They describe all of the symptoms well but do not explain how these things affect you in your day-to-day life or what you should do about them. I knew the diagnosis would teach us all we needed to know on the professional end, but I needed to come up with my own system that helped in the meantime. Similar to what I'd done in the classroom for so many years.

After buying multiple books off Amazon that were written by women who married autistic men, I only found one of them to be helpful. The spouses in the other books didn't remind me of Andrew, so I couldn't relate to what those women were going through. I hardly made it past the first couple of chapters.

The book I enjoyed is called *Life with a Partner or Spouse with Asperger Syndrome: Going Over The Edge? Practical Steps to Saving You and Your Relationship. By Kathy J. Marshack.* I highly recommend it as it's an insightful read. It helped me understand what parts of my life might be like down the road if Andrew and I get married, but it didn't help me understand anything from his perspective.

When you have a hard time understanding someone, it's extremely important to try to understand things from their perspective. Focus on what it must be like to be them while trying not to take anything personally. Sit and meditate on it. The world would be a better place if we all learned to do this from a young age. Take your emotions out of it, and do your best to imagine things from another's perspective. This is especially important when you're mad at them. One thing I can tell you for sure is that in any given situation, the story you are telling yourself is not the same story they are telling themselves. Neither one of you is right or wrong. You simply have different perspectives, given the lens you are looking through. When I was struggling with a student, I would do my best to imagine myself from their point of view. This helped me be more compassionate.

It's important to try to imagine your partner's lens on a regular basis. You are a team, after all, and how they see life and view your relationship consists of half your team. If you can't visualize things from their perspective, at best you're functioning at half capacity. You should understand your teammate, and your teammate should understand you in order to be a fully functioning unit. Naturally, you will disagree and challenge each other from time to time; that's healthy. But you should have a firm understanding of how they view the world. What type of lens they are using will affect every aspect of your relationship. Anything you can learn about it will be useful. How do they think? What are their blind spots? Where do they excel? What triggers them most? What makes them smile? The more you know, the better.

Anytime I attempt to put myself in Andrew's shoes, I'm at a loss. This is a big part of our disconnect. I never have any idea what he is thinking or what it's like to be him. The more I sit and try to visualize situations through his lens, the more I realize how little I understand him. It feels nearly impossible to do. I know I need to somewhat be able to see things from his point of view if our relationship is going to survive, so I keep trying. I dedicate some time every week to sit and imagine what it must be like to be him. After many attempts at this, I finally get somewhere.

I'm sitting on the floor of my room cross-legged in silence with my eyes closed.

I need to clear my mind and become present, sitting until my thoughts pass.

Once my mind is calm, I start thinking to myself, *What's it like to be Andrew? Show me what it's like to be Andrew.*

I'm now visualizing myself as Andrew walking down the street. It feels as if I am looking through his eyes as he's walking. After a block or so, I walk into a grocery store. It's a wooden-shelved store that looks like it's from the 50s. There's a nice man behind the counter who smiles at me. He is a cashier, but he's wearing an apron for some reason and looks like a baker (visualizations don't always make sense).

As I walk around the store, I see everything as fragments. It's as if I can only pay attention to the exact spot where I put my focus; everything else gets blurry and muffled. When I'm looking at the prices of vegetables, I can't hear the cashier talking to the customers that are paying him. It feels odd because I can normally do those two things at once. I grab a basket and look for some bread.

I walk around the store for a while to get more of a feel for my senses. Someone walks into the store, and there's a beep. The beep feels oddly loud, and it startles me. This causes my eyes to go blurry for a second. I feel very aware of my senses, but only one or two of them at once. It's a strange sensation.

I go to the cashier to pay for my bread when suddenly my perspective changes.

I'm no longer looking through Andrew's eyes. I'm now floating above him as he pays the cashier. I begin seeing images of file folders full of information opening and closing inside his mind. As soon as he opens one, the others snap shut. He can only see the details of each folder one at a time. It looks as though his mind is functioning like an actual computer.

That's it! I think to myself as I open my eyes. *He's like a robot.* (I realize this concept sounds a little ridiculous at first, but hear me out.)

Something clicks in my mind after that visualization, and I start imagining Andrew's mind working like a computer. It's all I can think about for days, and so many things feel like they add up.

A computer is only focused on what it's working on—"whichever window is activated," if you will. It can easily focus on smaller details, but it can't have all the windows open at once. I now understand why he forgets to check in with me when his plans change. The "Michelle window" isn't open because he is now focused on his new plans. I thought I understood this already, but visualizing Andrew as a robot makes it even more clear. He can't combine multiple windows at once to see the big picture; it's impossible. But he can quickly open and close folders to switch subjects, like when he is reading multiple books at once.

Now that I'm using the computer analogy, it becomes somewhat possible for me to put myself in Andrew's shoes. I sit and imagine what it must feel like to have a computer mind and how confusing that must be living in a world where most people are acting solely on their emotions. I do my best to imagine all of it: seeing the world in fragments, not having a strong sense of my emotions, not being able to visualize the future or anticipate what is going to happen, not really understanding people, the need for strong routines, always doing things in the same manner. For the first time, I feel like I can somewhat understand him.

I am a little anxious about Andrew's reaction. A part of me is worried that he will see it as a putdown when I don't mean it that way.

"So, I thought of something that is helping me understand you, but it's gonna sound weird," I say as we eat dinner at my place.

"Oh yeah, what's that?" Andrew replies as he takes a large bite of chicken.

"You're like a robot," I start off. "You know, by always taking things literally and not being able to relay your emotions. You're like my Robot Man."

Andrew thinks about it for a moment, then laughs. "Yeah, I guess that makes sense."

"I meditated on what life would be like as a robot, and it really helped me understand you," I explain. "So, I hope you are okay with me calling you that because I think it's adorable."

"I'm okay with it, and it makes sense, really," Andrew says as he chuckles. "If you can talk to me the same way you talk to Google, I will understand you better."

"Yes, exactly," I answer. "That's part of the problem. I don't talk to you like I would talk to Google. I'm a giant emotion. I speak feelings. I don't know how to speak robot."

It's short-lived, but this quickly becomes our favorite joke. It helps us bond and make light of our differences. We tend not to take life too seriously, and we enjoy teasing each other.

When we have a miscommunication or an awkward moment, we laugh and joke that "Andrew went full robot" and "Michelle doesn't speak robot." Or, we'd say that "Michelle is full of feelings today, and they are confusing Robot Man." Another one is, "Robot Man doesn't understand Michelle today. She is acting differently than usual, and it isn't in his programming. Robot Man is confused."

All of these statements help us make light of our arguments. We don't blame each other because we know that our miscommunications are due to the fact that I've never learned to speak "robot," and Andrew's never learned to speak "emotions." The problem is neither him nor me. The problem is that we have never been taught to merge these two ways of thinking that are so far removed from each other. Our best bet is to teach each other our own language, so we can hopefully meet somewhere in the middle. Once I begin thinking this way, it helps me not to take things so personally.

From this point up until the diagnosis, anytime I struggled to understand Andrew, I found myself coming up with more computer analogies and meditating on them.

A computer cannot anticipate what something will be like if it's never done it before because there's no programming encrypted in its memory (that must be terrifying). There have been many times I've tried to explain how something is going to happen to Andrew in an attempt to prepare him, and yet when we get there he is completely surprised. I've never understood why that is until this very moment. If it's never happened to him, he can't visualize it, no matter how much I explain. If it's not "programmed" in his system, he doesn't get it. My explanation doesn't help anything.

A computer understands feelings or emotions by their definitions. It takes words literally as they are defined and would not understand body language or a change in tone of voice. Of course, you can program in obvious things, such as *That person is talking loud and fast; therefore, they are likely excited or upset.* Or *Someone is staring at the floor, so they are shy/nervous or ashamed of themselves,* but factoring in all the smaller scenarios or tones people use is impossible. No two people are the same.

Sarcasm would also be really tough for a computer to understand. As would hypotheticals and small talk. A computer will not be at all focused on what other computers are doing because it doesn't care. I love this about Andrew. He rarely talks about others.

A computer won't know what to do when something happens out of routine as it hasn't been "programmed in yet," thus the rigidity. It's tough to change something once it has been programmed into a computer a certain way. It's why change is so hard for Andrew.

The more I visualize walking around this planet as a robot, the more Andrew makes sense. It must be so hard being him. As neurotypicals, we often don't say what we mean or stick to our word. We partake in much social small talk that doesn't make sense logically. We mostly do this out of habit or to feel safe around new people. "Hey, how about this weather?" really means, "Hey, I'm a friendly person, and it's safe to be around me," as opposed to anything actually being about the weather. Things like that must be tough for a robot to decipher because no two situations are the same.

We tell white lies to avoid hurting someone else's feelings. A robot would never tell you something it doesn't mean just to spare your feelings. I think that makes the robot honorable, even though it may come across as rude.

Another thing many of us do is cling to our beliefs when they aren't based on facts. No wonder Andrew is so confused all the time. None of us make sense to him (understandably so).

The longer we joke about it, the more I realize that having a robot man balances my personality. I have been dating men with too much magnetism, and I now understood why it never ended well. They were too much like me. When we were both on a high it was amazing, but inevitably we would disconnect because no one can rev high all of the time.

A robot is a constant, whereas I am a giant roller coaster of emotions. Andrew is my very levelheaded rock, and I can always depend on him to be him. He brings me back down to Earth. He thinks logically, and I think emotionally. Together, we can balance each other if we learn to communicate somewhere in between our two worlds.

When it comes to telling Andrew things that have been upsetting me, my approach has been flawed. I've been giving him broad suggestions that he can't make sense of. Asking him to check in with me more often wasn't enough. I had to be more specific and tell him in which scenarios to do so. Check in with me "if we have plans that day." Check in with me "when I am waiting for you." These are things Andrew can learn to understand if I keep what I want consistent.

My expectations for romance need to be adjusted. A robot isn't able to just "turn on the charm" because a robot doesn't have charm. A computer acts the same every day. It's really not a bad way to live when you are always being treated with respect. When I was telling Andrew I wanted more romance without giving him specifics, he was lost. I finally understand why I confused him so much. He has no idea where to start.

I should ask for specific things such as:

"I would like a date night once a week."

"Can we cuddle tonight at home?"

"If we go out somewhere, can you open doors for me so it feels like a date night?"

Andrew will easily understand these direct requests.

The specifics are what I should've been asking for, and I need to work on this skill. Ironically, I think all partners would benefit from people being more specific about their wants. But understanding how Andrew is wired helps me see this in a new light. It's absolutely needed. Hinting at anything is a waste of time. It will never be obvious to him. This means I need to work on my self-awareness to figure out which specific things will help me feel fulfilled in my relationship and learn to convey them directly.

There was a valid point in one of the books I read, and it stuck with me. The author said something along the lines of, "Sometimes I get upset that I always have to ask my husband to come to help me with the groceries. I wish he would just know to get up and help me when my hands are full and there's a toddler pulling at my leg. I wish he would just know to help me, but then I remember that I have a husband who will always help me when I ask. If I just ask, he will be more than willing to help." I've never forgotten that, and I'm doing my best to focus on it. I need to learn to ask for the things I want specifically and have the patience to do so in all scenarios. At least for now. Andrew is more than capable of learning the patterns of what I enjoy with time, if I keep them consistent.

Since I've made these simple adjustments, our relationship has improved. I'm confident that our time between now and the diagnosis will be bearable. We've had many small gains along the way. I now understand that Andrew cares; he just shows it differently. I've realized that I shouldn't attach my feelings to his blunt comments, and they are hurting me less. He's just like a robot pointing out an observation. He doesn't mean to be hurtful, he is just spitting out facts.

* * *

ANDREW'S TAKE

"It cannot anticipate what something will be like if it's never done it before because there's no programming encrypted in its memory (that must be terrifying)."

This was a big help for Michelle and me. I didn't feel like this was a putdown. This perspective helped us communicate better, and that's worth it to me.

Just like a computer, I do learn over time. It's a wonderful feeling when I realize that I've improved or I self-reflect and think. *Checking in made Michelle happy; gotta keep doing that.* It is hard to remember and learn from all of these little moments when we have communication problems.

Regarding the statement, *"A computer will not be at all focused on what other computers are doing because it doesn't care,"* I wanted to add more context to this quote. I am focused on what other people/computers are doing. It's just that I'm looking for information in different ways. It resonates with me when someone tells me exactly how they are feeling and what they want. It's next to impossible for me to pick up on subtle communicative cues that I don't have experience with. It's not that I don't care in the sense that I don't like you, it's in the sense that a computer does not care about information that is presented in the wrong format.

* * *

Period Girl

The robot analogy has helped me understand Andrew, but it hasn't helped him understand me. I still have some work to do. Operation Learn about Ourselves isn't just about Andrew. Holding up my end of this mission is important.

At my request, my doctor referred me to a psychiatrist to talk about hypomania. He said he didn't think I had it but agreed to refer me after I convinced him I needed to learn more about it. He then told me it could be a few months before I heard from anyone, and he wasn't lying. By the time the psychiatrist calls me, I've nearly forgotten about it. I take the first available appointment, which is shortly after the Christmas holidays.

When I arrive for my appointment, I'm greeted by a well-groomed older gentleman. He has an impressive haircut and an even more impressive suit. I have no idea what his name is as I only see him one time, so we will call him Dr. Nice Suit. This building is far removed from the offices I'm used to being in, and it feels out of my league. It's not a good day to be out in my sweatpants, but at least I'm warm. As I follow him into his office, I don't want to touch anything. Everything looks so fancy and pristine.

I speak with Dr. Nice Suit for nearly two hours. He makes me feel quite silly by the end of it. He says that although it does sound like I have some severe highs and lows in my life, it's nowhere near being considered a form of hypomania. He explains that in order for it to be considered a manic episode I'd have to do something that made zero sense in my life, like feeling the need to buy ten mattresses for no apparent reason. He goes on that a manic episode would likely cause me to be fired or lose my job. Given the fact that I've had the same employer for well over a decade, he doesn't believe it's possible. I apologize for wasting his time and thank him for explaining so much to me.

He makes a joke as I'm leaving that makes the entire experience worth it. At least I think he is trying to make a joke. In hindsight he may have been dead serious. He utters the words, "Yes, this really just sounds like a woman's regular period cycle," as he chuckles.

As I get in my car, I think to myself, *Could that be true? Are my highs and lows just from my period?* It seems unlikely.

Only a few days pass before a trainer at my gym brings up a book by Lisa Lister that she loves called *Code Red: Know Your Flow, Unlock Your Superpowers, and Create a Bloody Amazing Life. Period.* Because of the comment Dr. Nice Suit made, I ask her if I can borrow it. When something shows up more than once in a brief period of time, I pay attention to it. I believe it's life's way of nudging me to explore something important. And explore it, I do. I read *Code Red* cover to cover in two days. It gives me the same adrenaline rush I had when I was reading the "Autistic Echoes" chapter in *Shadow Syndromes*. This is even better, though, because it's about me.

Code Red explains that every period cycle has four phases: winter, spring, summer, and fall. It explains how your mood likely changes through those four phases and why. Oh my God, I can't believe it. Here I am, a 35-year-old woman finally learning about my period cycle. This book should be a requirement for every junior high student. Learning to track my period cycle is a game-changer in my relationship with Andrew and in my work-life balance.

Ladies, I highly recommend this book. Learning to plan and live according to my period cycle has improved my life significantly. Explaining it to Andrew also helps him understand me and my moods.

He appreciates it. He begins asking me what day of my period cycle I'm on. It helps to better prepare him for how I will be feeling.

Without venturing too deep into the subject, I'll give you a quick breakdown of what I've learned about myself simply by reading *Code Red* and tracking my period for three months. Of course, this is what I remember from reading the book and how my period cycle works. You may find your cycle to be different than mine and have different takeaways from tracking your period, which I highly suggest you do.

The first day you bleed is day one of your period cycle. Days 1–7 of your period cycle are the "winter season." During this season, you are on your period. Winter is a perfect time to relax and focus on yourself. It's not the best time to be socializing or doing high-intensity workouts. A walk, yin-yoga, or even just taking a break from exercise is good during this season. Bubble baths and meditations are also highly recommended. It's a great time to journal, turn inward, reflect on your month, get extra sleep, and make decisions. I eat a lot this season. On the first two days, I can down a whole pizza by myself. I do my best to have as little as possible in my schedule this week to allow for some rest while I'm on my period. No guilt for this. The body needs rest and nourishment during this time.

Days 7–14 of your cycle are the "spring season." This is when my mind tends to get what I would call somewhat manic. I get the urge to shop online for things I don't need or completely rearrange my house furniture. After the book tells me that spring is likely a high spending period, I go back through six months of my credit card statements to find out that is completely true. I consistently shop more in the same week every month. After I learn this, I tell myself I have to wait a week to buy anything in my online shopping cart. When I look back on it a week later, I often think, I totally don't need this. I can't believe I nearly bought more tights when I have thirty pairs already. My spending goes way down after implementing the waiting period.

Spring is a great time to channel your energy into workouts and creativity. It's also easier to stick to my diet and eat healthily. It's not a great time to make decisions because I'm quite erratic. I will likely agree to too many projects without thinking them through. When it comes to socializing, this is likely the week you will blurt out something rude to a friend; it's like your filter is gone. All your hormones are coming back after your period, and it feels like things happen quickly. I can hardly sleep in spring because I'm too busy overthinking. It's a good time to work a little extra or pull an all-nighter. It's also a good time to explore trying new things in the bedroom.

Then comes "summer season," days 13–21. Summer is my happiest time of the month. It's when I'm all-around at my best. I'm really on the ball. High energy levels, my skin looks great, and it's the easiest time to orgasm. Thank you! It's ovulation time, so mothering/nurturing instincts are on high alert. It's a great time to book an event, as I'll be more likely to nail it. All things are fantastic in summer, and days seem to go smoothly.

Then comes "fall season," days 22–28, the toughest week for many women. It's when your estrogen and testosterone levels are at their lowest. I'm cranky, irritable, and it seems all my self-confidence has taken a vacation. It's usually the week I will drink wine multiple times and make popcorn. Comfort food and comfort TV are needed. All the 90s rom coms and snacks to help ease my misery. It's highly likely I will take some anger out on Andrew.

In the book, the author makes a joke about how her husband didn't come home from work on day 25 because he knew how crabby she would be. Well, for me, it's days 22 or 23. Andrew and I will usually have an argument on one of those two days. I will have zero patience, and I won't be feeling good about myself, so naturally, I'll get mad at him for something. It really helps to give him a head's-up that I'll be feeling irritable. I know to take those two days to myself and have comfort food and movies ready. I also learn to stop giving myself a hard time for eating so unhealthily this week. It's inevitable, and I'll eat healthy for the next three weeks. So really, I call that balance.

So, it turns out Dr. Nice Suit was correct in making his smirky comment after all. I guess it wasn't a joke. I ended up learning a lot about myself and helping Andrew understand my moods. I've completed my mission, but not in the way I had originally thought. Life is funny that way.

ANDREW'S TAKE

I really appreciated it when Michelle explained her period cycle to me. This helps me to understand how Michelle's mood can change from week to week. I'm much less surprised and confused now.

* * *

OUR LOVE LANGUAGES

As an added bonus to completing our mission, I buy *The 5 Love Languages* by Gary Chapman. I've seen it mentioned many times on social media, and I want to learn what all the fuss is about. I order the book off Amazon, and when it arrives I'm surprised by how short it is. The book quickly engrosses me, and I end up reading the entire book and taking the love languages quiz all in one afternoon.

The 5 Love Languages puts many things into perspective for me. It gives many examples of relationships that are failing because people show love in their own ways when their partner may, in fact, need something entirely different to feel loved. My big takeaway is to learn to show love in the way that your partner needs it most, as opposed to only in the way you enjoy receiving it.

When I add my score to learn my love languages, I'm not surprised by the results. My top love language is acts of service, followed closely by quality time and physical touch. A distant fourth and fifth are words of affirmation and gifts.

Helping with the dishes, fixing my car, being responsible with bills, grocery shopping, cleaning, and taking care of me when I am sick are all things that matter most to me. It doesn't take me long to realize that Andrew has been lacking in this area but that he is rocking it in the quality time and physical touch departments. I have his full attention and all the cuddles I need when we plan our hangout nights, but he doesn't help much with daily tasks.

MICHELLE AND ANDREW PRESTON

The next day Andrew reads the book and takes the love language quiz as well. Comparing our scores and chatting about it is very enlightening. Andrew's top love language is words of affirmation, followed closely by physical touch and quality time, and then gifts and acts of service are way down at the bottom for him. Learning this puts a big spotlight on one obvious imbalance in our relationship.

Andrew needs words of affirmation and doesn't care much for acts of service. Whereas I need acts of service and don't care much for words of affirmation. We both highly value physical touch and quality time, which is why we are not having any issues in those areas.

"I watched a video where a girl was talking about love languages," I tell Andrew. "She explained that the love language you need most is probably the one you lacked as a child. This rings true for me; I was always doing things on my own growing up. It makes me feel loved to have help with everyday stuff."

"That makes sense," Andrew responds. "Everyone was always doing things for me in my house and buying me gifts. But they weren't really saying nice things."

"That's probably why it means so much to you," I explain. "In my house, everyone was always saying 'I love you,' but to me the words often felt meaningless. Probably why words aren't as important to me."

As we discuss words of affirmation, my mind immediately flashes back to my almost-marriage in my twenties and how my ex would complain that I didn't say 'I love you' enough. At the time I thought he was being ridiculous, but I realize now that he likely spoke a different love language than I did, but we never knew it. Mind blown.

"In my past relationships," I continue, "it was usually the men who said all the right things who ended up breaking my heart when I didn't see it coming. Especially in my early twenties. I guess that furthered my distaste for words. So many empty promises."

"Yeah, I'm not like that. Words are important to me. I would love it if you said 'I love you' more, and other nice things," Andrew explains.

"Absolutely, I'll make an effort now that I understand how important it is," I respond.

"Great, now how do I do more acts of service?" he asks. "I don't even know where to start."

"Well, I show you acts of service by doing your laundry, making you dinner, packing your lunch when we go hiking," I explain. "That's how I've been showing my love, by helping you where I can."

I'm taken aback by Andrew's response when he says, "Yeah, I mean those things are kind of nice, but I really don't need you to do any of those things. They aren't important to me."

At this moment, I realize how different our needs are. "Kind of nice"? Wow. I put so much effort into this area, and it's hardly being noticed.

We agree that I have been completely failing Andrew in the words of affirmation department and that he has been failing me in the acts of service department. We will both need to up our game to keep each other's love tanks full for the long haul.

We decide to take surprising each other with gifts out of the equation for the most part. Since we both don't value gifts highly, it doesn't make sense to stress about holidays or spend money unnecessarily. The focus and energy we take away from gifts will be better aimed where it matters most: on our top love languages.

It makes more sense for me to write Andrew a thoughtful card as opposed to getting him gifts on holidays. It makes more sense for him to do something nice for me and perform acts of service. Andrew is relieved since he never really knew what to buy me, and when I get him something, he feels bad when it isn't something he likes.

I make Andrew a specific list of things I always enjoy receiving or activities we can do if he ever wants to surprise me. If I'm craving a present for a holiday, I promise to give Andrew a head's-up, and he can just pick something off my list. He is happy that he will never have to guess or follow romantic societal norms that never made sense to him. We agree that I won't buy him anything unless I know it's something he likes. For the most part, I will opt to surprise him with thoughtful cards and love letters.

I explain to Andrew why acts of service are important to me. They make me feel cared for. They remind me that I'm not going through life alone and that someone else has my back. Andrew listens, but I can tell by the look on his face that he still doesn't know what to do. We decide that I will start pointing things out to Andrew that

I would like him to do for me. We agree that it will become much more important once we are living together. I will let him know specifically what I want help with. Then he will begin to understand my love language.

New habits are rarely formed overnight. It takes us many months to get the hang of each other's love languages. We both hit a few bumps along the way. I put a solid effort in for the first few weeks, but because it isn't a natural thing for me to do, it's only a matter of time before I begin failing in the words of affirmation department. I also make the mistake of saying "I love you" in a joking way a few times. For instance, if I asked Andrew to get up and do something for me when we were comfy on the couch, I'd say, "I loooove you" with a sarcastic tone. I was doing this in a playful manner as if to thank him for doing something I obviously didn't want to do. Andrew didn't take kindly to it, especially since I hadn't been saying "I love you" enough otherwise. Lesson learned.

This situation erupts during our one-year anniversary vacation. It's the first time Andrew gets mad at me, and we have a big fight about it. I haven't been filling his love tank, and he is hurting inside.

After this fight, I make a point of putting notes in my day planner reminding me to give Andrew words of affirmation. I write *Andrew Love Language* on random days every few weeks. On those days, I will send him a long text or an email telling him what a great boyfriend he is and how much I love him. Andrew becomes noticeably happier the more I focus on giving him his love language. Holidays become more enjoyable once I start writing him long positive notes as presents. It is a win-win. I avoid the malls and have a happy boyfriend. Our relationship improves. In a few months, I no longer have to set reminders. I'm now enjoying the flow of speaking in his love language.

Andrew learns in time how to speak my love language, and eventually, I rarely have to ask. At first he has no idea what I want help with. Every week I would ask for his help with something. He would help me get the groceries, pack the snacks for hiking, carry some of my stuff, or help clean my car. Over time he learned the things that I liked, and now I rarely have to ask him.

It's through this process that I truly fall in LOVE with Andrew. How committed he is to working on our relationship means everything to me. I know that no matter what life throws at us, we can handle it if we work together to meet in the middle.

* * *

ANDREW'S TAKE

How simple the five love languages are blew me away. Yet they are powerful. It's not perfect, but it puts things in a simple, easy-to-understand perspective. Once I noticed improvements in our relationship, I would think to myself, *Oh, this helps a lot. We need to keep doing this and never forget this.*

Reading the love languages book gives you the biggest "bang for your buck" as far as relationship advice goes. It's so simple yet so powerful. These concepts can be used with anyone—friends, family, coworkers, or offspring.

My main love language is words of affirmation. I've found when someone like my boss, supervisor, friend, coworker, or Michelle says to me, "Great job" or "I love you," I feel good. When I was growing up, words of affirmation were not spoken very often in my house. My family showed they cared through acts of service and gifts. Acts of service and gifts are very nice, but I didn't feel as much love as I feel when someone speaks very kindly to me.

I take things literally, so when you tell me how you feel, it really resonates deep inside me. Whereas if you do something nice for me, It just doesn't feel the same. I can't feel it deep inside unless they also say, "I did this for you because I love you." Otherwise, I might be confused as to why they performed an act of service or gave me a gift. Hearing someone say it, and mean it, feels so much stronger.

I've worked at a place where the boss will say, "If you don't hear from me about how well you're doing at your job, then that means you're doing a good job," and they think this is perfectly normal. I like to be told when I'm doing a good job, am improving, or if I've made mistakes. When I don't hear anything, I get anxious.

Once Michelle started to talk to me in my love language, I noticed that I felt happier. I would look forward to her notes and her loving words of affirmation. I still do.

* * *

18
THE DIAGNOSIS

The time has finally arrived for our intake session. We are ecstatic. It's February in Calgary, and there have been snowstorms all week. But even the weather can't keep us down.

We punch the address into Google Maps and are on our way. Nervous energy is vibrating off both of us. In part due to the crappy road conditions which are causing us to run late, but mainly because we are both feeling the gravity of the journey we are about to take. Our lives are about to change, regardless of how this session goes down.

We pull up to a house at 6:07 p.m. We are seven minutes late. There aren't many cars parked outside, and I'm surprised to be pulling up to a house in a residential area for an intake session. I'm worried that we are at the wrong address.

The address is correct, so we walk up and ring the bell. We wait in the bitter cold for a few minutes for someone to answer the door. As the door opens, I let out a sigh of relief. We are greeted by Doctor Baker, who welcomes us into the warmth.

"I'm so sorry we're late!" The words tumble out as we introduce ourselves and take our boots off. We are at the right place. I feel relieved.

Dr. Baker is a short man with long gray hair and a warm smile. He doesn't say much as he escorts us down a large carpeted staircase and hands us a clipboard full of forms.

"You can go find a seat," Dr. Baker says. "We will be starting shortly."

As we turn the corner, I'm shocked by how many people are seated in his basement. There are easily thirty people waiting, and yet the house feels quiet.

There aren't many seats left, but we manage to find two together in the front row near the far-left wall. We sit down and begin filling out our intake forms. An older couple arrives minutes later and fills up the last two seats, making me happy we aren't the last ones to arrive.

Before we finish filling out our forms, Dr. Baker begins his PowerPoint presentation at the front of the room. He begins by talking about the history of autism and Asperger's syndrome. He explains the original diagnosis criteria and what they understood about autism in the early days.

Dr. Baker explains how the criteria for autism changed in 1994 to include a wider range of people.

Andrew taps my leg as he says, "I went to the Mayo Clinic in 1992 before they changed the criteria."

"That explains your misdiagnosis of ADHD as a kid," I whisper back.

Andrew nods his head in agreement.

Dr. Baker's PowerPoint presentation is impressive, and it's clear that he is knowledgeable on the subject. He has clearly given this presentation many times and could likely give it with his eyes closed.

During the presentation, Dr. Baker makes an obvious joke about a social situation. An older gentleman in his sixties raises his hand and asks, "Are you being sarcastic?"

"Yes, I am being sarcastic," Dr. Baker answers, and then he goes on to give various definitions of sarcasm.

"Thank you so much for clarifying," the gentleman responds. "I get confused when people use sarcasm."

It's an adorable exchange as the man clearly feels he is in a safe space to speak.

After this moment, I begin looking around the room with a new perspective. It appears that 95 percent of the people here to be assessed are male, and most of them are easily over the age of forty-five. In our early thirties, we seem to be the youngest people here. These seemingly gentle souls have likely gone their entire lives not being understood by the world around them. I feel sad at the thought, yet it makes me happy that so many are about to find their answers and understand their differences.

Dr. Baker ends his presentation by explaining the diagnosis process to everyone.

"Please leave the top form with me today after you have finished filling it out. You will be contacted in the order which you registered on the website. It could be anywhere from two to four months, depending where you are on that list."

I give Andrew a little elbow nudge. "Sweet, two months. We must've been first or second," I whisper.

"The booklet is to be taken home to be completed and brought to your first session," Dr. Baker continues. "Loved ones can assist with the booklet, and they are welcome in the sessions as it helps give me a broader view of behaviors."

Andrew grabs my forearm with excitement. "Yay, you get to come!"

Dr. Baker continues, "The diagnosis assessment itself can take anywhere from two to five visits depending on the client. Each session will take two to four hours. As long as you have an Alberta Health Care number, the cost of the assessment is covered in full."

"OMG, this is amazing," I turn to Andrew and say. This statement obviously pleases the entire room, as we hear many others make similar comments of relief.

"This concludes the presentation, but I can stay and answer any questions you may have. Just make sure you leave that top form on the table on your way out," Dr. Baker concludes.

A few people choose to leave, but many stick around to ask questions.

"Let's stay and hear all the questions," I say to Andrew.

"For sure," he responds.

Andrew and I don't have anything to ask, but we enjoy watching the interactions of everyone around us and hearing their questions being answered. Dr. Baker has a great energy to him. He radiates patience and understanding as he answers questions I'm sure he's been asked a thousand times over. This impresses me. It can't be easy to keep enthusiasm when your services are in such high demand, and he makes it look effortless.

The dynamic conversation in the room feels interesting for both of us, so we stay until the very end. It's near 9 p.m. by the time we leave, and Dr. Baker escorts the last of us upstairs to say goodbye.

"Thank you so much for everything, Dr. Baker," I say as I put my boots on.

"Yes, thank you so much. We look forward to hearing from you," Andrew says as we walk out the door.

Two months go by.

Dr. Baker contacts us in April to book our first appointment. We choose an afternoon appointment in the month of May so that Andrew only has to take half a day off work. We dig out the booklet, which I had safely filed away, and Andrew begins filling it out. He takes a week to fill it out as it is quite extensive.

Once Andrew finishes the booklet, I go over it and make a few notes of my own. I highlight my comments in pink, so Dr. Baker can easily tell the difference.

The Diagnosis Booklet

The diagnosis booklet is fifteen pages long, and it begins with four different questionnaires. These tests can easily be found online for anyone who is curious about how they would score.

1. Autism Spectrum Quotient[5] This part is 50 situational questions where you have four possible answers for each question: *Definitely Agree, Slightly Agree, Slightly Disagree,* or *Definitely Disagree*. This test will score you with one click after you finish the test.

Andrew scores 35 out of a possible 50. Scores in the 33–50 range indicate significant autistic traits (autism).

---

[5] https://embrace-autism.com/autism-spectrum-quotient/

2. <u>Cambridge Behavior Scale Empathy Quotient.</u>[6] This test is composed of 60 questions where you have the same four possible answers for each question: *Definitely Agree, Slightly Agree, Slightly Disagree,* and *Definitely Disagree.*

Andrew scores 13 out of a possible 80. The threshold score for autism on this assessment is below 30.

3. <u>Executive Functioning – Skills Development – Self Rating Scale v3.1</u>

This test is composed of 50 questions in which you can answer Never, Occasionally, Often, or Very Often. It can be downloaded for free at www.neurodevelop.com. This test can also easily be done online, but you have to add up the results yourself.

It's separated into ten sections, and each section is scored on a scale from 1–15.
1–5 Normal/Mild   6–10 Moderate   11–15 Severe

Here is how Andrew scores:

1. Working Memory — (6) Moderate
2. Organization — (5) Normal/Mild
3. Initiation — (6) Moderate
4. Planning — (6) Moderate
5. Problem Solving — (5) Normal/Mild
6. Inhibition/Impulsivity — (7) Moderate
7. Shift (Adapting/Flexing) — (11) Severe
8. Self-Monitoring — (9) Moderate
9. Emotional Regulation — (10) Moderate
10. Communication — (7) Moderate

---

[6] https://embrace-autism.com/empathy-quotient/

4. <u>The Adult Repetitive Behavior Questionnaire</u> [7]

This questionnaire is composed of 20 questions that ask about specific repetitive behaviors. You answer each question twice, once in the present tense and once for when you were a child.

The question will ask you about a certain behavior, and then you choose one of the following: 1. *Never/Rarely* 2. *Mild or Occasional* 3. *Marked or Notable* (occasionally affects others) 4. *Serious or Severe* (affects others on a regular basis).

Andrew marked *Severe* in two areas:

1. Do you insist on doing things in a certain way or redoing things until they are "just right?" - *Severe*
2. Almost always choose from a restricted range of repetitive activities rather than having flexible interests. - *Severe*

Andrew marked *Notable* (occasionally affects others) in two other areas:

1. Do you play the same music, game, or video, or read the same book repeatedly? - *Notable*
2. Do you insist on eating the same foods or refuse to wear new clothes? - *Notable*

There are many questions on this test where Andrew marks *Hardly Ever* or *Mild*. This helps put a spotlight on Andrew's certain repetitive behaviors and areas where he struggles the most.

As I go over the booklet, it's helpful for me to see Andrew's answers. There are a handful of questions in which I'm surprised by what he selected.

For example, when asked, "It doesn't bother me too much if I am late meeting a friend." Andrew selected *Slightly Agree* when I would

---

[7] https://embrace-autism.com/rbq-2a/

have expected him to select *Definitely Agree,* as he seems completely unbothered when we are late. It's like he hardly even notices being late at all. Not a major difference, but I made small notes where I felt it was needed so that Dr. Baker could see my perspective.

I notice that Andrew left a few questions blank in the booklet.

"Andrew, can you come answer these questions, please?" I shout from the living room. "You left a few of them blank."

"Yeah, I know. I don't know how to answer those questions. They don't make sense," he responds.

"What do you mean they don't make sense?" I ask in a confused tone. "I answered them just fine."

"I don't like how they are worded. I can't answer them," he reiterates.

"Okay, well, I guess we'll just tell Dr. Baker that when we give it to him," I conclude.

I put a pink mark on what I think is the best answer for those questions and leave it at that.

The questionnaire is now ready, and I'm slightly nervous we are going to forget it on our first day. My glove box has a lock on it, so I decide that's the best place to leave it. I slide it in an envelope along with the notes I had taken about Andrew months ago and head to my car. I place the envelope in my glovebox, excited, knowing the big day is only weeks away.

MAY - FIRST SESSION WITH DR. BAKER

We ring Dr. Baker's doorbell and wait for him to answer, much like the first time we were there for our intake session.

He greets us at the door, and we follow him down to the basement. Only this time, we go into an office with his computer that sits across from a comfortable squishy sofa. The office is warm and welcoming. The many shelves are covered in various figurines.

"Here's our intake forms," I say as I pass the booklet to Dr. Baker. "It's all filled out except for a few questions Andrew left blank. I circled the answers I think they should be in pink, but Andrew didn't know how to answer them."

"Oh, perfect, we can start there," Dr. Baker says as he grabs the forms and sits down in front of his computer. "So let's see which questions you couldn't answer, Andrew."

"Yeah, there's a couple I think," Andrew says.

Dr. Baker studies the sheet for a moment before speaking. "The first question is, *In a conversation, I tend to focus on my own thoughts rather than what my listener might be thinking.*" Dr. Baker is a pro. He rarely takes his attention off of us while speaking and typing.

"Yeah, I don't know how to answer that because it's not always the same," Andrew explains.

"There are times I try to imagine what the other person is thinking, and times when I focus on my own thoughts."

"Okay, let's move on to the second question you left blank," Dr. Baker continues. "I would rather go to a library than a party."

"Yeah, I don't know how to answer that one either because it depends on multiple factors," Andrew says.

"I circled *Definitely Agree,*" I explain, "because Andrew rarely goes to parties. He's usually reading or learning about something on the weekends."

"But sometimes I like to go to parties," Andrew says, "I really don't like how these questions are worded."

"Yes, sometimes you go to parties, Andrew, but nine out of ten times, you would pick a library," I rebut.

"But that's not what the question is asking," Andrew says with confusion.

"Okay, I see what's going on here," Dr. Baker interjects as we listen intently. "What Andrew is displaying is an inability to generalize. This is common with autistic people."

Oh wow, he put that together quickly, I think to myself as I lean back on the sofa to get comfortable.

"The questions Andrew struggles to answer are all generalizations. So if he answers definitively, he will feel like he is lying. Autistic people tend to struggle in this area because they often have black-and-white thinking," Dr. Baker explains.

Then he turns to me and asks, "Would you say that Andrew thinks in absolutes? For people with black-and-white thinking, something either is or it isn't. They don't see the gray area. Does this sound like Andrew?"

"I've never thought of it that way before," I answer. "Yes, Andrew either does something 110 percent or not at all. Things seem to be either facts or nonsense in his eyes. Potential truths aren't a thing. I guess that's why he goes overboard with projects. He doesn't know how to "kind of" do anything or "kind of" believe anything."

"Yeah, I would agree with that," Andrew adds. "It sounds like me."

We all quickly conclude that Andrew thinks in black and white, and Dr. Baker begins to type notes on his computer.

My mind is blown. It seems so obvious now, and I'm surprised I didn't come to this conclusion on my own. If Andrew is my Robot Man, then obviously he won't be able to generalize. Robots either do something or they don't. "Kind of" doing something is not an option. Duh.

Throughout our relationship, I've said many things that confused Andrew, and it suddenly becomes clear as to why. I'm the queen of generalizations. I make them often. I don't speak matter of factly. I tend to leave room for interpretation.

Wow, we've hardly been here for ten minutes, and I've already learned something extremely valuable. Thank you, Dr. Baker, I think to myself.

After we collectively decide that Andrew has black-and-white thinking, Dr. Baker still needs Andrew to answer the questions he left blank so he can add his scores. I sit back and enjoy watching the exchange as Dr. Baker helps Andrew come to a conclusion. This process gives me more insight into how Andrew's mind works.

ADHD

"So, I see here that you have an official ADHD diagnosis from the Mayo Clinic?" Dr. Baker asks.

"Yes, I was diagnosed with ADHD as a child, but I've never really felt like I have ADHD," Andrew explains. "In your presentation, you said they changed the criteria in 1994, and I went to the Mayo Clinic just before that when I was seven."

Dr. Baker turns to me and asks, "Do you think Andrew has ADHD?"

"I'm not sure. I've never looked into it," I respond. "But he can focus longer than anyone I know when he's interested in something."

"My psychologist told me in 2008 that I do not have ADHD, and I've always wondered if she was right," Andrew adds. "She also tested my IQ, and it was above average. Before that IQ test, a part of me always felt like I was stupid."

Dr. Baker turns around and grabs some forms and a clipboard. "Well, Michelle knows you pretty well. Let's see if she thinks you have ADHD. And if you're neurodivergent, your IQ is likely higher than you tested because they wouldn't have factored in any social impairments which may have hindered your results."

"Oh wow," Andrew says. "That's interesting."

"You want me to fill these out?" I ask as I grab the forms from his hand.

"Yes, let's see how you would score Andrew for ADHD," Dr. Baker replies.

"Okay," I say as I unclick the pen and begin filling out the ADHD assessment forms.

"Yeah, awesome, let's find out," Andrew says. "I've always wondered."

As I check *No* or *Rarely* on most of the questions in the booklet, I'm assuming that Andrew's psychologist was likely right.

Dr. Baker asks Andrew about his work history, and Andrew tells him many stories about his struggles at past jobs, such as walking out due to anxiety and a story about how he got punched in the face by a coworker once.

Andrew and Dr. Baker talk for a good half hour while I sit back with my forms and enjoy their exchanges. Their topics change rapidly and randomly, but they both ride the wave with little effort. It's entertaining to watch because their topics jump all over the place and back again.

The same excitement and charm I love most about Andrew are also apparent in Dr. Baker. His face lights up as he explains the things he enjoys most in his office. It feels as if they are young friends showing each other their favorite toys at recess, and I eat it up.

"I hate to interrupt this delightful gab session, but I've finished the forms," I say as I sit up off the couch to hand them to Dr. Baker.

"Fantastic, I'll just go over these quickly," Dr. Baker says.

"Perfect, I need to excuse myself to go to the bathroom," I say as I stand up.

"Yup, it's just to the left of us," Dr. Baker explains.

As I wash my hands, I'm thinking to myself how I love that we are inside a house. It makes the entire experience feel a lot more comfortable and personable. When I go see my psychologist at his large office building, it feels much more intimidating.

It only takes Dr. Baker a matter of minutes to review the forms. By the time I sit down again, he is finished.

"According to Michelle, you most definitely do not have ADHD, not even close by any of these scores," Dr. Baker says as he throws the forms in a pile on his desk. "Now, let's get back to the rest of this booklet."

We continue to go over all of Andrew's answers to the questionnaire in detail until we run out of time.

"Wow, I can't believe it's already past 4 p.m," I say. "The hours flew by."

"Yup, that happens," Dr. Baker says. "I can book you in an afternoon just over a few weeks from now if that works?"

"Yes, any afternoon appointment works for us," Andrew responds. ''Thank you. I'm looking forward to coming back."

"Yes, it's been a pleasure," I add. "Thank you for taking so much time with us."

"No problem. You're all booked in," Dr. Baker says as he stands up to walk us to the door.

As we put our boots on, he adds, "I can't say for sure until we complete the entire booklet, but I'd say an ASD diagnosis is likely at this point."

"Thank you so much, Dr. Baker. We will see you next month," Andrew says as we walk out the door.

"That was fantastic," I say to Andrew as we get in my car. "He's so funny and easy to talk to."

"Yeah, I like talking to him," Andrew says before we drive off to get some food.

"I'm learning so much. The 'lack of generalization' statement alone was enough to make this entire process worth it, and we've only just begun," I say as I look up nearby restaurants on my phone.

"That made so much sense," Andrew reiterates. "Now, let's get some food."

June - Second Session with Dr. Baker

"Do you have issues making eye contact?" Dr. Baker asks Andrew.

"I can't look someone in the eye when I'm thinking deeply," Andrew explains. "I feel like I lose IQ points when I have to look someone in the eye."

"It's especially tough for him to look at me if we're talking about something emotional," I add.

"Did you just say that you feel like you lose IQ points when you look someone in the eye?" Dr. Baker chuckles as he looks at Andrew.

"Yeah," Andrew reiterates as he laughs along with Dr. Baker. "Is that weird?"

"I just can't say I've heard that one before," Dr. Baker says as he types his notes.

"Well, that's how it feels," Andrew explains. "If I have to look at someone, it's much harder to express my thoughts."

"Is that why you close your eyes when you're telling a story?" I ask.

"No. In that case, it's because I'm looking at a picture in my mind," Andrew answers.

"Oh, you've never explained it that way to me before," I reply. "That makes sense."

"Let me ask you this," Dr. Baker interjects. "Have you ever made a plan for making eye contact?"

"What do you mean by a plan?" Andrew asks.

"Have you ever come up with a strategy that you would use for making eye contact with people?" Dr. Baker explains the question further.

"Oh." Andrew clearly comes to a realization. "Yes, I've come up with a strategy where I will count to three, then break eye contact for six seconds and repeat. It seems to work."

"It's a neurodivergent trait to have a plan for eye contact," Dr. Baker explains. "If you ask a neurotypical if they've ever made a strategy for eye contact, they will usually say no."

"Really?" Andrew asks.

Dr. Baker looks at me. "Have you ever made a plan for eye contact?"

"Nope, " I answer as I sit up off the couch. "I didn't even know that was a thing."

"See?" Dr. Baker says with a smirk.

This is an interesting fact for us to learn. I immediately chime in by saying, "I've never in my life made a plan of how I would make eye contact."

Andrew follows this up with, "Oh, I most definitely have, more than once."

Our second session is similar to our first session. It lasts over three hours, and we enjoy chatting with Dr. Baker so much that we often venture off-topic. The hours pass quickly as the conversation never dries out.

As we go over the *Executive Functioning Booklet*, it helps shed light on the areas Andrew struggles most. He scores *Mild/Normal* or only *Slightly Moderate* in five out of the ten sections, so we don't discuss those much.

He scores highest (marked *Severe*) on his ability to shift/adapt. Followed closely by emotional regulation. Self-monitoring comes in third, and impulsivity and communication are tied for fourth. More of the puzzle begins to fall together as these are the areas where we most definitely struggle.

I'm filled with relief as Dr. Baker goes over Andrew's scores. Learning that he struggles so much with shifting and adapting makes me feel better about his reluctance to move in with me. Emotional regulation and self-monitoring are next, and this helps me realize why it took Andrew a year to be able to factor me into his life or express his feelings.

"You scored high on emotional regulation," Dr. Baker explains. "Have you guys heard of alexithymia? It can be closely related to ASD."

"I recognize the term from a text Andrew sent me months ago," I explain. "It's the only time I've ever heard of it."

"Yeah, I sent Michelle a text about it," Andrew says. "But I wasn't sure if I had it."

Wikipedia defines alexithymia as "a personality trait characterized by the subclinical inability to identify and describe emotions experienced by one's self. The core characteristic of alexithymia is marked dysfunction in emotional awareness, social attachment, and interpersonal relation. Furthermore, people with alexithymia can have difficulty distinguishing and appreciating the emotions of others, which is thought to lead to unempathetic and ineffective emotional responses."

We don't discuss alexithymia for long or do any kind of official diagnosis, but we all agree that it sounds like Andrew has alexithymia based on his scores.

After going over the four questionnaires, we cover a number of other subjects.

"Has anyone made comments about Andrew's tone of voice, facial expressions, or how he sits, stands, or walks?" Dr. Baker asks as he reads his computer screen.

Andrew immediately looks at me because he knows I'm the best one to answer this question.

"Oh man, I hardly know where to start," I announce. "There's so much to say."

"Start wherever you like," Dr. Baker says with a smile.

"Well," I begin, "if I whisper to him, he will answer in his full voice, even if we are in bed and he's right by my ear. Sometimes, he speaks in one long monotone sentence and changes subjects without pausing."

"Okay." Dr. Baker starts typing while speaking. "Speaks at odd volumes at the wrong times. What else?"

"He doesn't react to touch the same as anyone I've ever met. He can't tell me if he is enjoying a massage or not. When I try to loosen a knot on his back, he doesn't know if it is a knot or if kneading it is making it better," I explain.

"Strange reactions to touch, according to Michelle," Dr. Baker repeats as he continues typing. "Anything else?"

"Andrew is the least clumsy person I know, and he always has correct posture. He takes his time to do everything efficiently and doesn't seem to know how to rush. I hardly see him stumble or drop anything," I continue.

"Really? You're not clumsy?" Dr. Bakers sounds surprised as he turns to Andrew.

"No, I wouldn't say I'm clumsy," Andrew responds.

"I don't hear that often, and you don't seem to have much of a stim," Dr. Baker says. "Stimming is any repetitive movement people use to self-soothe. Examples of this include finger flicking or hand flapping."

"No, I don't think I stim," Andrew turns to see if I agree.

"There have been instances where he's verbally repeated something three times without realizing it, but other than that, I haven't noticed a stim," I explain. "Andrew is the most coordinated person I know, and he always uses good posture. I'm the clumsy one in our relationship."

"How often does he repeat himself three times?" Dr. Baker asks.

"Only a few times since we've been dating. It happens when he's really upset or gets triggered," I answer.

"Okay, what else?" Dr. Baker asks as he continues his notes.

"There have been times when he seems really upset, and he later tells me he was enjoying himself," I answer. "It's confusing. His facial expressions don't match his emotions."

"Okay." Dr. Baker turns to Andrew and asks, "Do you hear that often?"

"Yeah," Andrew responds. "People often tell me they can't read me."

"What are your special interests and hobbies?" Dr. Baker turns to Andrew.

"Well, I've read thirty-five books on finance, economics, investing, trading stocks, and the psychology behind investing," Andrew starts off. "I love Magic: The Gathering, Dungeons and Dragons, powerlifting, snowboarding, astronomy, and quantum mechanics."

Andrew pauses to think, so I add a little tidbit by saying, "He also loves fixing things."

"Yeah, I did not have much mechanical experience growing up, but I'm a good mechanic now," Andrew explains. "And learning about science and playing computer games is always a good time." I chuckle because Andrew's excitement is evident as he mentions science.

"Sounds like you have some pretty limited interests," Dr. Baker says.

"Pretty much," Andrew replies. "I've done hundreds upon hundreds of hours of research on these topics, and also economic, financial, and geopolitical topics. I love anything about the earth's history and human history."

This turns into a lengthy enjoyable discussion as Dr. Baker explains many of the interesting sci-fi figurines around his office. He and Andrew talk nerd for so long that we never do get to any more questions. They discuss many subjects I know little about, but their passion entertains me as I sit quietly. I love listening to people talk about what they enjoy most in life. Dr. Baker is lighting up the same way Andrew does when he explains the things he loves most, and I'm totally here for it.

By the end of their conversation, it's clear to me that most of Andrew's interests are quite typical for an autistic person. I had already known this, but this afternoon has clarified how deep this truth is.

It's past 4 o'clock by the time we leave.

"The next session will be our last. We don't have much left to discuss," Dr. Baker says as we walk upstairs.

"Thanks, Dr. Baker. We look forward to it," we say as we walk out the door.

July - Third Session with Dr. Baker

"How have you been?" Dr. Baker asks Andrew as we sit down on the comfy couch.

"Good. I think I'm getting a little better at most of these things," Andrew answers. "I've been having less anxiety."

Dr. Baker doesn't skip a beat as he replies, "No, you're not getting better, Andrew. Michelle is just accommodating you."

"Oh, is that what's happening?" Andrew replies.

"Yes, your brain is wired a certain way. That doesn't change. But if your environment is accommodating, you will feel much better." Dr. Baker explains. "Now that Michelle is understanding you more, I'm sure she's making many adjustments you don't realize."

"Yes, that's true," I chime in. "I also am getting less frustrated with certain things now that I understand them."

It feels nice to get validated by Dr. Baker for my efforts.

We don't have much left to cover in our last session. We mostly need to discuss sensory issues and go over the diagnosis after it is completed. This leaves time to go off-topic and enjoy some laughs.

"I don't like the show Friends," Andrew explains. "I have no idea why anyone would want to watch that show. It makes me cringe."

"I watch that show," I explain. "I find it comforting to have it playing in the background when I'm anxious or exhausted."

"I know you watch it, and I don't get it," Andrew explains.

Dr. Baker immediately knows why and makes an interesting point.

"It's because *Friends* plays off of body language and emotions," Dr. Baker explains. "It gives you all the good feelings with lots of smiles and exaggerated facial expressions."

Dr. Baker gives some examples of exaggerated facial expressions in between his sentences, and he nails them. His large smiles and grins are as impressive as they are comical.

"Without really understanding body language or needing to feel those social happy feelings, there really isn't much else to the show," Dr. Baker adds.

"OMG, is that what it is? Because I really hate that show," Andrew says.

"That's because you don't need emotional comfort the same way most people do," Dr. Baker adds.

"That's so true," I chuckle. "I totally watch it for the good feels."

We all have a good laugh before finishing the booklet.

"Are you bothered by certain lights, sounds, smells, how fabrics feel against your skin, being hot or cold, or being touched?" Dr. Baker asks Andrew as he reads off his computer screen.

"I absolutely hate being too hot. I couldn't stand being bundled up as a child," Andrew answers. "I would rather be chilled than hot in all circumstances."

"Yeah, he's pretty much always in T-shirts and shorts," I add. Then I tell the story about the first time we went shopping together and how I almost had a panic attack in the store.

"I hate tags touching my skin and any kind of rougher fabrics," Andrew explains. "I also hate the feeling of sunscreen being on my skin. I shower it off as soon as possible because it feels so icky."

"He mostly wears older clothes that he has had for years because they feel the most comfortable," I explain. "And he comments on things smelling bad when I don't notice a smell."

Dr. Baker is typing while Andrew and I begin talking to each other. "You really like your noise-canceling headphones and sunglasses, but I'd say your light and noise sensitivities are pretty mild," I say to Andrew.

"Yeah, I don't struggle too much with that," Andrew answers.

"Do you have an imagination?" Dr. Baker asks Andrew.

"I think I do," Andrew answers.

"Do you?" I ask. "Because it's tough for you to picture scenarios when I explain them to you."

"Yeah, I don't know. But I can play D and D, and that's all imagination," Andrew says.

"Tell me a story about a cat and some catnip," Dr. Baker says to Andrew.

"There was a cat who found some catnip on a Tuesday, and he brought it to his house," Andrew begins. "Then the cat showed off the catnip to his friends over some warm milk."

Dr. Baker sits back in his chair and folds his arms with a smile on his face. "Keep going," he says. "This is entertaining."

"Then they all started running around the house high on catnip. They were scratching chairs and knocking things over," Andrew continues.

"Okay, that's enough. You clearly have an imagination," Dr. Baker concludes as we all laugh.

It's a great way to wrap up the diagnosis process.

"I just need a few minutes to add up your final score and print your diagnosis letter," Dr. Baker explains.

"Sounds good," Andrew says as we wait patiently.

He explained that Andrew scored as a level 1, except for his rigidity and his ability to adapt, in which he scored as a level 2.

The Official Diagnosis Letter

The front page of Andrew's diagnosis letter reads like this:

July 17, 2019

To whom it may concern,

Andrew was diagnosed with Autism Spectrum Disorder today. The specific diagnosis is:

Autism Spectrum Disorder
Level 1 *Social Communication Severity - Supports needed*
Level 2 *Restrictive Repetitive Behavior Severity - Substantial Supports needed*

Without Developmental Speech Disorder
Without Intellectual Developmental Disorder

DSM 5 Severity is based on the level of support needed in each area
Level 1 - Supports needed
Level 2 - Substantial supports needed
Level 3 - Very substantial supports needed

Stapled to the diagnosis page are all of Andrew's test results, as well as Dr. Baker's observed symptoms.

In the area of social communication, Dr. Baker notes three out of five symptoms in Andrew. Three were required for an ASD diagnosis.

In the area of restrictive-repetitive (obsessive), Dr. Baker notes four out of five symptoms in Andrew. Three were required for an ASD diagnosis.

In the area of communication, Dr. Baker notes all five out of the five symptoms in Andrew.

Along with the diagnosis letter, Dr. Baker gives us a copy of his notes taken during the three sessions, as well as Andrew's printed scores from the questionnaire.

"So what do I do now? Do I tell people?" Andrew asks.

"Well, that's up to you," Dr. Baker replies. "Personally, I like to keep my diagnosis close to my heart. It's not for everyone to know."

"I'm not really sure what I'm going to do," Andrew ponders.

"Well, you don't need to decide right now," I say as I grab his hand. "You'll know what works for you, but I think it would help if the receptionists at your work understood this about you. Maybe they would be more direct with their email instructions, and you'd be less frustrated."

"What would I tell them?" Andrew asks.

"Well, technically, it's called Autism Spectrum Disorder. It's formally known as Asperger's syndrome," Dr. Baker explains. "But there's other things you can say if you don't want to tell people."

Dr. Baker hands us a form as he explains. "These are statements you can use as a different option: 'I'm the kind of person who…asks a lot of questions.' Or 'I'm the kind of person who…needs direct instructions.'"

"Oh, that makes sense," I say as I look over the form.

"'It would help me if…' is another one you can use. 'It would help me if you reworded your question.' Or 'It would help me if you explained this in more detail so I can understand,'" Dr. Baker continues.

"Okay, thanks," Andrew says as we stand up to leave.

"There's a support group that meets once a month to discuss different topics at the Autism Center. You're welcome to attend those if you like," Dr. Baker explains as he hands Andrew more information.

"Thanks so much. I'll check it out," Andrew says as he happily takes the form.

"Thanks for everything, Dr. Baker. We've really enjoyed this experience," I say as he walks us to the door.

"Yes, I'm sad we won't be coming back here," Andrew adds. "It's been great."

ANDREW'S TAKE

I remember this question: "In a conversation, I tend to focus on my own thoughts rather than what my listener might be thinking." My answer to this question would be the same today. I understand that it's trying to assess where your attention is while conversing with someone, but this question feels frustratingly ambiguous. The answer can vary based on the type of conversation I'm having. If I'm interested and want to hear what the other person is saying, then my attention is focused on them. I'm in a state of absorption and focused on what they are saying.

During other types of conversation, I'm trying to determine what kind of conversation I'm having and how I'm going to act. In these situations, my attention would be much more focused on my own thoughts.

I don't know how to answer questions like this in a general way. If it's not obvious which one to pick, then it feels like an explanation would be more appropriate.

The question "I would rather go to a library than a party" is also frustratingly ambiguous. I do like to go to parties, and I also like to nerd out on a Friday night. I have spent hours going down random Wikipedia rabbit holes. The answer to the question is context-specific. Is the party in question better than the library? Or do I want to learn about thermodynamics more than I would like to go to a possibly unfun party? The fulcrum is right in the middle. Might as well flip a coin.

This "not being able to generalize" extends to other areas in my life. I didn't get my passport for five years because I needed the signature of a guarantor. A guarantor is someone who is a professional and who has known you for five years or more. Well, I don't have that, so what do I do? I get frustrated that there is an impossible task on my passport application, and then I don't complete it, that's what I do. Guess I'm not leaving the country. This happens quite often when I'm filling out paperwork. Be it at work, at the bank, or at the airport.

"Things seem to be either facts or nonsense in Andrew's eyes. Potential truths aren't a thing. We all quickly conclude that Andrew thinks in black and white." Michelle mentions this earlier in the chapter, and I want to talk about it specifically.

This is true. I lump most things into a black or a white category. But there are many times when I don't know what category to put something in. I will mentally label something as: *Potentially true or false, white or black, and further information is required.* I would use this labeling method on countless ideas and concepts that I don't yet have an answer for. Questions don't become truths until at least 99 percent, but preferably when the subjective feeling of 100 percent is reached.

I was shocked when Dr. Baker explained the concept of being able to generalize and how I struggled significantly with this. I didn't think I struggled with generalization, but rather that I loved to add context and details. Surely, I could generalize? But alas, I struggled. My mind locked up when I was asked to generalize. Once I began to generalize, my mind would loop back to the details. Over and over, this would happen. This loop is hard to break out of, and in the end, I would have to use effort and discipline to come up with a generalization. Learning this about myself explained so many problems that I've had throughout my life.

While I was being diagnosed by Dr. Baker, I could feel the moments where we all realized that I likely have ASD. Whereas when I would do the online tests, I would still wonder, *Is this correct? Do I really have ASD?* I would ask Dr. Baker a question, and he would explain it to me, then I would feel a real sense of *Ah ha, I understand where I have a deficit.* This helped me to feel confident about my diagnosis.

I could feel that Michelle was getting a lot out of this too. This made me feel doubly good. Doubly good that I'm learning, feeling great about understanding myself, and Michelle is understanding me more too. I knew that this would definitely increase the odds of us having a long, happy, strong relationship.

* * *

19
THE AFTERMATH OF THE DIAGNOSIS

Hours after receiving Andrew's diagnosis, we head to the airport to catch a plane. We are going to visit his family in Thunder Bay for the second time as a couple. Throughout the first several days of that trip, Andrew is himself. We visit with his family, go for nice walks, and enjoy some delicious Persians.

Our enjoyment is short-lived. As the weekend approaches, Andrew becomes quieter and quieter. He is hardly engaging with anyone, including me. My initial thoughts are that it's the usual frustrations with his family that are getting to him. Andrew's family keeps the news playing on their living room TV constantly, and they worry about all the negative events happening around the world. This is tough on us. We don't watch the news or worry about things that are out of our control. We rarely keep our TV on, as we are not a fan of having constant background noise. I assume that is bothering Andrew, but I assume wrong.

By the weekend, complete overwhelm sets in, and Andrew is hardly functional. He is struggling to have even the simplest of conversations. Once he reaches this point, it takes him a few more days to explain what is bothering him.

He turns to me and says, "It's as if I've been going through my life looking through the wrong lens. I don't know how to think, and I don't know what I'm doing. I don't know who I am. I have to change my lens."

In this moment, I realize that his overwhelmed state is about the autism diagnosis and likely has little to do with his family. Keeping true to Andrew's form, it took a week for the diagnosis to sink in.

Throughout the diagnostic process with Dr. Baker, Andrew was in good spirits. He seemed to enjoy the entire experience. I didn't observe anything other than the excitement he had to learn more about himself. This sudden shift in his demeanor is not something I was expecting or prepared for.

He begins overthinking every single decision he makes, even the small ones. He doesn't know when he should eat, if he is tired, or what he wants to do. The final two days of the trip are a nightmare. Andrew is a mess, and being around his family isn't helping this matter.

Andrew's family has been missing him dearly since he moved away at nineteen, and they comment on this often. "We wish you would call more. We hardly see you, and we can't believe you are leaving so soon. You're not here enough. We never get to see you." It's tough for Andrew to listen to these comments on a good day, but in this state, it sends him over the edge. He can't think straight. I have to remind him to drink water and glance in his family's direction every once in a while. They will say something to him, and it's as if he doesn't even notice. His brain has completely checked out. He couldn't even be trusted to drive in this condition, and I can't wait to get him back home.

On our way to the airport, we sit in silence while squeezing each other's hands tight. We are both depleted and feel anxious to get on that plane. Andrew's mother surprises us at the airport to say goodbye. We sit at a table and grab a coffee to have a quick visit before going through security. We do our best to humor her during our visit, but we don't have much conversation in us. We are out of patience and in desperate need of some alone time.

Before we get up from the table, she gives us each a gift. They are pointy metal statues of wizards wrapped in bubble wrap. The look on Andrew's face shows that he doesn't want to take the statues, but his mother will be heartbroken if we reject the gifts.

Andrew and I travel with only carry-on luggage. Both of our bags were quite full, but there was a little bit of room in Andrew's bag. The statues barely fit. Andrew's anxiety nearly reached its maximum. I have to hold the top together as he zips it up. His eyes seem to be popping out of their sockets as we hug his mother goodbye.

Andrew travels with his CPAP machine and has to take it out at security every time we get on a plane. Andrew forgets about his CPAP and sends his bag through without removing it. It gets flagged and grabbed by a female security officer. "Can you come with me, sir?" she asks Andrew as she walks to the side counter.

As she opens it I hear her ask Andrew, "Is there anything sharp or dangerous in your bag, sir?"

"I don't know, maybe," Andrew replies.

She clearly wasn't expecting that response.

She doesn't seem to know what to do next. She freezes for a second and then asks, "Did you pack your bag yourself, sir?"

"Yes," Andrew replies.

"I'm going to ask you again: Is there anything sharp or dangerous in your bag, sir?" Her voice is getting firmer now.

"I don't know, maybe," Andrew repeats in the same tone.

My anxiety is now at epic levels. I'm rushing to put my shoes on as I hear this going down. I know exactly what is happening. The statues Andrew's mom just gave us could somewhat be considered sharp. They are magicians with pointy hats. Andrew doesn't know if she would consider them to be sharp, so he replies with, "I don't know, maybe."

The look on her face is a mixture of terror and confusion. It looks as if she is about to call for backup. I half expect her to unholster her gun and tell Andrew to get on the floor. I quickly make my way over with one shoe on and interject.

"There are some statues that are kind of sharp in his bag, but they have bubble wrap on them." I want to follow this up with, "And he's autistic, so he takes questions literally," but I don't know if we are telling people yet.

Understandably, she is still reluctant to open Andrew's bag. I do my best to cut the tension with some humor. "We've just had a long trip visiting family, and he's exhausted. You know how family can be. They really take a lot out of you." She chuckles a little and seems to relax as her shoulders drop. "Would you like me to open the bag for you?" I ask.

"No ma'am, that's okay. I'm just going to do it slowly," she responds.

Andrew and I stand silently while she slowly unzips the bag, removes the statues, and checks Andrew's CPAP machine. Andrew is so frozen still that he doesn't even make eye contact with me.

As the guard begins placing everything back in Andrew's bag, she says, "Okay, you are cleared to go."

"Thank you so much," I reply, feeling relieved.

* * *

ANDREW'S TAKE

Learning I have ASD, followed closely by overexposure to my family for seven days, was overwhelming. This caused me to have severe problems generalizing or responding to generalized questions. Especially when I'm in an unfamiliar, tense environment, such as airport security.

"Is there anything sharp or dangerous in your bag, sir?" she said to me. My mind processes her request like this: *What's the context? Like sharp sharp? What about pointy sharp? Do I say no even though there is a pointy sharp object in the bag? I can't lie to this person.*

Now imagine this loop on repeat fifty times within a span of four seconds, and no answer can be found. My mind has crashed. The input does not compute.

* * *

Back to Michelle

As we walk to our gate, I have an intense realization. I have been looking at the diagnosis as somewhat of an endpoint on our autism journey.

I'm wrong.

Andrew is not okay. He is not even a little bit okay. He told an airport security officer that there might be something sharp and dangerous in his bag. I've never seen him like this before.

It's an aftermath I'm not prepared for, and this is merely the beginning.

Photos for Chapter 19
Bellamimalifestyles.com/bookphotos

CONCLUSION

Well, you did it, bestie; you made it to the end. I'm so happy you stuck with us. It's time for us to start wrapping it up.

I am embarrassed that it took me until the age of thirty-three to try dating a guy like Andrew. I have an inkling that many people out there will relate to overlooking someone like him for similar reasons, particularly the clothes and the fact that we split nearly every check.

Many people struggle with social anxiety and are terrible at romance. With these types of people, the first few dates may feel awkward, but that doesn't mean they don't make fantastic life partners. If I would've had this perspective through my many years of online dating and failed relationships, I would have taken a second date more often than I did.

I want you to open your eyes to the quiet person in the corner with the pocket protector and special interests. The person you might have to make the first move on because they may be too shy to ask you out. The person who dresses for function over style. The one who won't promise you the world until they know they can give it to you (which may take a long time). The person you can most be yourself with, that's the partner you want. They may feel more like a friend than a lover, but I assure you this can be a huge blessing in the long run.

Romance and special occasions are grossly overrated. Many people brag about the gifts they were given on a special occasion, while they feel neglected by their partner all the other days of the week. That is just silly. What we should be paying the most attention to is the other days of the week. Daily life is much more important than special occasions.

How do they greet you when they get home? How do they act when you are having a tough day? Do you like the person you are becoming while you are with them? Can they admit to their shortcomings? Are you both self-aware enough to realize how your habits affect each other? These are the things that matter most; these are the things that movies should be about.

The world needs all sorts of people to keep it running smoothly. We need extroverts, introverts, people who are good with people, and people who excel at working with machines. Often where we excel in one area, we lack in another; that's just how it works. There's only so much bandwidth available in the brain, and you can't be a genius at everything. Whoever you are in this world, own it and know that it's exactly who you are meant to be.

I will get more into this in a later book, but I am terrible at pretty much everything Andrew is great at. If my life depended on my figuring out how to fix a car to get myself to safety, I'd be dead. In many ways, his skills are more useful than mine, and yet he is often made to feel lesser than by society. Words cannot express how much this bothers me. I make sure to remind him of his talents when he's feeling down on himself.

I feel nerds are misunderstood because they do not mirror our behaviors back to us in the same ways we are accustomed to. To me, this makes them awesome. The fact that they will stick to what they're interested in, regardless of whether it's popular or not, is admirable. The problem is we live in a society that is trying to make everyone the same, and we aren't taught to appreciate neurodiversity.

Wikipedia defines a nerd as the following: *"a nerd is a person seen as overly intellectual, obsessive, introverted or lacking social skills. Such a person may spend inordinate amounts of time on unpopular, little-known, or non-mainstream activities, which are generally either highly technical, abstract, or relating to topics of science fiction or fantasy, to the exclusion of more mainstream activities. Additionally, many so-called Nerds are described as being shy, quirky, pedantic, and unattractive."* I don't mind

Wikipedia's definition so much, but when I typed "nerd" into google dictionary, I got a definition that felt much more negative, *"a foolish or contemptible person who lacks social skills or is boringly studious."* I do not like this definition at all.

Personally, I would describe a nerd as, *"Someone who doesn't exist to please others. Who follows their own interests regardless of what is mainstream, and who pays attention to minute details and aims to share their knowledge."* Also, from my experience, they are trustworthy people who stick to their word. I find them much more interesting to spend copious amounts of time with. I love my nerd. It is refreshing not to be living to impress anybody, as I used to be. I also love the fact that with him, I am constantly learning. I want to encourage more people to take a second date with someone who felt "awkward" because I am so glad that I did. The nerds are where it's at; we just need to understand them better.

I look at my early days with Andrew much differently now. How he was dressed when I met him to play squash makes perfect sense. His socks were pulled up and folded over because it feels comfortable on his calf, and they don't fall down. (He wears his socks like that to this day). His shorts were pulled up just a little too high because he does not want to deal with them falling down mid-game. He wants everything to be as functional as possible so that he can play the game optimally. I respect this about him now, and after a year of dating, I've even begun dressing more like him.

When I look back at our first hike together when he wore that terrible t-shirt with holes in it, I realize there was something magical about that day. We learned a significant amount about each other in a matter of hours, but I never gave it much thought. I revealed my true self without being guarded, even though I hardly knew him. I suppose I am glad he chose to wear that hideous almost yellow t-shirt that day. Otherwise, I may have thought he was cute, and talking wouldn't have been so effortless. I never saw him wear that shirt again, and I threw it out shortly after he moved in when I noticed it hanging on his side of the closet.

It was not Andrew's clothes, sunglasses, or the hole in his smile that was keeping me from being attracted to him. That's just what I defaulted to picking on him for because something more important was missing. He lacked the basic social skill set that I needed in order to feel attracted to him. It was about feeling cared for and protected. Little things can make all the difference, even something as simple as asking me if I want anything. Once Andrew gave me a glimpse that he was capable of this by getting me a coffee, my attraction began to blossom because it felt as though he considered my needs ahead of his own.

Now that I understand how Andrew's mind works, I realize that he would have never made a move on me. I had verbally told him when we first met a year prior that I was only interested in friendship, so until I verbally told him otherwise, he would act as such. He did not notice that things were changing between us. He actually didn't notice. Things would have continued like that for months or possibly years had I not taken action. Because Andrew sees each day as an individual event, the shift in our friendship was not obvious to him.

For months, I ached for Andrew to be able to express how he felt about me, and yet in the end, he ended up expressing more emotion than anyone I had ever been with when he wrote that list about me. He didn't write it to impress me, or to get any credit. He didn't even bother to show it to me. He wrote it for himself, to express gratitude for his life. He didn't do it because I was mad at him, or because it was some cheesy holiday. He did it because he wanted to, and that made me feel loved in a way I never knew was possible.

My hope is that this book helped to change the way you look at others regardless of if they are autistic or not. Here are some of the lessons that I hope you take away from this:

- Observe people without trying to change them.
- Stop taking everything personally. Assume others' personality traits have absolutely nothing to do with you.
- Take the time to learn about your loved ones. Notice how their mind works and figure out a way to compromise in areas that are tough. Begin to ask more questions when they say or do something you do not understand, rather than immediately getting upset. If professional help is unavailable to you, there is

still much you can learn on your own by doing some research. Get creative and be relentless.
- Communication is everything. Often, behavior has nothing to do with how much someone loves or cares about us and everything to do with how their brain is wired. Acknowledge your differences and make light of them, rather than placing all the blame on your partner.
- Once you've learned more about your partner, see if you can adjust your expectations in certain areas to make both your lives easier.
- Design a relationship that works for both of you. Figure out the best way your puzzle pieces fit together without the worry of how it's perceived by others.
- Mainstream media has put the spotlight on grand romantic gestures and physical attraction, neither of which will make for healthy day-to-day life in the long term. Little emphasis is put on what makes a solid foundation for a long-lasting relationship.
- Let's change the narrative. The first year of your relationship doesn't need to be all about romance. What if the beginning stages of love were the hardest part as you put the work into learning about each other, and it only got better from there? A spark isn't needed because it inevitably fizzles out, anyway. Having a strong foundation through understanding is much more important.
- Relationships are about two people with different backgrounds and issues coming together and communicating. Don't be that couple that spends decades arguing about directions because they have not figured out that one of them is a visual thinker and the other is not. Learn how your partner's mind works and be aware of your own. Put the work in now, rather than spending a lifetime being frustrated.

There were likely parts throughout this book where you thought to yourself, *Really, Andrew, that's all you have to say?* All I can say to that is, welcome to my life. Getting him to open up as much as he did was like pulling teeth. It's not easy for Andrew to express his emotions, and I'm proud of him for being so vulnerable.

Don't worry, our journey isn't over; it is just beginning. This is the first of a five-book series. We still have plenty of topics to cover, and the best is yet to come.

Our next book is entitled *Before Love & Autism,* and it has many full chapters written by Andrew. You will learn about his childhood as well as mine. It will highlight all the trauma, adventure, heartbreaks, and healing we went through in our lives before we fell in love.

* * *

ANDREW'S TAKE

Michelle summed this up pretty well, but I disagree with one thing she said. "A spark isn't needed, because it inevitably fizzles out, anyway." I think a spark is needed, just not the kind of spark that sets off tons of fireworks within six weeks and then fizzles into a hazy mess.

Be open to new ways of navigating relationships. Just by being open to new ideas about how "things are" or "should be," your life might take a turn for the better that you never imagined possible.

Core character attributes that help to create and cultivate this approach:

- Patience, tolerance, self-care, being self-aware and loving toward yourself and your partner.
- Knowing what you want and allowing what you want to change. In a sense, being rigid enough to protect yourself, your self-worth, or whatever it is that makes you awesome. Yet flexible, and adaptable enough to ebb and flow with the relationship and not damage it.

How do you integrate these approaches into your life? Step one - Do you love yourself? Yes / No

If you answered no to step one, then take the next several weeks or years to learn how to love yourself. Good luck.

Otherwise, move on to step two.

Step two - There is no step two. Once you learn to love yourself, you will know what to do.

We will get into this subject further in our next book. In the meantime, I hope you follow us on social media, take the time to review this book, and check out our relationship course as well as our other publications linked below.

* * *

Bellamimalifestyles.com

ENDNOTES

Notes I wrote about Andrew the night I read *Shadow Syndromes*:

- Sensitive to textures, smells, air quality, noises (how something fits is extremely important)
- Incapable of breaking a routine to "hurry" (only has one speed)
- Must put his shoes on a certain way (everything has a process that must remain the same)
- Delayed when it comes to reactions & processing emotions (often Takes 9-12 days to figure out how he feels about something)
- Breaks eye contact when he talks about feelings (or can't talk about feelings at all)
- Often closes his eyes when telling a story or looks away from you
- Extremely literal in speech (takes everything I say literally)
- Often tells fragments of a story and "misses the point" he was trying to make
- Unable to give proper context when recounting conversations with people
- Sometimes speaks in one long, monotone sentence
- Speaks at odd volumes at the worst times (if I whisper at him, he will answer back in his full voice)
- Expressions don't match his face (will look bored when he's really enjoying something)

- Will become overwhelmed and abort social situations without saying anything (Where did Andrew go?)
- Awkward demeanor
- Unaware when he is "wound up" and needs a break (takes him days to figure out why he was wound up)
- Wants to be told exactly what he is doing right or wrong (doesn't take offense, just sees it as useful information)
- Can't sort relevant information from irrelevant information (if you ask a vague question, he will tell you about his entire day instead of important parts)
- Rules need to apply in all situations the same (doesn't seem to grasp that the context might be different)
- So micro-focused that he can't see the whole picture (will become obsessed with one thing and let everything else fall apart)
- Unable to understand someone else's viewpoint (or how what he is doing is affecting you)
- Doesn't tie situations together or realize how they affect each other (sees them as individual events)
- Unable to tell me what mood someone is in after he spends time with them
- Loyal to a fault (often to people with ill intent)
- Unable to estimate how long something will take him (cannot give you any approximations)
- Needs to figure out how to do something by making his own mistakes or reading the instructions (you can explain it to him in detail, but it won't help; he needs pictures or to make the mistakes to learn himself)
- If you can explain something to him, he will seem to fully understand what to do, but then when the moment happens, he can't connect it to the conversation you had (it feels as if you had the conversation for nothing)
- Small things that take him away from his microfocus can really ruin his day. (Example: getting a phone call while at work. It will take his brain quite a while to get back to the level of focus it was at before the call.) It really affects him when he needs to break focus.

- Will do what I ask, but at the wrong time and place. Doesn't seem to have any concept of bad timing
- Black and white thinking (he's either really worried or not worried enough)
- Very impulsive without thinking things through
- Starts large projects with no concept of how much time they will take
- If something is not where it's supposed to be, it's like he's incapable of guessing where it might be (he doesn't think to check in the obvious places it might be; he will just be confused)
- Does not understand embellishing (sees it as a lie)
- Hates small talk (often just doesn't engage)
- Can't seem to tell what affects his life in a negative way when it comes to people. Can tell immediately with objects, almost too well too quickly ("I hate this, throw it away")
- On a few occasions has panicked and repeated things three times while shaking his head ("I bought it for you, I bought it for you, I bought it for you.")
- Basically seems incapable of understanding the effect people have on his life or recognizing bad influences that he doesn't need
- Doesn't like pets (doesn't need the companionship)
- His brain is like file folders (can switch subjects with one click and read multiple books at once)
- His text messages are often backwards and not what he's meaning to say
- Extremely attentive and present (I have all his focus, or none of it)
- Doesn't seem to pick up on obvious social cues or know when he's angering someone
- Doesn't like team sports aside from dodgeball (because he can just use his own strategy)
- Has no concept of time or how much he can fit into his schedule (overbooks himself without realizing he will run out of time or energy)

- He can't play Scrabble—at all—it was surprising to me how he was trying to spell the words backwards or diagonal even after I explained it twice
- He hurts my feelings with blunt statements that can sometimes feel like they are stuck on repeat as he will say them multiple times in one day
- He will tell me he's fine one day before a huge meltdown because he thinks he is fine. It's as if he has little understanding of how he's feeling.
- He thinks in pictures (visual thinker), especially with directions, He needs to see the picture in his head; you can't just tell him where to turn. He also sometimes describes a picture when he tells a story.

www.ingramcontent.com/pod-product-compliance
Lightning Source LLC
Chambersburg PA
CBHW051707160426
43209CB00004B/1055